Jesus was entombed on the late morning of the 11th day and raised on the morning of the 15th day and was therefore entombed three days and three nights as required by prophesy and would have come forth on Sunday, the first day of the week.

Copyright © 2024 Gordon L. Ormesher

ISBN (Hardback): 979-8-89381-036-3
ISBN (Paperback): 979-8-89381-037-0
ISBN (eBook): 979-8-89381-038-7

All rights reserved. No part of this book may be reproduced or transmitted in any form or by any means, electronic or mechanical, including photocopying, recording, or by any information storage and retrieval system, without permission in writing from the copyright owner.

The views expressed in this work are solely those of the author and do not necessarily reflect the views of the publisher, and the publisher hereby disclaims any responsibility for them.

508 West 26th Street KEARNEY, NE 68848
402-819-3224
info@medialiteraryexcellence.com

PREFACE

Atonement

The most important single event ever to occur in human history, is the atoning sacrifice of our Lord and Savior Jesus Christ. There is nothing in the entire plan of salvation that compares with this most transcendent event. Consequently, it is the rock foundation upon which the gospel and all other things rest. One prophet wrote: "and this is the gospel, the glad tidings, which the voice out of the heavens bore record unto us— That he came into the world, even Jesus, to be crucified for the world, and to bear the sins of the world, and to sanctify the world, and to cleanse it from all unrighteousness; That through Him all might be saved whom the Father had put into his power and made by Him." On many occasions the Savior stated very clearly that He had come into the world to do the will of His Father, because his Father had sent Him that He might be lifted up upon the cross.

The plan of salvation was adopted in the heavens before the foundation of the world was laid. Part of the great plan of salvation, was that our Father Adam was appointed to come to earth and stand at the head of the whole human family. Because of the Adam's transgression, Jesus, the only begotten Son of the Father, had been appointed to come and redeem the world from the consequences of the fall.

"Wherefore, redemption cometh in and through the Holy Messiah; for he is full of grace and truth. Behold, he offereth himself a sacrifice for sin, to answer the ends of the law, unto all those who have a broken heart and a contrite spirit; and unto none else can the ends of the law be answered. Wherefore, how great the importance to make these things known unto the inhabitants of the earth, that they may know that there is no flesh that can dwell in the presence of God, save it be through the merits, and mercy, and grace of the Holy Messiah, who layeth down his life according to the flesh, and taketh it again by the power of the Spirit, that he may bring to pass the resurrection of the dead, being the first that should rise. Wherefore, he is the first fruits unto God, inasmuch as he shall make intercession for all the children of men; and they that believe in him shall be saved." (2 Nephi 2:6–9)

"…As in Adam, or by nature, they fall, even so the blood of Christ atoneth for their sins. Moreover, I say unto you, that there shall be no other name given nor any other way nor means whereby salvation can come unto the children of men, only in and through the name of Christ, the Lord Omnipotent. For behold he judgeth, and his judgment is just; … but men drink damnation to their own souls except they humble themselves and become as little children, and believe that salvation was, and is, and is to come, in and through the atoning blood of Christ, the Lord Omnipotent. For the natural man is an enemy to God, and has been from the fall of Adam, and will be, forever and ever, unless he yields to the enticings of the Holy Spirit, and putteth off the natural man and becometh a saint through the atonement of Christ the Lord, and becometh as a child, submissive, meek, humble, patient, full of love, willing to submit to all things which the Lord seeth fit to inflict upon him, even as a child doth submit to his father. And moreover, I say unto you, that the time shall come when the knowledge of a Savior shall spread throughout every nation, kindred, tongue, and people." (Mosiah 3:16–20)

It is essential to understand two great truths about the doctrine of salvation: 1. The fall of Adam; and 2. The divine Sonship of our Lord. Adam's fall brought spiritual and temporal death into the world.

Spiritual death is to be cast out of the presence of the Lord and to die as pertaining to the things of righteousness, or in other words, things of the Spirit.

Temporal death or natural death is the separation of the body and the spirit, the body going back to the dust from which it was created and the spirit, to a world of waiting spirits to await the day of the resurrection.

To atone is to ransom, reconcile, expiate, redeem, reclaim, absolve, propitiate, make amends, pay the penalty. Thus the atonement of Christ is designed to ransom man from the effects of the fall of Adam in that both the spiritual and temporal death are conquered; their lasting effect is nullified. The spiritual death of the fall is replaced by the spiritual life of the atonement, in that all who believe and obey the gospel law gain spiritual or eternal life—life in the presence of God where those who enjoy it are alive to the things of righteousness or things of the Spirit. The temporal death of the fall is replaced by the state of immortality which comes because of the atonement and the resurrection of our Lord. The body and spirit which separated, incident to what men call the natural death, are reunited in immortality in an inseparable connection that never again will permit the mortal body to see corruption.

Immortality comes as a free gift, by the grace of God alone without works of righteousness. Eternal Life is a reward for "obedience to the laws and ordinances of the Gospel."

"Adam fell that men might be; and men are, that they might have joy, and the Messiah cometh in the fullness of time, that he may redeem the children of men from the fall." & "The atonement was prepared from the foundation of the world for all mankind, which ever were since the fall of Adam, or who are, or whoever shall be, even unto the end of the world."

And thus the Lord says that because of the atonement, and following the "natural death," man is "raised in immortality unto eternal life, even as many as would believe; And they that believe not unto eternal damnation; for they cannot be redeemed from their spiritual fall, because they repent not."

If there had been no atonement of Christ (their having been a fall of Adam!), then the whole plan and purpose connected with the creation of man would have come to naught. If there had been no atonement, temporal death would have remained forever, and there never would have been a resurrection. The body would have to remain forever in the grave, and the spirit would have stayed in a spirit prison to all eternity. If there had been no atonement, there never would have been spiritual or eternal life for any persons. Neither mortals nor spirits could have been cleansed from sin, and all the spirit hosts of heaven would have wound up as devils, angels to a devil, that is, as sons of perdition.

Christ is the only person ever to be born in the world who had power to bring to pass the resurrection of himself or anyone else, and to atone for the sins of any living being. This is because he had life in himself; he had the power of immortality by divine inheritance. The atonement came by the power of the God and not of man, and to understand it one must believe that our Lord was literally the son of God (an immortal Personage) and of Mary (a mortal woman). From his mother he inherited mortality, the power to lay down his life, to die, to permit body and spirit to separate. From his Father, he inherited the power of the immortality, the power to keep body and spirit together, or voluntarily had been permitted them to separate, a power to unite them again in a resurrected state. The Prophet John quoted Jesus when he said "I lay down my life, that I might take it again, no man taketh it from me, but I lay it down myself, I have power to lay it down, and I have power to take it again. This commandment have I received of my Father.",

Because of the atonement and by the obedience to gospel law men have power to become the sons of God. In that, they are spiritually begotten of God and adopted as members of his family. They become the sons of God and joint heirs with Christ of the fullness of the Fathers kingdom. It behooves us to try and understand how He exactly accomplished this great sacrifice for us.   (MD 60)

THE 𝔄tonement of 𝔍esus 𝔆hrist

𝔗he 𝔗ruth about the 𝔓assober

A compilation regarding the Saviors fulfillment of the Law of Moses

according to the Holy Testaments, both ancient and modern,

including the studies & writings of Apostles and

credible historians of today and yesterday.

The conversation of scholarship of this particular

time, is examined for a comparison of precepts of

men against the teachings of the scriptures.

This work has been compiled by Gordon L. Ormesher, a simple Elder of the Church of Jesus Christ of Latter Day Saints. Gordon is a retired carpenter and lays no claim to scholarship, except to be a disciple of Jesus Christ. The views contained herein, were obtained from study, prayer, inspiration, and promptings of the holy spirit and do not reflect any official the position of the church. This work is the sole responsibility of the author and reserves all rights to the same. It would be preferred that you do not use this work without permission, but if you should, please contact info@medialiteraryexcellence.com

My thanks to a dear friend, Doug Marks who has been an inspiring contributor and counsel as to the preparation for printing of this work.

Introduction

The scope of the subject in this book about the Passover is basically set forth on this title page. Christian teaching generally centers around the New Testament, as it should be, but has its basis in the Old Testament. These Testaments were given to us by Gods' holy servants the Prophets, so as His children we may know clearly where we came from, why we are here and how we may return to our once heavenly home.

In the preexistence, we existed as spirit children with our exalted Father and Mother in the heavens, and they diligently taught us the principles of the plan of salvation. While we were still in spirit form, we longed for the time when we could come to an earth and fulfill the purposes our Father had intended for us. The purpose of the plan was to enable us to have the opportunity to receive a body, and to eventually gain immortality and hopefully eternal life. However, since we range in intelligence from the least to the greatest and are given our agency. The degrees in glory we may obtain are as numerous as the stars in the heavens. This plan rewards us according to our obedience to principles of personal righteousness. Therefore, it would be expected there would be a disparity in the powers of heaven that could be granted to each individual.

A great war in heaven resulted, and Satan, wanting to have the power of God and the glory, championed the cause of equality by controlling the agency of all and thereby rewarding everyone equally under his dominion and direction. Jesus the Christ championed the cause of freedom of choice between good and evil, with the glory to be to the Father, and each of us to be rewarded by our choices. In the finality, 2/3rds of the spirits waiting to come to earth chose the plan of our Father and His Son Jesus, while Satan and 1/3rd of the spirits rebelled, and consequently were cast out of heaven without the opportunity to obtain a body and progress as we do. Each of us come to earth to gain our mortal body and engage in life's pursuits to determine our eventual glory. Satan and his spirits are here and are the appointed tempters to induce us to choose evil and engage in those activities which ultimately prove our true character.

Our loving Father knew that under these circumstances, none of us would be able to accomplish the task of becoming immortal and rising to the level of being exalted with Him in the Celestial World. While there are many who have the embryo of perfection within us, our Father knew it would be necessary to have someone to guide us and pay the price for our imperfections, so we might rise to the required stature required to return to Him. That someone, who was selected and foreordained in the Grand Council before the world came in to existence, was His only begotten Son, Jesus the Christ.

Before the earth was formed, Jesus the Christ was chosen to be the only begotten Son in the flesh and the Lord and Savior over this great plan of salvation. The earth was then organized and our opportunity was established and set into motion, so each of us may be tested in our physical body and procure a suitable degree of glory in relationship in the kingdom of Heaven to come. Since no unperfected thing can enter into the Celestial Kingdom of Heaven, a plan of sacrifice was required to pay for our imperfections, and Jesus agreed to pay that price, and thus we are indebted to Him for the opportunity as we start on the path to our Eternal life.

To the very first man on earth, Adam, the priesthood was conferred with the commandment to offer the firstling of the flocks, as an offering unto the Lord. Adam was informed by an angel that this action is a similitude of the sacrifice to be offered by the Only Begotten of the Father, which is full of grace and truth. Even though Adam observed to do all in the name of the Son, there were those of his generations who perverted the ordinances and sacrifices which resulted in heresies before God.

When God looked down upon the earth and saw all the corruption, it grieved Him and He decided to destroy all flesh by bringing on a flood of waters. However, Noah and his immediate family were spared and instructed to build an ark so they might escape this judgement, because Noah was a just man and perfect in his generations, and walked with God. After the flood, many in the following generations began to corrupt and distort the truth, never-the -less the priesthood and the proper ordinances were mainly preserved through the loins of Shem, one of the sons of Noah. Through generations of time, these histories were kept and brought forth so we might know how the Lord dealt with His covenant people.

Through covenants made with Abraham and ultimately through Israel, the priesthood and the plan were preserved, never-the-less, individual short comings and strife caused the tribes of Israel to be forced into bondage to the Pharaohs of Egypt. Foreknowing and establishing the circumstances and the components of the plan of salvation required at this time in history, Jehovah, the Great I Am, brought forth Moses from out of the chains of slavery and prepared him to establish a great work. After being raised as a Prince of Egypt, Moses was faced with a set of events which caused him to flee into the desert, where he came to reside with Jethro his future father-in-law. It was from Jethro that Moses received the Priesthood and became tutored in the ways of God.

Moses first encounter with God was in the appearance of a burning bush, and subsequently Moses was informed that the Lords' children were crying to heaven for relief from their grievous burdens under the Pharaohs. Moses rejected in every way he could at the idea that the Lord told him, he was expected to deliver the people out of the hands of the Egyptians. It appears quite evident that our Father in Heaven knows all that will happen and has the ready solution for the problem. In particular, it is clear in reading Exodus, the strife and bondage facing the children of Israel was occasioned and foreordained for the purpose of instituting the Law of Moses (Passover). Jehovah set His hand to extricate His covenant people from the slavery to the Egyptians to which they found themselves bound.

At this time, the Passover was instituted with all of its performances and ordinances and the people of Israel were required to remember and observe them forever. However, the law was not just for a remembrance, it was given as a similitude of what the Savior would accomplish in bringing about the immortality and offer of eternal life to all mankind, and deliver them from the bondage of death brought about by the fall of Adam. When Jesus celebrated this last Passover with His disciples, He very plainly declared He had not come to destroy the Law but to fulfill that part which concerned His Atonement. The Prophets of God have declared all through time just how Jesus would fulfill the Law right down to the method and details of His death, as well as many of the words uttered and actions taken by His friends and enemies involved in His atoning sacrifice.

There has been many false Christs and prophets but only one true Christ capable of accomplishing every last jot and tittle of the Law and thus fulfilling the requirements of the Passover as revealed. Jesus of Nazareth fulfilled every detail of the correct chronology of the Passover Law and redeemed us from the fall and thus we may identify and recognize our true Savior. He is the first fruits of the resurrection! He is the Only Begotten of the Father in the flesh and is the Redeemer of the world! He has established a true order of law by which we may gain salvation and eternal life!

The Passover Law with all the performances and ordinances pertaining to it, as commanded by Jehovah in Exodus 12, was celebrated in precisely 12 days, and was observed in that manner until the Jews were driven out of Israel in 70 AD. When Jesus and the Apostles were in Jerusalem to celebrate this last Passover, it was a 12-day occasion with all its' pageantry, and not a 7-day occurrence such as we celebrate today. Even after Jesus died and was resurrected the apostles continued to keep the feasts, as it gave them opportunity to make converts by explaining how the Law had been fulfilled by the Savior. The Apostles knew, however, there would be an apostasy from the gospel when they were gone, and many of the plain and precious truths would be perverted. By the time of the council of Nicaea in 325 A.D., the Passover had morphed into the erroneous 7-day celebration and remains as such today. As a consequence of the false codification of the Law of Moses, and many other false practices, the world sank into a period called the dark ages.

It's easy to see how this occurred. When the Jews were forced out of Jerusalem in 70 A.D., they had to discontinue the sacrifices leading up to the 7-day feasts and the simultaneous days of unleavened bread. When the council of Nicaea convened in 326 A.D., the evolving hierarchy of theologians and scholars and the new universal church chose to ignore, or in ignorance ignored, the Old Testament teachings and the customs of the Jewish observation of the Passover. The Constantine council in their attempt to deal with the Coptic Christians and other various splinter groups of claimed authority, codified the 7-day logic.

For over 1800 years, since and because of the prophesied apostasy, there has been a continued scholarly effort to explain the details of the Saviors' fulfillment of the Passover. To this day there is still an ongoing conversation in scholarship and, in order to get gain, the scholars and religionists bring forth the precepts of men mingled with scripture and try to convince everyone that their interpretations are correct. However, there remains the same controversy and confusion regarding the Passover and it stems from the false narratives and machinations of men.

When the reformation began in these latter days, all the scholars of the offshoots of the Christian religion continued to maintain a 7-day logic concerning the Passover. Consequently, all of the apologists for their particular sect have become very intricate and inventive in their explanations of trying to convince their congregations how Jesus fulfilled of the Law of Moses.

In their conversation of scholarship these apologists reach this conclusion: *"Readers of the New Testament have always faced the issue of having four separate witnesses to the same events and of dealing, in certain situations, with four witnesses who do not always agree among themselves. The synoptic Gospels, Matthew, Mark, and Luke, are significantly different from the Gospel of John. Though the synoptic Gospels often agree among themselves, they do not always agree with John's account. The modern student of the Bible, therefore, is met with a wide array of possible solutions. In any given instance, the possibility exists that in some way the accounts can be harmonized, that one account is more historically more accurate than another, or that a combination of certain elements from each account is the best course to pursue."* **These apologists all agree that it is essential to understand the synoptics and John, but** *"they must be studied in the light of plain reading of their respective narratives and no attempt should be made to harmonize the synoptics and the Johannine traditions."* **These apologists claim that**, *"with improved scholarly method and greater accessibility to primary sources, they can expose us to methods of form, redaction, and literary criticism--- students will be able better to identify such things as interpolation, alteration, and editing of biblical texts"*. *(The Life & Teachings of Jesus Christ.)* BYU

When we abandon our understanding to precepts taught by self-serving apologists of conflicting faiths, then controversy is the end result. We are grateful for all of the divergent views and research presented by the apologists of these last days and for latter day prophets and the accumulated history which is available for our study. **However, unless content is applied in the proper context**, such teachings usually only become the precepts of men and usually do not achieve the perfection and exactness needed for our personal advancement. In order to attain the stature of our Father in heaven and return to Him, we eventually must attain as much clarity and exactness as we possibly can to be able to qualify to enter Gods Kingdom.

The Author (Skousen) asked, "Can you outline the major events in the last week of the Savior's life, and indicate on which day you think each event occurred?" While this question is correct and valid, but is an impossibility, when we try to place all of the scriptures pertaining to the Atonement into 7 days, and thus we can only end up in the confusion and be embroiled in the controversy that currently exists. Is it any wonder the majority of the world cannot accept Christianity when the different sects disagree and cannot provide the exactness of the details regarding their declared Redeemers death and resurrection? The Apostles were men of God and knew what they were writing about and what it meant, they were there.

One prophet proclaimed, *"For it shall come to pass in that day [the last days] the churches that are built up and not unto the Lord, ...they have all gone astray save it be a few, who are the humble followers of Christ; nevertheless, they are led, that in many instances they do err because they are taught by the precepts of men"*. (2

Nephi 28). Isaiah saw our day as well: *"... Forasmuch as <u>this people draw near me with their mouth, and with their lips do honor me, but have their heart far from me, <u>and their fear toward me is taught by the precept of men:</u> Therefore, behold, I will proceed to do a marvelous work among this people..."*: (Isaiah 29:13) Theological scholars completely ignore the Exodus 12-day time frame as given to Moses by Christ, even as partially practiced by the Jews to this day, and attempt to force the actual events of 15 days into the precept of an apostasy time frame of 7 days. Controversy and confusion can be all that will ever come out of trying to force 15 days of scripture into 7 days.

God is not the author of confusion, but the ultimate source of truth and harmony, and He has established performances and ordinances in the gospel, which He expects us to follow as precisely as humanly possible. In the Passover portion of the Law to Moses we find not only details of the similitude, but also the day by day chronology that Jesus would precisely fulfill to the last "Jot and Tittle", when He came in the meridian of time. However, the 12day celebration as given by Jehovah to Moses has morphed into a 7day observance and, because of this apostasy, the Passover has been rife with controversy ever since.

Joseph Smith was a man raised up in these last days and the stick of Ephraim placed in his hand was the book of Mormon. Speaking of the Bible and the Book of Mormon and others, Joseph Smith said:

> *"<u>Who is it that writes these Scriptures? Not the men of the world</u> or mere casual observers, <u>but Apostles</u>—men who knew one gift from another, <u>and of course were capable of writing about it;</u> ------No man knows the things of God but <u>by the Spirit of God</u>."*

He further stated,

> *"Now taking it for granted that* **the scriptures say what they mean, and mean what they say,** <u>we have sufficient grounds to go on</u> **and prove from the bible that the gospel has always been the same; the ordinances to fulfil its requirements, the same; and the officers to officiate, the same; and the signs and fruits from the promises, the same."*[1]

The study in this book not only harmonizes the four gospels into the proper chronology given to Moses, but also includes the supportive evidence of ancient history, modern revelation from authors and prophets and even research from the apologists of the different sects. You will be able to see that God has given us abundant prophetic information regarding the Passover, that's not the problem. The problem of controversy can only be solved when correctively organizing all of the information in the proper God given time frame of the 12-day Passover of the Law of Moses. When properly organized within the correct logic, it becomes plain that Jesus is the Christ and He did fulfill every last jot and tittle as He declared.

True, we know we cannot come to a state of complete righteousness in this world, but Jesus the Christ paid the price for our short comings, if we will make the honest effort to live up to the standards required, and eventually, in the millennium and remaining time, we may be blessed to find the path to become perfect, as our Father in heaven is perfect.

The following chapters focus not so much on the controversy of scholarship, which for centuries has plagued the Passover, but what have men of God written to us by their direct revelations. There is no attempt to be totally comprehensive in this effort, as that would fill many volumes, so we will center our discussion essentially on the written scriptural events and prophetic teaching pursuant to the fulfillment of the Passover

Before you start reading chapter #1, we suggest you study the following:

After this Introduction is **a Map of Jerusalem**, which shows the exact route and chain of events which occurred, from the Last Supper...to the arrest in Gethsemane...to the supposed night trials...to the morning trial

---

[1] JST p.614

(6am)…to the trial before Pilate…to the trial before Herod…to another trial before Pilate, 6th hour (noon)…to the release of Barabbas…to the solders for scourging…to the crucifixion, 3rd hour (9am). The scholars dismiss the evidence of these time frames, as revealed by the scriptures, and claim them to be simply in error because they don't fit their 7day logic. Except for the 3rd hour (9am).

After the table of contents there are three different calendars: **The Exodus Calendar**….Jehovah established this Passover part of the Law of Moses, which began on the10th of Nissan and went through the 21st of Nissan, (12 days). He further established two High days and the ordinances pertaining to them. The 1st high day on the 6th day of the Passover and the 2nd High Day on the 12th day of the Passover, with a preparation day before each High Day. Scholars tend to pay this little or no attention as it does not conform to their precepts, yet it is undeniably true. These same scholars expound only briefly on different segments of the events of the Passover story but ignore the time line.

The Calendar of the Passover, as Jesus fulfilled it day by day…In the back index you will find a complete harmonization of all 4 gospels, day by day for fifteen days, every passage and verse leaving none out, and you will clearly see they completely show a total context regarding all prophecy regarding the Saviors' fulfillment of the Atonement. The scriptures say what they and mean what they say and have no need of adjustment, and the content actually describes and establishes the context of a 15-day time frame.

The Calendar of current Christian version of Passover fulfillment: …For over 1800 years, all of the apologists of the different sects of Christianity have had a conversation in scholarship in attempting to correct or adjust all the seeming discrepancies they claim to be found in the pages of the scriptures. It can be respectfully suggested that any such error comes from the same conversation in scholarship that attempts to fit 15 days of scripture into 7 days. Impossible to do.

Truth is harmony, and the truth is that all 4 gospels are the word of God and they are in complete harmony with one another. The Synoptic and the Johannine Traditions harmonize perfectly and do not need to be rearranged and twisted to accommodate dozens of false narrative and teachings of the precepts of men.

The Passover was instituted for two reasons. First, it was to commemorate the day the destroying angel passed over Israel's households and spared their firstborn children, as well as their subsequent hasty exodus of Israel from Egypt. Second, it is the similitude of the sacrifice and death of Jesus Christ. which He fulfilled. Jews accept the first meaning, but, in this day, they do not accept our claim that it has been fulfilled.

One of the reasons Jews cannot accept the fulfillment (and consequently, cannot accept Christ as their Messiah) is because Christians have for many centuries taught that Jesus performed the Atonement on Passover night and that he was crucified and died the next day, with his resurrection following on the second day after his death. (Yes, we teach that Christ died on Friday and was resurrected Sunday morning.)

If Christ is a fulfillment of the Passover, His atonement and death must match up with Passover observances as outlined in Exodus: 12. But, under the timeline currently taught by Christians, including the LDS Church and its scholars, very little about Christ's atonement and death correspond with the actual time line of the revelation of the Passover. Thus, it is easy to see why Jews cannot accept Christ as their Messiah.

This is an unfortunate situation, because the Atonement of Jesus is the exact fulfillment of this Passover. When one reads the Bible with a mind enlightened by the teachings of the Book of Mormon and modern prophets, it becomes evident that everything about Christ's last days on earth correspond exactly with Passover events, as observed by Jews at the time of Christ.

This summary explains how Christ entered Jerusalem on the 10th day of Nissan, the very day that Exodus Chapter 12 required the Jews to select the lamb that was to be sacrificed.

It explains how the four days spent establishing Christ's divine heritage and claiming to the world that he was the very Son of God, corresponds exactly with the days the sacrificial lamb was kept up in preparation for the Passover sacrifice.

It explains how the actual physical similitude part of the Atonement began on the evening and early morning after partaking of the Passover, and that over the next several days (not in just a few hours, as current Christians theorize), Christ, who was the leaven of righteousness, was shuffled from one tribunal to another and kept apart from the people while he was judged and persecuted.

It explains how Christ's trials, suffering and eventual crucifixion occurred over a six-day period after the Passover meal, not less than a single day as Christians currently teach, and establishes a parallel between the Passover night and Christ's eventual Atonement and death. While Christ was kept apart from the House of Israel between the Passover meal and His death, the House of Israel was truly without leaven.

It explains how, in accordance with the teachings of all the holy prophets, Christ's body remained in the grave for a full three days and three nights before resurrection, not a mere night (Friday night), 1 day (Saturday), and early morning (Sunday morning).

What is a Day? 1. One period of the earth's revolution on its axis (24 hours) is called a day. (Gen.7:24) **Hebrew days were calculated "from even unto even"** (Lev. 23:32)., Meaning from sunset to sunset. The Lord's Day is the first day of the week. (D'&C 59:9-14). **2.** That period between dawn and dark is the day as distinguished from the night. (Gen.8:22; Ps. 19:2). **"Are there not twelve hours in the day?"** (John 11:9). **3.** A day is a specified age, time or period.... (Job 19:25) .... This must be correct in calculating the days of the Atonement.

It's important to understand that the Jewish day is from 6pm to 6pm the next day, 24 for hours. The night before is included in the following day, thus 24 hours. Therefore, 6am is "when it was day"; the scriptural 1st hr. is 6am to 7am... 2nd hr. is 8am;... 3rd hr. is 9am; ....6th. hr. is 12noon.... 9th hr. is 3pm. These are specific times given by the scriptures in chapters 13 and 14. The Jewish hours cited in the scriptures do not correspond to our A.M.-P.M. structure.

It is important to understand the Correct Timeline: The reason for the confusion surrounding these events of the Passover, was caused by Apostasy, (Chapter 1). Apostasy from what? The established time line of the Passover as given to Moses by Jehovah in Exodus: 12 (this book Chapter 2).

A brief discussion of the generally accepted current Christian version of the Passover, that has evolved over the passage of the ages, is presented in Chapter 3.

To obtain a little better understanding of the significance of the Passover, the exactness of some of the details surrounding the sacrifices of the Passover, as well as some of the many prophesies pertaining to Saviors fulfillment of the Passover, refer to Chapter 4.

Jesus entered Jerusalem on the 1st day, 10th of Nissan, or the day on which the pascal lamb was to be held up for the sacrifice. Jesus was anointed by Mary the night of the 10th day (at the end Chapter 4), and the triumphal entry occurred the next morning, at which time He was accepted as the Messiah by His followers and He declared His mission. Returned to Bethany. (Chapter 5).

On the 2nd day, 11th of Nissan, Christ entered the temple and declared it as His house and began to throw out the leaven in preparation of the Passover. (Chapter 5) Returned to Bethany.

On the 3rd day, 12th of Nissan, Christ returned to the Temple and challenged the Jewish Authorities, so as to further purify His house. (Chapters 6 & 7).

On the 4th day, 13th of Nissan, the Passover regulations required that the lamb be held up and final preparations made for its sacrifice. The New Testament says nothing about what Christ did on that day. It can be assumed that He was with His family and quietly preparing himself for what was to come. (Chapter 8).

On the 5th day, 14th day of Nissan, the lamb was to be sacrificed. It should be understood that this lamb is not the sin sacrifice, but the commemorative sacrifice denoting the deliverance of Israel from Egyptian bondage. This is the first preparation day. (Comparison Calendar, insert before Chapter 1).

Beginning of that night, which is the night of the 6th day (feast day) – 15th of Nissan, Jesus and the apostles partook of the Passover supper and He instituted the Sacrament. (Chapter 8). After they has partaken of the supper, Jesus and the apostles proceeded to the Mount of Olives and they were instructed as to many things that would happen to them after He left them, and finally terminated their walk at the Garden of Gethsemane. (Chapter 9).

Sometime before dawn of the 6th day (feast day), Jesus was arrested and brought before Annas and Caiaphas for a preliminary hearing and was bound over for trial. (Chapter 10)

Early on the morning of the sixth day, now, here's where it gets interesting, the official Christian version teaches that between Christ's arrest early in the morning of the second day of the Passover and the moment He was placed on the cross, the following events occurred. (Remember that these all had to occur before the 3rd hour (9am) in the morning, because that is when he was on the cross.) (Mark 15:25)

1. He had a formal trial before the Sanhedrin, -- then across town,
2. He went to Pilate and was cross examined, ------------then across town,
3. He went to Herod & was cross examined at length, --then across town.
4. He went back to Pilate, who also tried him again, the people were called together, and after the trial they called for Christ's crucifixion.
5. Pilate tried to release Jesus at the 6th hour (Noon)
6. He was scourged,
7. He traveled to Golgotha, carrying his own cross

It becomes quite obvious, upon a close reading of the scriptures, this is not what actually occurred. Rather than being sent around, examined, judged, scourged, and crucified all in a matter of 3 hours, Christ actually endured these events over the space of a 6 days, (Chapter 11). He was not crucified the day after the Passover meal, but on the preparation day of the final sacrifice, six days later. (Chapters 12 & 13). There are not any scriptural references to any night trials, but only hearing before the Judges to establish an information in order to legally bind Jesus over for trial. Jesus was then confined to the jail cell below the palace for two days, the 6th and 7th, the High Convocation day (Friday) and the day of the First Fruits, which was also the7th day Sabbath (Saturday). The 15th & 16th of Nissan.

The Jewish hierarchy would not have crucified Christ on the Holy Convocation day, and did not do so because they were afraid it would start an uprising. (Matt 26:5, John 14:2) Chapter 11 establishes the exact day of the crucifixion.

Then on the 8th day, 17th of Nissan, when it was day, the men who held Jesus in jail brought Him forth to the Jewish council and a formal trial was held, (Luke 22:63-71). Chapter 12 explains how such a trial is conducted.

The next day, the 9th day, 18th of Nissan, Jesus was taken before Pilate. Pilate soon believed that Jesus was under Herod's jurisdiction and sent Him across the city to Herod's Palace. After a lengthy trial, Herod determined Jesus to be of no threat to him and turned Him over to the Jewish Priesthood for further harassment, and finally over to the soldiers for mockery, and then returned Him to Pilate that same day. (Chapter13)

On the 10th day, 19th of Nissan, Pilate called all the people together and proceeded to try to release Jesus two more times, but ultimately failed and finally, in the afternoon, turned Jesus over to the soldiers who scourged Him through the night. (Chapter 13)

He was placed on the cross at the 3rd hr. of the 11th day of the Passover (9am), 20th day of Nissan, (Wednesday) and all the events describing that day occurred, not the day after the Passover, but a full 6 days after the Passover meal, thus, the final sin sacrifice of the seven-day Passover observance. At precisely the 9th hour, 3pm our time, that the final sin sacrifice was made, as Jesus gave up the ghost. Unwittingly, the Jews were feasting on their pascal lambs on the very days their Messiah was suffering for the sins of the world and again on the day he was crucified on their behalf. (Chapter 14)

Having died on Wednesday Christ actually had three days for his body to remain in the tomb: part of Thursday night and Thursday – 21st day Nissan, all night and all-day Friday -- 22nd day Nissan, all night and all-day Saturday – 23rd day Nissan, most of the night on Sunday – 24th day Nissan, a full three days and three nights, 72 hours, thus fulfilling the prophecies that had been spoken regarding his death and resurrection. (Matthew 12:40). (Details in Chapters 15 & 16).

Jesus' resurrection was in the early morning hours of Sunday morning – 24th Nissan (Chapter 16).

Ministry and ascension (Chapter 17).

…….. *the scriptures say what they mean, and mean what they say, we have sufficient grounds to go on and prove from the bible that the gospel has always been the same; the ordinances to fulfil its requirements, the same; and the officers to officiate, the same; and the signs and fruits from the promises, the same.*

It is indeed unfortunate that there was to be an apostasy before His coming the second time. However, it is prophesied that the day of His coming, "shall not come, except there come in a falling away first:" (2 Thes: 2: 3). Because, "some having swerved have turned aside: (1 Tim.1:6) …. "giving heed to seducing spirits:" (1 Tim. 4: 1). Even those who have received the truth in this day, "who concerning the truth had erred:" (2 Tim. 2: 18), having entered into a conversation in scholarship, and mistakenly continue to teach the precepts of men.

This book addresses those precepts.

MATTHEW 12:40 for as Jonah was three days and three nights in the belly of the great fish, so will the Son of Man be three days and three nights in the heart of the earth.

JERUSALEM AT THE TIME OF JESUS

MAP 12

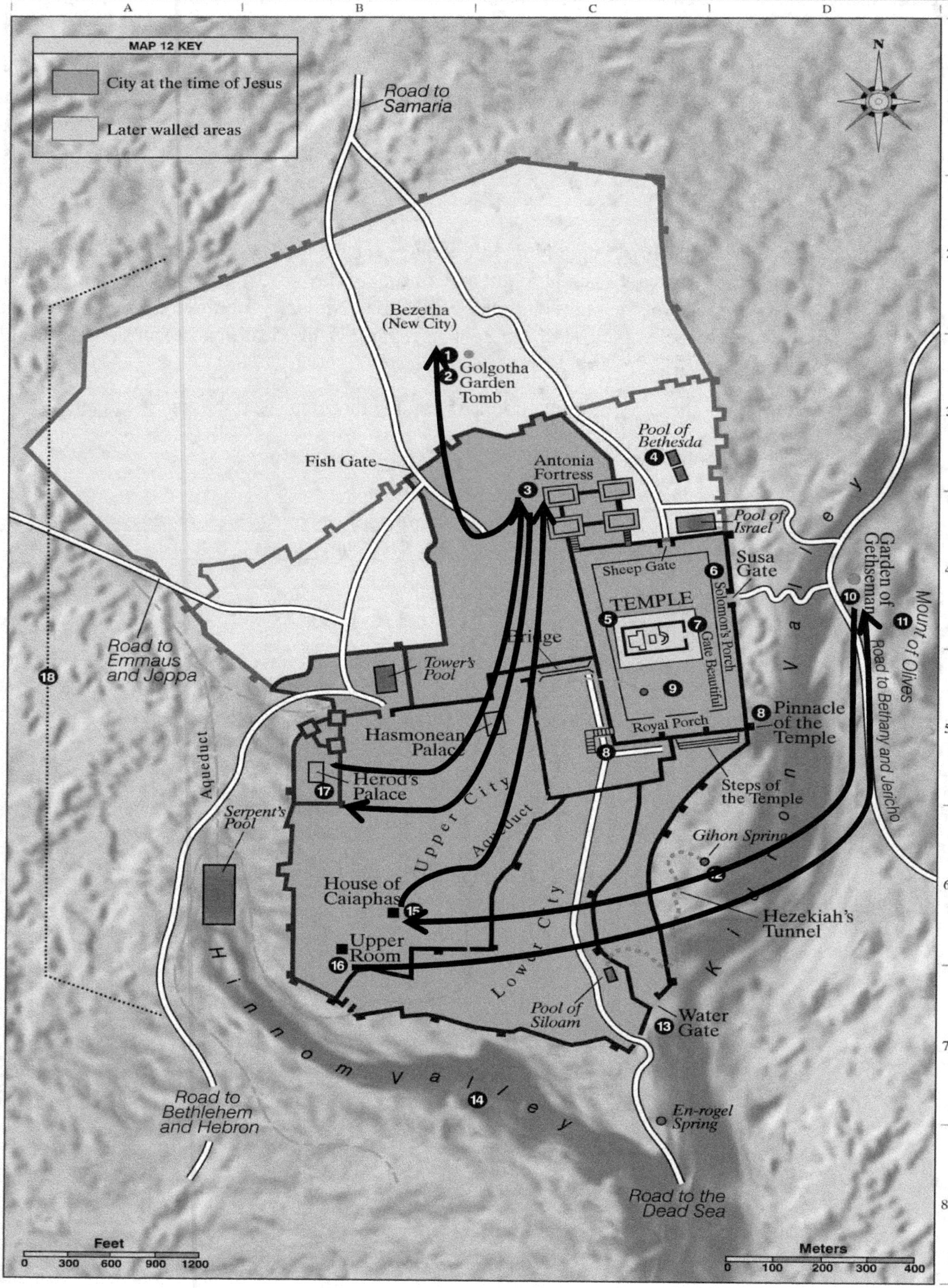

MAP 12 KEY
- City at the time of Jesus
- Later walled areas

Road to Samaria

Bezetha (New City)

1
2 Golgotha Garden Tomb

Fish Gate

Pool of Bethesda

3 Antonia Fortress

Pool of Israel

Sheep Gate

6 Susa Gate

TEMPLE

5 Solomon's Porch

7 Gate Beautiful

Royal Porch

9

8 Pinnacle of the Temple

Steps of the Temple

Bridge

Tower's Pool

Road to Emmaus and Joppa

18

Hasmonean Palace

17 Herod's Palace

Aqueduct

Serpent's Pool

Gihon Spring

12

Hezekiah's Tunnel

Kidron Valley

10 Garden of Gethsemane

11 Road to Bethany and Jericho

Mount of Olives

Upper City

House of Caiaphas 15

16 Upper Room

Lower City

Pool of Siloam

13 Water Gate

Hinnom Valley

14

En-rogel Spring

Road to Bethlehem and Hebron

Road to the Dead Sea

Feet: 0 300 600 900 1200

Meters: 0 100 200 300 400

CONTENTS

CHAPTER		Page
1	*Apostasy & Type of things to come*	1
2	*Passover Revealed*	10
3	*Discussion on the week of the atoning sacrifice*	24
4	*The Final Passover*	32
5	*Triumphal Entry*	39
6	*Day of Authority*	46
7	*Afternoon 3rd Day*	56
8	*Passover Meal*	65
9	*Mount of Olives*	75
10	*Gethsemane & Arrest*	85
11	*Establish Crucifixion Day*	92
12	*Formal Trial*	100
13	*Final Trials*	108
14	*Crucifixion*	118
15	*Burial*	129
16	*Resurrection*	135
17	*Ministry & Ascension*	146
	Harmony of Passover Gospels	152
	Law of Moses	159

1-Cor	1-Corinthians	Matt	Matthew
D&C	Doctrine & Covenants	MD	Mormon Doctrine
DNTC	Doctrinal New Testament Commentary	M&A	Mediation & Atonement
Ex.	Exodus	MM	Mortal Messiah
Gal	Galatians	Mo	Moses
Gen	Genesis	Ne	Nephi
Isa	Isaiah	2 Pet	2 Peter
I.V.	Inspired Version	Philip	Philippians
JCT	Jesus Christs Teachings	SM	Student Manual
JTC	Jesus the Christ	Teachings	Teachings of Joseph Smith
JST	Joseph Smith Translation	TGK	The Gospel Kingdom
JA	Josephus Antiquities	2 Thes	2Thessalonians
JW	Josephus Wars	2 Tim	2Timothy
Lev	Leviticus	Zech	Zechariah

After the crucifixion of the Savior and the death of the apostles, there arose a number of apostate apologists who started a great conversation of scholarship. Having already lost and twisted many of the scriptures to suit their purpose, these ecclesiastical ministers were able to convince the people, both educated and the ignorant, that their teachings were the way to Christ. For over 1800 hundred years Christianity entered the dark ages and thus remained until the reformation.

Even though there has been a reformation and a restoration of the teachings of the gospel of Jesus Christ, the conversation in scholarship remains, as the representatives of the different sects continue to teach the precepts of men that they get gain. These religious scholars maintain, (as previously stated) that the gospels are discordant with one another and cannot be read without us first being exposed to their improved scholarly methods of greater accessibility to primary sources, and they need to expose us to proper methods of form, redaction and literary criticism, thus we will better understand such things as interpolation, alteration, and editing texts.

We submit this question to you, - aren't these the very teachings and methods that brought about the original apostasy and led to the dark ages?

This book is not an attempt to prove any particular sect correct, but is a compilation of scriptures, history and inspirational common sense, and guided by prayer we may better understand and appreciate how and what the Savior went through the last two weeks of His mortal life. By reading clearly the book of Exodus, as given to Moses by the very mouth of God, we are able to discover the precise time frame of the Passover. Once this is properly established, we are easily able to discover that the Gospels of the synoptics and John in the New Testament are in exact and a perfect harmony one with another. The last pages of this book reveal the organization and harmony of these gospels and how they are in total alignment one with the other.

These scriptures have been given to us by Prophets who knew what they were writing about as they came in contact with the Savior and His teachings and had the Holy Ghost as their guide as they wrote. Any attempt to subject the works of the Prophets to man-made methods of form, redaction, and literary criticism, will inherently only lead to improper interpolation, as well as unnecessary alteration and editing of text.

This book simply compiles the scriptures, associated materials and history with as little commentary as possible, so as not to distract from the words and the teachings of God given to man.

If there be error it is mine, for the scriptures are true and are from men of God.

There is much more that could be incorporated into this discussion, but there is sufficient written here that will hopefully help you appreciate more fully what really transpired in the final two weeks of the Saviors' mortal life.

The discussed items pointed out above might seem confusing, but the following chapters will go into each one in detail.

<u>The Prophets knew</u>!!!

WORKSHEET

Comparison Calendar,

top – Exodus Calendar, middle Calendar – Jesus Actual Fulfillment of Passover, bottom Calendar – Christian Version of fulfillment

*Days of Nissan   **Days of week

Top — Exodus Calendar (Days of Nissan)

*10	Select Lamb
11	
12	
13	
14	Prepare Lamb
15	Passover feast — Sacrifice lamb day & even meal, Passover @ night — 1st day of unleavened bread — Convocation
16	2nd day feast of first fruits
17	3rd day unleavened bread — Sacrifice
18	4th day unleaven-bread — Sacrifice
19	5th day unleaven-bread — Sacrifice
20	6th day unleaven-bread — Preparation day — Final Sacrifices
21	7th day of unleavened bread — High Day — Convocation
22	
23	
24	

Middle — Jesus fulfilled Passover, Law of Moses, as confirmed by New Testament

**Day	Event
Sunday	Triumphal Entry
Monday	*Cleansed* Temple
Tuesday	*Questioned* Authority
Wednesday	Prepare Lamb. *Savior prepared Himself and family*
Thursday	Sacrifice lamb 9hr–11hr, Last supper, Passover night, Garden, Arrest & Hearings
Friday	Passover Feast Prep. Day; Sacrifice lamb and 1st day of unleavened bread, Convocation day, High day, *Jesus in cell*
Saturday	2nd day feast of first fruits — *Saturday, 7th day Sabbath, Jesus in cell*
Sunday	3rd day Sacrifice — *Formal Trial by Sanhedrin*
Monday	4th day Sacrifice — *Pilate Trial, Herod Trial*
Tuesday	5th day Sacrifice — *Pilate Trial 6th hr., Scourging*
Wednesday	6th day Preparation day, Lamb of Goat-Sin Sacrifice 9th hr, *Crucifixion 3rd hr, gave up ghost 9th Hr.*
Thursday	7th day of unleavened bread — Convocation day, *High day*
Fri.	Prepare oils & Spices
Saturday	*Saturday, 7th day* Sabbath
Sun.	Resurrection

Bottom — Christian version of fulfillment (Regular Jewish days of the week)

#	Day	Event
1	Sunday	Triumphal Entry
2	Monday	*Cleansed* Temple
3	Tuesday	*Questioned* Authority
4	Wednesday	Silence
5	Thursday	Sacrifice 9hr., even meal — Passover @ night
6	Friday	*Arrest* Trials Crucifixion — Preparation day — Burial
7		Passover Sabbath
1		Resurrection

This tear out worksheet in the book is for the purpose of allowing you to follow along more easily the narrative presented. If used with the har- mony of the four gospels in the back of the book, and those harmonies at the beginning of some chapters, without question, you will be able confirm the day by day events surrounding the Saviors' atonement.

Since the Jewish nation was driven out of Israel in 70 A.D., they were no longer able to make the sacrifices necessary to celebrate the 12 day Passover. Therefore, they simply celebrated the 7days of the feast week of unleavened bread and, as a consequence, they omitted the 5 days of preparation which preceded that week.

The Christian movement, already falling into a state of apostasy, picked up on the 7-day time frame and eventually codified this idea around the time of the council of Nicaea. The disciples dutifully recorded the events of 12 days and it is impossible to squeeze them into 7 days. However, since the apostasy began, a conversation in scholarship has ensued, that continues to find more inventive ways to advance the precepts of men in a deluge of books and fables, in order to convince blissful congregations that their interpretations of the scriptural contents are pure. When these apolo- gist scholars try to accomplish the task of incorporating 12 days of scriptures into 7 days, they end up in controversy with each other, the scriptures, the disciples that wrote the scriptures, the ancient record keepers, as well as all the different versions of the bible on the market today. Yet, they conver- se with each other, use each other's research and still each one claims they have the correct interpretation.

Most of these authors claim the scriptures surrounding the Passover cannot be harmonized or at the least not enough to be dependent on the con- text to any degree. However, there is no difficulty in harmonizing the content of all four gospels when placed in the context of 12 days. In this book, we do not attempt to interpret the scriptures but to listen to what they say and, when we do, we find the Holy Ghost will lead us to a bright understan- ding. The authorities and information we use speaks for themselves and there is no need to create narratives out of the precepts of men.

Chapter 1
The Apostasy & types of things to come

"Apostasy: an abandoning of what one believed in, as a faith, etc."[2] The definition of apostasy is simple, however the study of it as applied to religion fills volumes. As we proceed we will see how apostasy has affected the observance of the Passover.

In the Book of Exodus Chapter 12 we find the Law given to Moses concerning the Passover was a 12-day celebration, and not a 7-day observance as now celebrated by general Christianity.[3]

"James E. Talmage, Jesus the Christ, Ch.33, p.618 - p.619

> "**1. The Day of the Passover Feast. -- Controversy has been rife for many centuries as to the day of the Passover feast in the week of our Lord's death.** *That He was crucified on Friday, the day before the Jewish Sabbath, and that He rose a resurrected Being on Sunday, the day following the Sabbath of the Jews, are facts attested by the four Gospel-writers.* **From the three synoptics we infer** *that the last supper occurred on the evening of the first day of unleavened bread, and therefore at the beginning of the Jewish Friday. That the Lord's last supper was regarded by Himself and the apostles as a Passover meal appears from Matt. 26:2, 17, 18, 19 and parallel passages, Mark 14:14-16; Luke 22:11-13; as also from Luke 22:7, 15. John, however, who wrote after the synoptics and who probably had their writings before him, as is indicated by the supplementary character of his testimony or "Gospel," intimates that the last supper of which Jesus and the Twelve partook together occurred before the Feast of the Passover (John 13: 1, 2); and the same writer informs us that on the following day, Friday, the Jews refrained from entering the Roman hall of judgment, lest they be defiled and so become unfit to eat the Passover (18:28). It should be remembered that by common usage the term "Passover" was applied not only to the day or season of the observance, but to the meal itself, and particularly to the slain lamb (Matt. 26: 17; Mark 14: 12, 14, 16; Luke 22:8, 11, 13, 15; John 18:28; compare 1 Cor. 5:7). John also specifies that the day of the crucifixion was "the preparation of the Passover" (19:14), and that the next day, which was Saturday, the Sabbath, "was an high day" (verse 31), that is a Sabbath rendered doubly sacred because of its being also a feast day.*
>
> **Much has been written by way of attempt to explain this seeming discrepancy.** *No analysis of the divergent views of Biblical scholars on this subject will be attempted here; the matter is of incidental importance in connection with the fundamental facts of our Lord's betrayal and crucifixion;* **for brief summaries of opinions and concise arguments the student may be referred to Smith's Comprehensive Bible Dictionary,** *article "Passover";* **Edersheim's** *Life and Times of Jesus the Messiah, pp. 480-2, and 566-8;* **Farrar's** *Life of Christ, Appendix, Excursus 10;* **Andrews'** *Life of Our Lord,* **and Gresswell's** *Dissertations. Suffice it here to say that the apparent inconsistency may be explained by any of several* **assumptions**.*"*

It seems difficult to believe in this day and age of enlightenment and understanding, controversy and inference still surrounds the topic of the Passover. We appear to be content with the authoritative-sounding opinions and assumptions of apologists of various religious sects. Might this be a case of the blind leading the blind?

The truth of the matter is this: throughout the whole history of the world, from Adam to the present, there has been one instance of personal or group apostasy after another. The Lord gives the true gospel and government to His people, and almost immediately they forsake the principals contained therein.[4]

---

[2] Webster
[3] Ex 12
[4] MD p43

In the meridian of time the Savior personally came crying repentance and preaching the gospel, and through His apostolic ministry offered the saving truths.[5] Jesus did not restore the government and kingdom of Israel at this time, but indicated it was for another season.[6]

Even though the ancient apostles witnessed the atoning sacrifice of our Lord and Savior, they recognized the false prophets and teachers who brought in damnable heresies, even to go as far as to deny the Lord.[7] Paul warned of a great falling away would take place before the second coming.[8] Paul also warned us in the last days there would be perilous times and men would be lovers of their own selves … having a form of godliness but, denying the power thereof … ever learning but never able to come to the knowledge of the truth.[9]

Paul further stated:

2 Timothy 4:3 **For the time will come when they will not endure sound doctrine;** *but after their own lusts shall they heap to themselves teachers, having itching ears;*

4 And they shall turn away [their] ears from the truth, **and shall be turned unto fables**

In the Book of Mormon, the prophet Nephi gives a very apt description of the apostasy from the true gospel and the loss of the precious truths contained there-in, all of which occurred as soon as these great written revelations left the hands of the twelve apostles.

*"**1 Nephi 13:26** And after they go forth by the hand of the twelve apostles of the Lamb, from the Jews unto the Gentiles, thou seest the formation of that great and abominable church, which is most abominable above all other churches; for behold, they have taken away from the gospel of the Lamb many parts which are plain and most precious; and also many covenants of the Lord have they taken away.*

*27 And **all this have they done that they might pervert the right ways of the Lord**, that they might blind the eyes and harden the hearts of the children of men.*

*28 **Wherefore, thou seest that after the book hath gone forth through the hands of the great and abominable church**, that there are many plain and precious things taken away from the book, which is the book of the Lamb of God.*

*29 **And after these plain and precious things were taken away it goeth forth unto all the nations of the Gentiles;** and after it goeth forth unto all the nations of the Gentiles, yea, **even across the many waters which thou hast seen with the Gentiles which have gone forth out of captivity**, thou seest--because of the many plain and precious things which have been taken out of the book, which were plain unto the understanding of the children of men, according to the plainness which is in the Lamb of God--**because of these things which are taken away out of the gospel of the Lamb, an exceedingly great many do stumble, yea, insomuch that Satan hath great power over them.**"*

Nephi tells us the reason for us not being able to come to a clear understanding including the few followers are misled; **"they have all gone astray save it be a few, who are the humble followers of Christ; nevertheless, they are led, that in many instances they do err because they are taught by** the precepts of men."[10]

Many books have been written about the great apostasy. Without exception most all authors agree, after the death of the apostles the world sank deep into the dark ages.

---

[5] Mark 1:14-15; 16: 14-18
[6] Acts 1: 6-8
[7] 2Pet. 2:1-2
[8] 2 Thes. 2:1-3
[9] 2 Tim. 3:1-7
[10] 2 Nephi 28:14

Apostasy was well under way by the year 200 AD and history shows in 325 AD the Roman emperor Constantine assembled a council of Bishops to meet at Nicaea. The purpose of the council was to solidify the empire politically, civically, and religiously and settle the explosive problem of Arianism.

There is really no way of knowing when the current chronology of the celebration of the "week of the atoning sacrifice" or "passion week" took its final form, however the present ideology has been handed down from 325 AD, or before, as the tradition of our fathers.

Are we forever to be plagued with controversy and are we doomed to simply accept the precepts of men?

Moses and others gave us some direction as we struggle with our perplexing questions regarding the "Law of Moses":

> *"Moses 1:41 And in a day when the children of men shall esteem my words as naught and take many of them from the book which thou shalt write, behold, I will raise up another like unto thee; and they shall be had again among the children of men--among as many as shall believe.*

Paul explains we should be able to rely on the scriptures to guide us:

> *2 Timothy 3:16 All scripture [is] given by inspiration of God, and [is] profitable for doctrine, for reproof, for correction, for instruction in righteousness:*
>
> *17 That the man of God may be perfect, thoroughly furnished unto all good works.*

The Lord tells us in these end days we can expect to receive additional help from the scriptures of Ephraim:

Ezekiel 37:15 ¶ The word of the LORD came again unto me, saying,

> *16 Moreover, thou son of man, **take thee one stick, and write upon it, For Judah,** and for the children of Israel his companions: **then take another stick**, and write upon it, **For Joseph, the stick of Ephraim, and [for] all the house of Israel his companions:***
>
> *17 And join them one to another into one stick; and they shall become one in thine hand.*
> *18 And when the children of thy people shall speak unto thee, saying, wilt thou not **shew us what thou [meanest] by these**?*
>
> *19 Say unto them, Thus saith the Lord GOD; Behold, **I will take the stick of Joseph, which [is] in the hand of Ephraim, and the tribes of Israel his fellows, and will put them with him, [even] with the stick of Judah, and make them one stick, and they shall be one in mine hand.***
>
> *20 And the sticks whereon thou writest shall be in thine hand before their eyes.*

Joseph Smith was a man raised up in these last days and the stick of Ephraim placed in his hand was the book of Mormon. Speaking of the Bible and the Book of Mormon and others,

Joseph Smith said:

> **"Who is it that writes these Scriptures? Not the men of the world** or mere casual observers, **but Apostles—men who knew one gift from another, and of course were capable of writing about it;** ------**No man knows the things of God but by the Spirit of God**."[iii]

He further stated,

> "Now taking it for granted that **the scriptures say what they mean, and mean what they say,** we have sufficient grounds to go on **and prove from the bible that the gospel has always been the same; the ordinances to fulfil its requirements, the same;** and **the officers to officiate, the same; and the signs and fruits from the promises, the same.**"[11]

He also gives a helpful tool to use in our studies:

> "I have a key by which I understand the scriptures. I enquire, what was the question which drew out the answer, or caused Jesus to utter the parable? To ascertain its meaning, we must dig up the root and ascertain what it was that drew the saying out of Jesus."[12]

Can we at the very least agree with Joseph Smith, the scriptures say what they mean, and mean what they say, and we should be to able rely on them for the truth of the ordinances and the signs and fruits from the promises and thus be able to prove it from the bible?

It comes, as no surprise, the Lord preserved enough of the Bible scriptures for us to be able to reach a correct conclusion, if properly applied. When coupled with the book of Mormon, our standard works, and prophets as a source of unadulterated information to draw upon, with prayer and effort, we can proceed with confidence. As you will see as we study the Passover, we can ascertain a correct logic of the Passover and the veil of controversy will be lifted from our eyes.

Jesus was in Jerusalem to partake of the Passover, and Paul said:

> "For even Christ our Passover is sacrificed for us: Therefore, **let us keep the feast,**"[13]

and Paul further stated;

> "**wherefore the law was our schoolmaster to bring us unto Christ ......**"[14] and

JESUS himself declared **"for behold, by me redemption cometh, and in me is the law of Moses fulfilled.**[15]

Since Jesus was in Jerusalem to fulfill the Law of the Passover, it behooves us to try and understand it more fully. We find in the Book of Mormon, Nephi agreed with Joseph Smith, as he used the scriptures to prove to his people Christ would fulfill the Law of Moses.

> "2 Nephi 11:4 Behold, my soul delighteth in **proving unto my people the truth of the coming of Christ; for, for this end hath the law of Moses been given**; and **all things which have been given** of God from the beginning of the world, unto man, **are the typifying of him.**"

Many have and will come and claim to be Christ, but only He who fulfills every jot and tittle of the Law of Moses is the true Christ. What does it mean the Law of Moses has been given to the end of showing His coming and it is a <u>typifying</u> of Him?

If we look in the dictionary we find the meaning of the word
<u>Type:</u>
"a person, thing, or event that represents another, especially another that is to come".
<u>Typify:</u>
"to have or show the distinctive characteristics of, ...".

---

[11] JST p.614
[12] JST p. 367
[13] 1 Cor 5:7,8,
[14] Gal 3:24
[15] 3 Nephi 9:17,

A study of the scriptures carefully identifies the actual characteristics of the Passover and what Jesus must accomplish in order to bring about our redemption and salvation. Fulfilling the exact details of the Passover is essential because these represent the credentials of the true Christ.

"This is essential because untold millions have worshiped before the thrones of false Christs. Some deluded fanatics have bowed before persons professing to be saviors or to have power to confer salvation. Other hosts of misguided souls have trekked to desert monasteries, to mountain hermitages, to Jesuit retreats, and to meeting places of secret cults—all acting under the specious assumption that in the place of their choice they would find Christ. Still others have made money, power, worldly learning, political preferment, or the gratification of sensual lusts, their God. And virtually millions of apostate Christendom has abased themselves before the mythical throne of a mythical Christ whom they vainly suppose to be a spirit essence who is incorporeal, uncreated, immaterial, and three-in-one with the Father and Holy Spirit.[16]"

Alma explains how and why the people in the western world obeyed the Law of Moses:

"Alma 25:15 Yea, and they did keep the law of Moses; for it was expedient that they should keep the law of Moses as yet, for it was not all fulfilled. But notwithstanding the Law of Moses, they did look forward to the coming of Christ, considering that the Law of Moses was a type of his coming, and believing that they must keep those outward performances until the time that he should be revealed unto them.

*Alma 25:16 Now they did not suppose that salvation came by the law of Moses; **but the law of Moses did serve to strengthen their faith in Christ;** and thus, they did retain a hope through faith, unto eternal salvation, relying upon the spirit of prophecy, **which spake of those things to come.***

As we can see, Alma stated the **Law of Moses was a type of the Saviors atoning sacrifice** and the people kept the **outward performances in anticipation of Christ to come.** By keeping the performances of the law, it did strengthen their faith in Christ.

King Benjamin, in the Book of Mosiah, states the Lord God sent his holy prophets to every kindred, nation and tongue so the people might anticipate the coming of Christ for the purpose of receiving a remission of their sins and rejoice with great joy.[17]

However:

*Mosiah 3:14 Yet the Lord God saw that his people were a stiff-necked people, and **he appointed unto them a law, even the law of Moses.***

*15 **And many signs, and wonders, and types, and shadows showed he unto them, concerning his coming;** and also, holy prophets spake unto them concerning his coming; and yet they hardened their hearts, and understood not that **the law of Moses availeth nothing except it were through the atonement of his blood.***

Even though the people were shown signs, and wonders, and types, and shadows in regard to the fulfillment the Law of Moses, they still hardened their hearts. The law is a schoolmaster and a shadow of things to come.

Abinadi, in the book of Mosiah taught, the people who were keeping the Law of Moses, salvation does not come by the law.

*Mosiah: 13:28 ...but I say unto you, that **the time shall come when it shall no more be expedient to keep the law of Moses........; and were it not for the atonement, which God himself shall make for the sins and iniquities of his people,** that they must unavoidably perish, notwithstanding the law of Moses.*

---

[16] MD p. 269
[17] Mos 3:13

>29 And now I say unto you that **it was expedient that there should be a law given to the children of Israel,** yea, even a very strict law; for they were a **stiff-necked people**, quick to do iniquity, **and slow to remember the Lord their God;**
>
>30 Therefore there was a law given them, yea**, a law of performances and of ordinances, a law which they were to observe strictly from day to day**, to keep them in remembrance of God and their duty towards him.
>
>31 But behold, I say unto you, that **all these things were types of things to come**.[18]"

The people kept the Law of Moses with performances and ordinances <u>strictly</u> from day to day, but did they understand it? "Nay, they did not all understand the law; and this because of the hardness of their hearts;"![19] Because of this, they seemed to be unable to make the connection between Jesus being the God who would come down and make a literal sacrifice.[20]

Abinadi goes on to show the people what some actions the Savior will endure in regard to the fulfilling of the Law of Moses:

>"*Mosiah 14:7* **He was oppressed, and he was afflicted, yet he opened not his mouth; he is brought as a lamb to the slaughter**, and as a sheep before her shearers is dumb so he opened not his mouth.
>
>8 **He was taken from prison and from judgment**; and who shall declare his generation? **For he was cut off out of the land of the living**; for the transgressions of my people was he stricken.
>
>9 **And he made his grave with the wicked, and with the rich in his death; because he had done no evil, neither was any deceit in his mouth."**

The Testaments are replete with descriptions of the literal actions and words which would all be fulfilled by Jesus at the last official Passover in Jerusalem. We will discuss many of them in later chapters, but for now we are examining the Law of Mosses:

>"*Mosiah 16:14* **Therefore, if ye teach the law of Moses, also teach that it is a shadow of those things which are to come—**
>
>15 *Teach them that redemption cometh through Christ the Lord, who is the very Eternal Father. Amen."*

It's abundantly clear the people in the new world kept the Law of Moses in all of its ordinances and performances. They continually had been informed the Law was a shadow of the trials and the suffering Christ would submit himself to, and all things, even to the last jot and tittle would be fulfilled in Him.

In the Book of Alma, Amulek testifies in detail about the necessity that requires the greater sacrifice:

>"for according to the great plan of the Eternal God there must be an atonement made, or else all mankind must unavoidably perish;" …. "For it is expedient that there should be a great and last sacrifice…. but it must be an infinite and eternal sacrifice." and "; then shall the law of Moses be fulfilled; yea, it shall be all fulfilled, every jot and tittle, and none shall have passed away."

---

[18] Mos 13:27-31
[19] ibid 13: 32
[20] ibid 13: 32-37

Amulek explains the meaning of the sacrifice:

> "And behold, **this is the whole meaning of the law, every whit pointing to that great and last sacrifice; and that great and last sacrifice will be the Son of God, yea, infinite and eternal.**"[21]

There is no ambiguity in the fulfillment of God's plan, which requires the infinite and eternal sacrifice of the Son of God. Abraham was commanded to sacrifice his son, as the Father in Heaven would sacrifice His Son. When Isaac asked where the lamb was for the burnt offering,

Abraham replied,

> "My son, God will provide himself a lamb for a burnt offering."[22]

John the Baptist saw Jesus coming to him, and said:

> "Behold the Lamb of God, which taketh away the sins of the world...
>
> ...and I saw, and bare record that this is the Son of God."[23]

At the time of the great and last sacrifice, the people on the American continent had suffered great destruction and had been in great darkness for three days and three nights: *"And it came to pass that there was a voice heard among all the inhabitants of the earth..."* a voice out of the darkness declaring the nature and amount of destruction, and identifying Himself as Jesus Christ and this is His testimony:

> *"3 Nephi 9:15 Behold,* **I am Jesus Christ the Son of God.** *I created the heavens and the earth, and all things that in them are. I was with the Father from the beginning. I am in the Father, and the Father in me; and in me hath the Father glorified his name.*
>
> **16 I came unto my own, and my own received me not. And the scriptures concerning my coming are fulfilled.**
>
> *17 And as many as have received me, to them have I given to become the sons of God; and even so will I to as many as shall believe on my name, for behold,* **by me redemption cometh, and in me is the law of Moses fulfilled.**
>
> **18** *I am the light and the life of the world. I am Alpha and Omega, the beginning and the end.*
>
> *19 **And ye shall offer up unto me no more the shedding of blood; yea, your sacrifices and your burnt offerings shall be done away, for I will accept none of your sacrifices and your burnt offerings.**"*

Indeed Jesus Christ, and without hesitation or equivocation, declared the scriptures concerning his coming and the redemption in the Law of Moses as being now fulfilled.

Later, as He was ministering to them in the body, He perceived they did not fully understand.

> *"3 Nephi 15:2 And it came to pass that when Jesus had said these words he perceived that there were some among them who marveled, <u>and wondered what he would concerning the law of Moses</u>; <u>for they understood not the saying that old things had passed away, and that all things had become new.</u>*
>
> *3 And he said unto them: Marvel not that I said unto you that old things had passed away, and that all things had become new.*
>
> *4 **Behold, I say unto you that the law is fulfilled that was given unto Moses.** 5 **Behold, I am he that gave the law, and I am he who covenanted with my people Israel; therefore, the law in me is fulfilled, for I have come to fulfil the law; therefore, it hath an end.***

---

[21] Alma 34: 9-14
[22] Gen 22:7-13
[23] John 1:29-36

6 Behold, I do not destroy the prophets, for as many as have not been fulfilled in me, verily I say unto you, shall all be fulfilled.

7 And because I said unto you that old things have passed away, I do not destroy that which hath been spoken concerning things which are to come.

8 For behold, the covenant which I have made with my people is not all fulfilled; **but the law which was given unto Moses hath an end in me.**

9 **Behold, I am the law,** *and the light. Look unto me, and endure to the end, and ye shall live; for unto him that endureth to the end will I give eternal life.*

10 Behold, I have given unto you the commandments; therefore, keep my commandments. And ***this is the law and the prophets, for they truly testified of me."***

Jesus declared to the people the law that was given to Moses is now fulfilled. There is no doubt the law of the Passover is now fulfilled, and who fulfilled it.

Jesus declared He was the one who gave the law, He was the one who made the covenants, He is the one who fulfilled the law and in Him it has an end. There are other portions of the law which have been given by the Prophets and are yet to be fulfilled, but the Passover law is fulfilled in Him.

What we have discussed thus far has been a confirmation of a portion of the patriarchal-Mosaic covenant or testament done away in Christ. However, the law of carnal commandments, the law of performances and ordinances revealed through Moses, was an old covenant as compared with the gospel restored by Jesus and his apostles. The New Testament or covenant, this restored gospel, was the same testament in force between God and his people from Adam to Mosses in both the old and the new worlds.[24] Modern revelation confirms the truth of ancient revelation.

Some people maintain these performances and ordinances are **mere symbols** of the Savior's sacrifice, and in reality, He never literally fulfilled the Law in every detail. If we look up the meaning of the word symbol we find: Symbol – an object used to represent something abstract -

Abstract – thought of apart from any particular instances or material objects. Not easy to understand; abstruse. Loosely theoretical; not practical.

We fail to find the use of the word "symbol" in the Bible, the Book of Mormon or the D & C. We feel those who use the word "symbolism" have mistakenly or deliberately interchanged it with the word "similitude".

"*Moses 6:62 And now, behold, I say unto you: This is the plan of salvation unto all men,* **through the blood of mine Only Begotten, who shall come in the meridian of time.**

63 And behold, ***all things have their likeness, and all things are created and made to bear record of me****, both things which are* ***temporal, and*** *things which are* ***spiritual****; things which are in the heavens above, and things which are on the earth, and things which are in the earth, and things which are under the earth, both above and beneath: all things bear record of me.*

Earlier on he said:

"*Moses 5:7 And then* **the angel spake**, *saying:* **This thing is a similitude of the sacrifice of the Only Begotten of the Father,** *which is full of grace and truth.*

And Aaron and Miriam complained against Moses and the Lord called them out and came down to them in the pillar of a cloud:

"*Numbers 12:6 And he said, Hear now my words:* **If there be a prophet among you,** *[I] the LORD will make myself known unto him in a vision, [and] will speak unto him in a dream.*

---
[24] MD p. 542

7 My servant Moses [is] not so, who [is] faithful in all mine house.

*8 With him will **I speak mouth to mouth**, even apparently, and not in dark speeches; **and the similitude of the LORD shall he behold**: wherefore then were ye not afraid to speak against my servant Moses?"*

The Lord confirmed to Aaron, He spoke to Moses face to face and showed Moses the **similitude** of what He the Lord would do to fulfill the law he was about to receive.

In Hosea we find:

*"Hosea 12:9 And I [that am] the LORD thy God from the land of Egypt will yet make thee to dwell in tabernacles, **as in the days of the solemn feast**.*

*10 I have also spoken by the prophets, and I have multiplied visions, **and used similitudes, by the ministry of the prophets.***

And in the day of solemn feast:

"Exodus 12:1 ¶ AND the LORD spake unto Moses and Aaron in the land of Egypt, saying..."

We now see in the 12th Chapter of Exodus, the Lord spoke directly with Moses and the law was established.

And in Jacob we find:

*"Jacob 4:5 Behold, **they believed in Christ and worshiped the Father in his name,** and also we worship the Father in his name. **And for this intent we keep the law of Moses,** it pointing our souls to him; and for this cause it is sanctified unto us for righteousness, even as it was accounted unto Abraham in the wilderness to be obedient unto the commands of God in offering up his son Isaac, **which is a similitude of God and his Only Begotten Son."***

<u>Webster's Dictionary:</u>

Similitude – A person or thing resembling another; counterpart. Form; image. Similarity; likeness.

Counterpart -- A person or thing that corresponds to or closely resembles another. A thing that completes or complements another.

It now becomes apparent, the Lord spoke directly with Mosesit is ptistand gave to us the Law of Moses with its performances and ordinances. These performances are not just a symbolic representation of the Eternal sacrifice to be made, but is a <u>similitude</u> revealed to us concerning the Lord's sacrifice as the Lamb slain from the foundation of the world and the keystone in the plan of salvation. The law of the Passover is <u>not just a symbol, but a counterpart,</u> that Jesus promised He would personally complete and fulfill and Jesus was the **prototype** of the Law. A clear understanding will begin to erase the controversy that surrounds the Passover with confusion.

The Lord had commanded his people to keep the feast of the Passover and, it was during the time of this feast 1500 years later, Jesus had partaken of the feast along with his disciples and He was betrayed and ultimately crucified. It was on the occasion of the last supper He instituted the ordinance of the sacrament to the church. (Matt, Mark, & Luke)

Paul said: *"**Let us keep the feast**, not with old leaven, neither leaven of malice or wickedness; but with the unleavened bread of sincerity and truth."*[25]

Clearly, we are instructed to remember, with love and faith in our hearts, the sequence of events associated with the Passover and how the Savior had fulfilled the Law of Moses with His Eternal sacrifice for us.

---

[25] 1 Cor. 5:6-8

Chapter 2
Passover Revealed

The Passover is a commemoration of Israel's deliverance from Egyptian bondage, and points particularly to the fact the destroying angle passed over the homes of the faithful sons of Jacob, when the first-born in all the families of Egypt were slain.[26]

Forty years had passed since Moses fled from Egypt and, while tending his father-in-law's flock, he observed a burning bush, but was not burned, and he turned aside to see. God spoke to Moses, out of the bush, and told him of the affliction His children in Egypt were enduring and He desired to free them from bondage.[27]

"For" said God *"they shall inhabit this happy land which your forefather Abraham inhabited, and shall have the enjoyment of all sorts of good things;* **and thou, by thy prudence, shalt guide them to those good things."**[28]

God began to instruct Moses about what He expected him to do:

Exodus 3:10 Come now therefore, and **I will send thee unto Pharaoh, that thou mayest bring forth my people the children of Israel out of Egypt.**

11 ¶ And Moses said unto God, **Who [am] I, that I should go unto Pharaoh,** *and that I should bring forth the children of Israel out of Egypt?*

Moses felt totally unworthy and inadequate to accomplish what the Lord wanted him to do and he found many excuses and reasons not to go. The Lord identifies himself as the God of Abraham, Isaac and Jacob and as the Great I AM, and reveals the plan to smite Egypt and bring the people out with great wealth.[29]

Exodus 4:1 ¶ AND Moses answered and said, But, behold, they will not believe me, nor hearken unto my voice: for they will say, The LORD hath not appeared unto thee.

2 And the LORD said unto him, **What [is] that in thine hand? And he said, A rod.**

3 And he said, **Cast it on the ground**. *And he cast it on the ground*, **and it became a serpent;** *and Moses fled from before it.*

4 And the LORD said unto Moses, **Put forth thine hand, and take it by the tail**. *And he put forth his hand, and* **caught it, and it became a rod in his hand:**

5 That they may believe that the LORD God of their fathers, the God of Abraham, the God of Isaac, and the God of Jacob, hath appeared unto thee.

6 And the **LORD said furthermore unto him, Put now thine hand into thy bosom.** *And he put his hand into his bosom: and when he* **took it out, behold, his hand [was] leprous as snow.**

7 And he said, **Put thine hand into thy bosom again**. *And he put his hand into his bosom again;* **and plucked it out of his bosom, and, behold, it was turned again as his [other] flesh.**

8 And it shall come to pass, if they will not believe thee, neither hearken to the voice of the first sign, that they will believe the voice of the latter sign.

9 And it shall come to pass, **if they will not believe also these two signs, neither hearken unto thy voice**, *that thou shalt take of the water of the river, and pour [it] upon the dry [land]: and the* **water which thou takest out of the river shall become blood upon the dry [land].**

10 ¶ And Moses said unto the LORD, O my Lord, I [am] not eloquent, neither heretofore, nor since thou hast spoken unto thy servant: but I [am] slow of speech, and of a slow tongue.

Moses was concerned the people in Egypt would not believe him, so the Lord gave Moses certain sings and wonders to convince them otherwise. Moses tried to excuse himself from the task by claiming to be slow of speech and slow of tongue, and thus, the anger of the Lord was kindled against Moses. The Lord informs Moses his brother Aaron will be sent to be his mouthpiece.[30]

---

[26] Ex. 12
[27] Ex. 3:1-9
[28] JA. 2-12-1
[29] Ex. 3:12-22
[30] Ex 4:14-18

Moses, with signs and wonders to perform, is finally convinced and makes arrangements with his family to head to Egypt to serve the Lord.[31]

> *Exodus 4:27 And* **LORD said to Aaron, go into the wilderness to meet Moses**. *And he went, and met him in the mount of God, and kissed him.*
>
> *28 And* **Moses told Aaron all the words of the LORD** *who had sent him, and all the signs which he had commanded him.*

Moses, Aaron and all that were with them went into Egypt and entered Goshen and the word spread throughout, "Moses is back! Moses is back!"

> *Exodus 4:29 And Moses and Aaron went and gathered together all the elders of the children of Israel:*
>
> **30 And Aaron spake all the words which the LORD had spoken unto Moses, and did the signs in the sight of the people.**
>
> **31 And the people believed**: *and when they heard that the LORD had visited the children of Israel, and that he had looked upon their affliction, then they bowed their heads and worshipped.*

As spokesman, Aaron laid out the sacred plan of the Lord to liberate Israel. Moses came forth and declared in the name of the Great "I AM", and to witness that he did not come as a self-appointed liberator, he threw his staff to the ground and it transformed into a writhing, living serpent. Moses grasped it by the tail and retrieved a simple shepherds' staff. He thrust his hand into his robe and brought forth a white hand ulcerated with dreaded plague of leprosy. He thrust his hand back into his robe, drew it forth, cleansed and healed with radiance of healthy flesh. "The people believed".

But, the real challenge was now to face Pharaoh:

> *Exodus 5:1 ¶ AND afterward* **Moses and Aaron went in, and told Pharaoh**, *Thus saith the LORD God of Israel,* **Let my people go, that they may hold a feast unto me in the wilderness.**
>
> **2 And Pharaoh said, Who [is] the LORD, that I should obey his voice** *to let Israel go? I know not the LORD, neither will I let Israel go.*
>
> *3 ¶ And they said, The God of the Hebrews hath met with us: let us go, we pray thee, three days' journey into the desert, and sacrifice unto the LORD our God; lest he fall upon us with pestilence, or with the sword.*
>
> *4 And* **the king of Egypt said unto them, Wherefore do ye, Moses and Aaron, let the people from their works? get you unto your burdens**

Pharaoh decides the Jewish slaves have too much time on their hands when they petition him with a contemptible plot for freedom. Therefore, he orders his officers and taskmasters to have the slaves gather the straw themselves to make the bricks, and the tally will remain the same.[32]

Within two days the situation became too grievous to bear and the officers of the children of Israel cried unto Pharaoh for relief, but to no avail.[33]

As the officers left the palace:

> *Exodus 5:20 And they met Moses and Aaron, who stood in the way,* **as they came forth from Pharaoh:**
>
> *21 And they said unto them, The LORD look upon you, and judge; because ye have made our savor to be* **abhorred in the eyes of Pharaoh, and in the eyes of his servants, to put a sword in their hand to slay us.**

Moses and Aaron, somewhat puzzled and disappointed by this turn of events, attempted to make contact with the Lord:

> *Exodus 5:22 And* **Moses returned unto the LORD, and said**, *Lord, wherefore hast thou [so] evil entreated this people? why [is] it [that] thou hast sent me?*

---

[31] Ex 4:18-21
[32] Ex. 5-14
[33] Ex. 5:15-19

       23 For since I came to Pharaoh to speak in thy name, he hath done evil to this people; **neither hast thou delivered thy people at all.**

    The Lord replied and reassured Moses of what was about to happen and why.

       Exodus 6:1 ¶ THEN the LORD said unto Moses, **Now shalt thou see what I will do to Pharaoh***: for with a strong hand shall he let them go, and with a strong hand shall he drive them out of his land.*[34]

Then Moses was reassured by the Lord that He was indeed Jehovah and instructed how they must again go before Pharaoh:

       Exodus 7:1 ¶ AND the LORD said unto Moses, See, **I have made thee a god to Pharaoh: and Aaron thy brother shall be thy prophet.**

       2 Thou shalt speak all that I command thee: and **Aaron thy brother shall speak unto Pharaoh,** *that he send the children of Israel out of his land.*

       3 **And I will harden Pharaoh's heart**, *and multiply my signs and my wonders in the land of Egypt.*

       4 **But Pharaoh shall not hearken unto you, that I may lay my hand upon Egypt**, *and bring forth mine armies, [and] my people the children of Israel, out of the land of Egypt by great judgments.*

In spite of the hardships they were about to encounter, the Lord told them they must move on.

       Exodus 7:8 ¶ And the LORD spake unto Moses and unto Aaron, saying,

       9 When Pharaoh shall speak unto you, saying, **Shew a miracle for you***: ...*

    So, Moses came again to the new king and told him how much he, Moses, had done for the good of Egypt when he had been commander of the armies during the war with the Ethiopians. He told the king how he had faced great danger, but he had fought for the Egyptians as if they were his own people, without ever receiving any proper returns he deserved. Moses informed Pharaoh distinctly what God had said to him on Mt. Sinai, and showed the king the signs he had been given to prove his authority. Moses then exhorted the king to believe what he told him and not oppose the will of God.

    Yet was the king very angry with him and called him an ill man, who had formerly run away from his Egyptian slavery, and now come back with deceitful tricks, and wonders, and magical arts to astonish him. The king derided Moses even more, and said, **I will shew a miracle for you**, and commanded the priests to throw down their rods, and they became serpents.'[35]

    'But Moses was not daunted at it; and said, "O king, I do not myself despise the wisdom of the Egyptians, but I say what I do is so much superior to what these do by magic arts and tricks, as Divine power exceeds the power of man:…[36]'

       Exodus 7:12 For they cast down every man his rod, and they became serpents: but **Aaron's rod swallowed up their rods**.

    Never the less:

       13 And he hardened Pharaoh's heart, that he hearkened not unto them; as the LORD had said.

As the Lord commanded Moses, the next morning the plagues that were to be inflicted on Egypt began, and are as follows:

1. The water turned into blood.
2. The plague of the frogs.
3. The plague of the lice.
4. The plague of flies (insects).
5. The plague of murrain among the cattle.

---

[34] Ex: 6:1-30
[35] JA. 2-13-2&3
[36] JA. 2-13-3; Ex 7: 9-12

6. The plague of boils and blains.
7. The plague of fire mingled with hail.
8. The plague of locusts.
9. The plague of thick darkness.
10. The slaying of the first-born.

First Plague: Water becomes blood

Exodus 7;17 Thus saith the LORD, In this thou shalt know that I [am] the LORD: behold, ***I will smite with the rod that [is] in mine hand upon the waters*** *which [are] in the river, and they shall be turned to blood. , and in the sight of Pharaoh, and in the sight of his servants;* ***and all the waters that [were] in the river were turned to blood.***

'For the Egyptian river ran with bloody water at the command of god, insomuch that it could not be drunk, and they had no other spring of water neither; for the water was **not only the color of blood, but it brought upon those who ventured to drink of it, great pains and bitter torment**. Such was the river to the Egyptians; **but it was sweet and fit for drinking to the Hebrews**, and no way was it different from what it naturally used to be. As the king therefore knew not what to do under these surprising circumstances, and was in fear for the Egyptians, he gave the Hebrews leave to go away; but when the plague ceased, he changed his mind again, and would not suffer them to go.[37]'

Exodus 8:1 ¶ AND the LORD spake unto Moses, ***Go unto Pharaoh, and say*** *unto him,* ***Thus saith the LORD, Let my people go, t****hat they may serve me.*

2 And ***if thou refuse*** *to let [them] go, behold,* ***I will smite all thy borders with frogs:***
Pharaoh, however did not let them go!

Second Plague: Frogs

Exodus 8:5 And the ***LORD spake unto Moses, Say unto Aaron, Stretch forth thine hand with thy rod over the streams, over the rivers, and over the ponds, and cause frogs*** *to come up upon the land of Egypt.*

6 And Aaron stretched out his hand over the waters of Egypt; ***and the frogs came up, and covered the land of Egypt.***

'An innumerable multitude of frogs consumed the fruit of the ground; the river was also full of them, insomuch that those who drew **water had it spoiled by the blood of these animals**, as they died in, and were destroyed by, the water; and the country was full of filthy slime, as they were born, and as they died; they also spoiled the vessels in their houses which they used, and **were found among what they eat and what they drank, and came in great numbers upon their beds.** There was also an **ungrateful smell, and a stink** arose from them, as they were born, as they died therein. The king ordered Moses to take the Hebrews with him, and be gone. Upon which the whole multitude of frogs vanished away; and both the land and the river returned to their former natures. But as soon as the Pharaoh saw the land free from this plague, he forgot the cause of it, and retained the Hebrews.[38]'

Accordingly, God punished his falseness with another plague, added to the former:[39]

Third Plague: Lice

Exodus 8:16 ¶ And the LORD said unto Moses, Say unto Aaron, Stretch out thy rod, and smite the dust of the land, that it may become lice throughout all the land of Egypt.

'The **magicians of Pharaoh tried to duplicate this feat but they could not do so**, and concluded this **must truly be the finger of God.**[40] Pharaoh's own magicians turned against Pharaoh, but he would not listen and once again hardened his heart against Moses.

Accordingly, God punished his falseness with this plague, added to the former; for there arose out of the bodies of the Egyptians an innumerable quantity of lice, by which, wicked as they were, they miserably perished,

---

[37] JA. 2-14-1; Ex. 7: 15-25
[38] JA. 2-14-2, Ex. 8:5-14
[39] JA. 2-14-3
[40] Exodus 17-19

as not able to destroy this vermin either with washes or ointments. …upon fear into which Pharaoh reasoned himself, least his people should be destroyed…. for he gave leave for Hebrews themselves to depart. However, once the plagued ceased Pharaoh once again hardened his heart, hereby he provoked God to be more vehemently angry at him. [41]'

Fourth Plague: Insects

Exodus 8:20 ¶ And **the LORD said unto Moses, Rise up early in the morning, and stand before Pharaoh;** *lo, he cometh forth to the water; and say unto him,* **Thus saith the LORD, Let my people go, that they may serve me.**

21 Else, **if thou wilt not** *let my people go, behold,* **I will send swarms [of flies] upon thee,** *and upon thy servants, and upon thy people, and into thy houses: and* **the houses of the Egyptians shall be full of swarms [of flies], and also the ground whereon they [are].**

22 And I will sever in **that day the land of Goshen, in which my people dwell, that no swarms [of flies] shall be there; to the end thou mayest know that I [am] the LORD in the midst of the earth.**

23 And I will put a division between my people and thy people: tomorrow shall this sign be.

24 And the LORD did so; **and there came a grievous swarm [of flies]** *into the house of Pharaoh, and [into] his servants' houses, and into all the land of Egypt: the land was corrupted by reason of the swarm [of flies].*

25 And Pharaoh called for Moses and for Aaron, and said, Go ye, sacrifice to your God in the land.

But as usual, Pharaoh bargained with Moses to finally convince him to lift the plague of flies and Moses did so. But as before, Pharaoh hardened his heart and would not let the people go.[42]

Fifth Plague: Murrain

Exodus 9:1 ¶ THEN *the LORD said unto Moses,* **Go in unto Pharaoh, and tell him, Thus saith the LORD God of the Hebrews, Let my people go, that they may serve me.**

2 For **if thou refuse** *to let [them] go, and wilt hold them still,*

3 Behold, **the hand of the LORD is upon thy cattle which [is] in the field, upon the horses, upon the asses, upon the camels, upon the oxen, and upon the sheep: [there shall be] a very grievous murrain.**

4 And the LORD shall sever between the cattle of Israel and the cattle of Egypt: and there shall nothing die of all [that is] the children's of Israel.

5 And the LORD appointed a set time, saying, To-morrow the LORD shall do this thing in the land.

6 **And the LORD did that thing on the morrow,** *and all the cattle of Egypt died: but of the cattle of the children of Israel died not one.*

7 And Pharaoh sent, and, behold, **there was not one of the cattle of the Israelites dead. And the heart of Pharaoh was hardened, and he did not let the people go.**

Even though the men of Egypt underwent this plague of distemper, Pharaoh would not yield to the will of God.[43]

Sixth Plague: Boils & Blains

Exodus 9:8 ¶ *And the* **LORD said unto Moses and unto Aaron, Take to you handfuls of ashes of the furnace, and let Moses sprinkle it toward the heaven in the sight of Pharaoh.**

9 And it shall become small dust in all the land of Egypt, and shall be a boil breaking forth [with] blains upon man, and upon beast, throughout all the land of Egypt.

---

[41] JA. 2 -14:3
[42] Ex. 8:25-32
[43] JA. 2-14-3

*10 And they **took ashes of the furnace**, and stood before Pharaoh; **and Moses sprinkled it up toward heaven; and it became a boil breaking forth [with] blains upon man, and upon beast.***

*11 And the magicians could not stand before Moses because of the boils; for the **boil was upon the magicians, and upon all the Egyptians**.*

*12 **And the LORD hardened the heart of Pharaoh**, and he hearkened not unto them; as the LORD had spoken unto Moses*

But when the king was not brought to reason by this plague:

*Exodus 9:13 ¶ And **the LORD said unto Moses, Rise up early in the morning, and stand before Pharaoh, and say unto him, Thus saith the LORD God of the Hebrews, Let my people go, that they may serve me.***

14 For I will at this time send all my plagues upon thine heart, and upon thy servants, and upon thy people; that thou mayest know that [there is] none like me in all the earth.

But Pharaoh disregarded the warning of Moses:[44]

Seventh Plague: Hail

*Exodus 9:22 ¶ And the **LORD said unto Moses, Stretch forth thine hand toward heaven, that there may be hail in all the land of Egypt**, upon man, and upon beast, and upon every herb of the field, throughout the land of Egypt.*

23 And Moses stretched forth his rod toward heaven: and the LORD sent thunder and hail, and the fire ran along upon the ground; and the LORD rained hail upon the land of Egypt.

*24 **So there was hail, and fire mingled with the hail, very grievous, such as there was none like it in all the land of Egypt since it became a nation.***

*25 And the hail smote throughout all the land of Egypt all that [was] **in the field, both man and beast; and the hail smote every herb of the field, and brake every tree of the field.***

*26 **Only in the land of Goshen, where the children of Israel [were], was there no hail.***

"Hail was sent down from heaven ; and such hail it was, as the climate of Egypt had never suffered before, nor was it like to that which falls in other climates in winter time, but was larger than that which falls in the middle of spring to those that dwell in the northern and north-western regions. This hail broke down their boughs laden with fruit."[45]

*Exodus 9:27 **And Pharaoh sent, and called for Moses and Aaron, and said unto them**, I have sinned this time: the LORD [is] righteous, and I and my people [are] wicked.*

*28 **Intreat the LORD (for [it is] enough) that there be no [more]** mighty thunderings and hail; and I will let you go, and ye shall stay no longer.*

*29 And **Moses said unto him, As soon as I am gone out of the city, I will spread abroad my hands unto the LORD; [and] the thunder shall cease, neither shall there be any more hail; that thou mayest know how that the earth [is] the LORD'S.***

30 But as for thee and thy servants, I know that ye will not yet fear the LORD God.

Mosses did as he said he would and he raised his hands and the plague of ceased.

*34 And **when Pharaoh saw that the rain and the hail and the thunders were ceased, he sinned yet more, and hardened his heart, he and his servants.***

35 And the heart of Pharaoh was hardened, neither would he let the children of Israel go; as the LORD had spoken by Moses.

With Egypt virtually in ruins, and all hopes of the future fruits of the ground, Pharaoh could still not make a wise or sensible decision which would be to his advantage.

*Exodus 10:3 And **Moses and Aaron came in unto Pharaoh**, and said unto him, Thus saith the LORD God of the Hebrews, **How long wilt thou refuse to humble thyself before me? let my people go, that they may serve me**.*

---

[44] Ex. 9:14-21
[45] JA. 2-15-4

*4 Else, **if thou refuse** to let my people go, behold, tomorrow will **I bring the locusts into thy coast:***

Moses proceeded to describe the plague that was about to be visited upon them and having done so, left his presence.[46]

*Exodus 10:7 And **Pharaoh's servants said unto him, How long shall this man be a snare unto us?** let the men go, that they may serve the LORD their God: **knowest thou not yet that Egypt is destroyed?***

*8 And **Moses and Aaron were brought again unto Pharaoh: and he said unto them, Go, serve the LORD your God: [but] who [are] they that shall go?***

Pharaoh then proceeds to dictate the terms of their leaving by limiting the religious ceremonies to just the men, and when Moses and could not agree to the conditions which were being placed upon them, they were driven out from Pharaoh's presence.[47]

Eighth Plague: Locusts

*Exodus 10:12 ¶ And **the LORD said unto Moses, Stretch out thine hand over the land of Egypt for the locusts,** that they may come up upon the land of Egypt, **and eat every herb of the land, [even] all that the hail hath left**.*

*13 And **Moses stretched forth his rod** over the land of Egypt, and the LORD brought an east wind upon the land all that day, and all [that] night; [and] when it was morning, the east wind brought the locusts.*

*14 And the locusts went up over all the land of Egypt, and rested in all the coasts of Egypt: **very grievous [were they]; before them there were no such locusts as they, neither after them shall be such.***

*15 **For they covered the face of the whole earth, so that the land was darkened; and they did eat every herb of the land, and all the fruit of the trees which the hail had left: and there remained not any green thing in the trees, or in the herbs of the field, through all the land of Egypt.***

After this a tribe of locusts consumed the seed which was not hurt by the hail: so that to the Egyptians all hopes of the future fruits of the ground were entirely lost.[48]

*Exodus 10:16 **Then Pharaoh called for Moses** and Aaron in haste; and he said, I have sinned against the LORD your God, and against you.*

*17 Now therefore forgive, I pray thee, my sin only this once, and **intreat the LORD your God, that he may take away from me this death only**. 18 And he went out from Pharaoh, and intreated the LORD.*

*19 And **the LORD turned a mighty strong west wind, which took away the locusts**, and cast them into the Red sea; there remained not one locust in all the coasts of Egypt.*

*20 But the **LORD hardened Pharaoh's heart, so that he would not let the children of Israel go**.*

But Pharaoh, being led not so much by his folly as by his wickedness, even when he saw the cause of his miseries, still contested with God, and willfully deserted the cause of virtue.[49]

Ninth Plague: Darkness

*Exodus 10:21 ¶ And **the LORD said unto Moses, Stretch out thine hand toward heaven, that there may be darkness over the land of Egypt, even darkness [which] may be felt**.*

*22 And Moses stretched forth his hand toward heaven; and there was **a thick darkness in all the land of Egypt three days:***

---

[46] Ex. 10:5-6
[47] Ex. 10:9-11
[48] JA 2-14 -4
[49] JA 2-14 -5

> *23 They saw not one another, neither rose any from his place for three days: but all the children of Israel had light in their dwellings.*

'The thick darkness, without the least light, spread itself over the Egyptians, whereby their sight being obstructed, and their breathing hindered by the thickness of the air, they died miserably, and under terror lest they should be swallowed up by the dark cloud.'[50]

The same kind of darkness and length of time was descended on the Nephites in the New World when the Savior gave up the ghost on the cross:

> *3 Nephi 8:20 And it came to pass **that there was thick darkness upon all the face of the land, insomuch that the inhabitants thereof who had not fallen could feel the vapor of darkness;***
>
> *21 And there could be no light, because of the darkness, neither candles, neither torches; neither could there be fire kindled with their fine and exceedingly dry wood, so that there could not be any light at all;*
>
> *22 And there was **not any light seen, neither fire, nor glimmer, neither the sun, nor the moon, nor the stars, for so great were the mists of darkness which were upon the face of the land.***

When the darkness finally lifted from the face of the land:

> *Exodus 10:24 And Pharaoh called unto Moses, and said, **Go ye, serve the LORD; only let your flocks and your herds be stayed**: let your little ones also go with you.*
>
> *25 And Moses said, **Thou must give us also sacrifices and burnt offerings**, that we may sacrifice unto the LORD our God.*
>
> *26 Our cattle also shall go with us; there shall not an hoof be left behind; for thereof must we take to serve the LORD our God; and we know not with what we must serve the LORD, until we come thither.*
>
> *27 But the **LORD hardened Pharaoh's heart, and he would not let them go.***

When Moses told Pharaoh these terms were unacceptable and said to him: "How long wilt thou be disobedient to the command of God? For he enjoins thee to let the Hebrews go; nor is there any other way of being freed from the calamities you are under, unless you do so."[51]

> *Exodus 10:28 And **Pharaoh said unto him, Get thee from me, take heed to thyself, see my face no more; for in [that] day thou seest my face thou shalt die.***
>
> *29 And Moses said, Thou hast spoken well, **I will see thy face again no more.***

Moses leaves the presence of Pharaoh and returns to Goshen and the Lord desires to prepare Israel for the Passover which is to come.

> *Exodus 11:1 ¶ AND the **LORD said unto Moses, Yet will I bring one plague [more] upon Pharaoh, and upon Egypt; afterwards he will let you go hence**: when he shall let [you] go, he shall surely thrust you out hence altogether.*
>
> *2 Speak now in the ears of the people, and <u>**let every man borrow of his neighbor, and every woman of her neighbor, jewels of silver, and jewels of gold.**</u>*
>
> *3 <u>**And the LORD gave the people favour in the sight of the Egyptians**</u>. Moreover, the man **Moses [was] very great** in the land of Egypt, **in the sight of Pharaoh's servants, and in the sight of the people**.*
>
> *4 ¶ And Moses said, **Thus saith the LORD, About midnight will I go out into the midst of Egypt:***
>
> *5 **And all the firstborn in the land of Egypt shall die**, from the firstborn of Pharaoh that siteth upon his throne, even unto the firstborn of the maidservant that [is] behind the mill; and all the firstborn of beasts.*
>
> *6 And **there shall be a great cry throughout all the land of Egypt**, such as there was none like it, nor shall be like it any more.*

---

[50] JA. 2-14-5
[51] JA. 2-14-5

*7 **But against any of the children of Israel shall not a dog move his tongue, against man or beast**: that ye may know how that the LORD doth put a difference between the Egyptians and Israel.*

8 And all these thy servants shall come down unto me, and bow down themselves unto me, saying, Get thee out, and all the people that follow thee: and after that I will go out. And he went out from Pharaoh in a great anger.

9 And the LORD said unto Moses, Pharaoh shall not hearken unto you; that my wonders may be multiplied in the land of Egypt.

10 And Moses and Aaron did all these wonders before Pharaoh: and the LORD hardened Pharaoh's heart, so that he would not let the children of Israel go out of his land.

President John Taylor said; "In regard to the offering of sacrifices, it is very evident that in the days of Moses the children of Israel were quite familiar with the rite, as also were the Egyptians. … It is further stated, that after a time, when all other judgments had failed to bring about the desired effect on Pharaoh, that the tenth plague was about to take place".[52]

In order to prepare the children of Israel for the exodus from Egypt that was also about to take place, the Lord instituted the Passover and the feast of unleavened bread.

The Lord desired to commemorate this great event by instructing Moses to memorialize the month by making it the first month of the year, to memorialize the day by celebrating it with the "feast of Passover", to memorialize the flight from Egypt with the "feast of unleavened bread", and to memorialize their freedom from bondage by collecting from the Egyptians vast quantities of gold, silver and raiment. And God gave Moses explicate instructions on the Passover and the feast of unleavened bread:

Exodus 12:1 ¶ ***AND the LORD spake unto Moses and Aaron** in the land of Egypt, saying,*

*2 **This month** [shall be] unto you the beginning of months**: it [shall be] the first month of the year to you.***

*3 Speak ye unto all the congregation of Israel, saying**, IN THE TENTH [DAY] OF THIS MONTH** they **shall take to them every man a lamb,** according to the house of [their] fathers, a lamb for an house:*

*4 And if the household be too little for the lamb, let him and his neighbor next unto his house take [it] according to the number of the souls; **every man according to his eating shall make your count for the lamb.***

*5 **Your lamb shall be without blemish, a male of the first year**: ye shall take [it] out **from the sheep, or from the goats**:*

*6 And ye shall **keep it up until the FOURTEENTH DAY OF THE SAME MONTH:** and the whole assembly of the congregation of Israel shall kill **it in the evening.***

7 And they shall take of the blood, and strike [it] on the two side posts and on the upper door post of the houses, wherein they shall eat it.

8 And they shall eat the flesh in that night, roast with fire, and unleavened bread; [and] with bitter [herbs] they shall eat it.

9 Eat not of it raw, nor sodden at all with water, but roast [with] fire; his head with his legs, and with the purtenance thereof.

*10 And **ye shall let nothing of it remain until the morning; and that which remaineth of it until the morning ye shall burn with fire.***

11 And thus shall ye eat it; [with] your loins girded, your shoes on your feet, and your staff in your hand; and ye shall eat it in haste: it [is] the LORD'S Passover.

*12 **For I will pass through the land of Egypt this night, and will smite all the firstborn in the land of Egypt, both man and beast; and against all the gods of Egypt I will execute judgment: I [am] the LORD.***

---

[52] TGK Chap. 13

> *13 And the blood shall be to you for a token upon the houses where ye [are]: and when I see the blood, I will pass over you, and the plague shall not be upon you to destroy [you], when I smite the land of Egypt.*
>
> *<u>14</u> **And this day shall be unto you for a memorial; and ye shall keep it a feast to the LORD throughout your generations; ye shall keep it a feast by an ordinance for ever.***
>
> *15 **SEVEN DAYS SHALL YE EAT UNLEAVENED BREAD; EVEN THE FIRST DAY** ye shall put away leaven out of your houses: for **whosoever eateth leavened bread from the first day until the seventh day, that soul shall be cut off from Israel.***
>
> *16 **AND IN THE FIRST DAY [THERE SHALL BE] AN HOLY CONVOCATION, AND IN THE SEVENTH DAY THERE SHALL BE AN HOLY CONVOCATION TO YOU**; **no manner of work shall be done in them,** save [that] which every man must eat, that only may be done of you.*
>
> *17 And ye shall observe [the feast of] unleavened bread; **for in this selfsame day have I brought your armies out of the land of Egypt: therefore, shall ye observe this day in your generations by an ordinance forever.***
>
> *18 In the first [month], **ON THE FOURTEENTH DAY OF THE MONTH AT EVEN, YE SHALL EAT UNLEAVENED BREAD, UNTIL THE ONE AND TWENTIETH DAY OF THE MONTH AT EVEN.***
>
> *19 **Seven days shall there be no leaven found in your houses**: for whosoever eateth that which is leavened, even that soul shall be cut off from the congregation of Israel, whether he be a stranger, or born in the land.*
>
> *20 Ye shall eat nothing leavened; in all your habitations shall ye eat unleavened bread.*

As we have earlier discovered in the Book of Mormon of the study of the Law of Moses, this was a law of performances and ordinances that were to be strictly observed.[53]

'God commanded Moses to tell the people they should **have a sacrifice ready,** and they should prepare themselves **on the tenth day of the month Xanthicus, against the fourteenth**, (which month is called by the Egyptians Pharmuth, Nisan by the Hebrews; but the Macedonians call it Xanthicus) and that he should carry the Hebrews with all they had. Accordingly, he having got the Hebrews ready for their departure, and having sorted the people into tribes, he kept them together in one place: **but when the fourteenth day was come, and all were ready to depart they offered the sacrifice…**'[54]

> *Exodus 12:21 ¶ Then Moses called for all the elders of Israel, and said unto them, **Draw out and take you a lamb according to your families, and kill the Passover.***
>
> *22 And ye shall take a bunch of hyssop, and dip [it] in the blood that [is] in the basin, **and strike the lintel and the two side posts with the blood that [is] in the basin; and none of you shall go out at the door of his house until the morning.***
>
> *23 **For the LORD will pass through to smite the Egyptians; and when he seeth the blood** upon the lintel, and on the two side posts, the LORD will pass over the door, and **will not suffer the destroyer to come in unto your houses to smite [you].***
>
> *24 **And ye shall observe this thing for an ordinance to thee and to thy sons forever.***
>
> *25 And it shall come to pass, when ye be come to the land which the LORD will give you, according as he hath promised, that ye shall keep this service.*
>
> *26 **And it shall come to pass, when your children shall say unto you, What mean ye by this service?***
>
> *27 That ye shall say, It [is] the sacrifice of the LORD'S Passover, who passed over the houses of the children of Israel in Egypt, when he smote the Egyptians, and delivered our houses. And the people bowed the head and worshipped.*

---

[53] Mosiah 13:30
[54] JA. 2-14-6

28 And the children of Israel went away, and did as the LORD had commanded Moses and Aaron, so did they.

On the fourteenth day they offered the sacrifice:

"So, these high priests, upon the coming of their feast which is called the Passover, when **they slay their sacrifices, from the NINTH HOUR TILL THE ELEVENTH,** but **so that a company not less than ten belong to every sacrifice (for it is not lawful for them to feast singly by themselves), and many of us are twenty in a company.**"[55]

…and purified their houses with the blood, using bunches of hyssop for that purpose; **and when they had supped, they burnt the remainder of the flesh, as just ready to depart.**[56]

"**On the fourteenth day of the lunar month, when the sun is in Aries**, the law ordained that we should every year slay that sacrifice which I before told you we slew when we came out of Egypt, and which is called the Passover; and so do **we celebrate this Passover in companies**, leaving nothing of what we sacrifice till the following day. **The feast of unleavened bread succeeds that of the Passover, and falls on the fifteenth day of the month and continues seven days,** wherein they feed on unleavened bread. …

… But on the **second day of unleavened bread, which is the sixteenth day of the month, they first partake of the fruits of the earth**, for before that day they do not touch them."[57]

The Logic of the Passover, with its performances & ordinances, has now been established.

Tenth Plague: Death of the First Born

*Exodus 12:29 ¶ And it came to pass, that **at midnight the LORD smote all the firstborn in the land of Egypt**, from the firstborn of Pharaoh that sat on his throne unto the firstborn of the captive that [was] in the dungeon; and all the firstborn of cattle.*

*30 And **Pharaoh rose up in the night, he, and all his servants, and all the Egyptians; and there was a great cry in Egypt; for [there was] not a house where [there was] not one dead.***

*31 And **he called for Moses and Aaron by night**, and said, **Rise up, [and] get you forth from among my people, both ye and the children of Israel; and go, serve the LORD, as ye have said.***

32 Also take your flocks and your herds, as ye have said, and be gone; and bless me also.

*33 And the **Egyptians were urgent upon the people, that they might send them out of the land in haste;** for they said, We [be] all dead [men].*

34 And the people took their dough before it was leavened, their kneading troughs being bound up in their clothes upon their shoulders.

*35 And the children of **Israel did according to the word of Moses; and they borrowed of the Egyptians jewels of silver, and jewels of gold, and raiment:***

36 And the LORD gave the people favour in the sight of the Egyptians, so that they lent unto them [such things as they required]. And they spoiled the Egyptians.

"**Whence it is that we do still offer this sacrifice in like manner to this day**, and call this festival Pascha which signifies the feast of the Passover; because on that day God passed us over, and sent the plague upon the Egyptians; for the destruction of the first-born came upon the Egyptians that night, so many of the Egyptians who lived near the king's palace persuaded Pharaoh to let the Hebrews go. Accordingly, he called Moses, and bid them be gone; as supposing, that if once the Hebrews were gone out of the country, Egypt would be freed from its miseries. They also honored the Hebrews with gifts; some, in order to get them to depart quickly, and others on account of their neighborhood, and the friendship they had with them."[58]

*Exodus 12:37 ¶ And the children of **Israel journeyed from Rameses to Succoth, about six hundred thousand on foot [that were] men, beside children**.*

---

[55] JW 6-9-3
[56] JA. 2-14-6
[57] JA. 3-10-5
[58] JA. 2-14-6

38 And a mixed multitude went up also with them; and flocks, and herds, [even] very much cattle.

"So, the Hebrews went out of Egypt, while the Egyptians wept, and repented that they had treated them so hardly. Now they took their journey by Letopolis, a place at the time deserted, but where Babylon was built afterwards, when Cambyses laid Egypt to waste; but they went away hastily, **on the third day they came to a place called Beelzphon, on the Red Sea**; and when they had no food out of the land, **because it was a desert, they eat of loaves kneaded of flour, only warmed by a gentle heat;** ... Whence it is that, in memory of the want we were in, **we kept a feast of eight days, which is called** *the feast of unleavened bread.* Now the entire multitude of those that went out, including women and children, was not easy to be numbered, **but those that were of and age fit for war, were six hundred thousand.**"[59]

Exodus 12:39 And they baked unleavened cakes of the dough which they brought forth out of Egypt, for it was not leavened; because they were thrust out of Egypt, and could not tarry, neither had they prepared for themselves any victual.

40 Now the sojourning of the children of Israel, who dwelt in Egypt, [was] four hundred and thirty years.

41 And it came to pass at the end of the four hundred and thirty years, even the selfsame day it came to pass, that all the hosts of the LORD went out from the land of Egypt.

*42 **It [is] a night to be much observed unto the LORD for bringing them out from the land of Egypt: this [is] that night of the LORD to be observed of all the children of Israel in their generations.***

Insight by John Taylor:

From the above quotations, amongst other important matters, it appears, that when the destroying angel passed by the houses of the children of Israel he found the blood of a lamb sprinkled on the door post; which was a **type** of the blood of Christ, the Lamb of God. The angel who was the executor of justice could not touch those who were protected by that sacred symbol; **because that prefigured the sacrifice of the son of God, which was provided at the beginning of creation for the redemption of the human family, and which was strictly in accordance with provisions than made by the Almighty for that purpose—"the Lamb slain from before the foundation of the world"**—and accepted in full as an atonement for the transgressions of mankind, according to the requirement of justice, which proposal is accepted by the contracting parties, all these contracting parties being satisfied with the arrangement thus made. Hence it is said by one of the prophets: "Then he is gracious unto him, and saith, deliver him from going down to the pit: I have found a ransom."—Job 33:24.

John Taylor, Mediation and Atonement, Ch.13

And further: "Therefore the redeemed of the Lord shall return, and come with singing unto Zion; and everlasting joy shall be upon their head: they shall obtain gladness and joy; and sorrow and mourning shall flee away."—Isaiah, l, 11.

John Taylor, Mediation and Atonement, Ch.13

Who are the redeemed, except those who have accepted the terms of the ransom thus provided? **The ransom being provided and accepted, the requirements of justice are met, for those contracts are provided and sanctioned by the highest contracting parties that can be found in the heavens, and the strongest, most indubitable and infinite assurances are given for the fulfillment of that contract, and until the contract is fulfilled the sacrifices are offered as a token and remembrance of the engagements and covenants entered into.** God gave a token to Noah, of a rainbow, which should be a sign between Him and mankind he would nevermore destroy the earth by water**; He accepted these sacrifices as a token of the covenant that the messiah should come to take away sin by the sacrifice of Himself, and thus, fulfill the covenant, pertaining to this matter, made before the world was**.

---

[59] JA. 2-15-1

THE ACT OF THE ATONEMENT OF CENTRAL IMPORTANCE.

In reality, this act of the atonement was the fulfillment of the sacrifices, of the prophesying, of the Passover, and of all the leading, prominent acts of the patriarchs and prophets relating thereto; and having performed this, the past and the future both centered in him. **Did these worthies offer sacrifices? They prefigured his appearing, and atonement. Did they prophecy? It was of him, for the testimony of Jesus is the spirit of prophecy. Did they keep the Passover? He himself was the great expiatory offering. Were the people called upon afterwards to commemorate this event?** They did it in remembrance of him, as a great memorial among all of his disciples in all nations, throughout all time; **of the sacrifice of his broken body and spilt blood; the *antitype* of the sacrificial lamb slain at the time of the Passover;** of him; as being the Mediator, the Messiah, the Christ, the Alpha and Omega, the Beginning and the End: the Son of the living God. MA, 126.

John Taylor, The Gospel Kingdom, p.116

THE SHEDDING OF BLOOD. —Again, there is another phase of this subject that must not be forgotten. From the commencement of the offering of sacrifices the inferior creature had to suffer for the superior. Although it had taken no part in the act of disobedience, **yet was its bloodshed and its life sacrificed, thus prefiguring the atonement of the Son of God, which should eventually take place.** The creature indeed was made subject to vanity not willingly, but by reason of him who hath subjected the same in hope. **Millions of such offerings were made, and hecatombs of these expiatory sacrifices were offered in view of the great event that would be consummated when Jesus should offer up himself**. With man this was simply the obedience to a command and a given law, and with him might be considered simply a pecuniary sacrifice. With the animals it was a sacrifice of life.

John Taylor, The Gospel Kingdom, p.116

But what is the reason for all this suffering and bloodshed, and sacrifice? We are told without shedding of blood there is no remission of sins. This is beyond our comprehension. Jesus had to take away sin by the sacrifice of himself, the just for the unjust, but, **previous to this grand sacrifice, these animals had to have their blood shed as types, until the great anti-type should offer up himself once for all.** And as he in his own person bore the sins of all, and atoned for them by the sacrifice of himself, so there came upon him the weight and agony of ages and generations, the indescribable agony consequent upon this great sacrificial atonement wherein he bore the sins of the world, and suffered in his own person the consequences of an eternal law of God broken by man. Hence his profound grief, his indescribable anguish, his overpowering torture, all experienced in the submission to the eternal fiat of Jehovah and the requirements of an inexorable law. —MA, 149-150.

Thus, the celebration of the Passover and unleavened bread was started and is still, in a reformed version, practiced by much of the remaining Jewish nation today.

Exodus Passover Calendar (as memorialized in old testament)

Abib (later Nissan) the 1st month of the year (days of month in 1st row Passover days in 2nd row

*10	11	12	13	14	15	16	17	18	19	20	21
**1st day	2nd	3rd	4th	5th	6th	7th	8th	9th	10th	11th	12th
Select the lamb			Prepare the lamb	Passover sacrifice in the even	Passover day & 1st day of unleavened bread Convocation					Sacrifice in even	7th day of unleavened bread Convocation
					1st day	2rd day	3rd day	4th day	5th day	6th day	7th day

Chapter 3
Discussion on the "Week of the Atoning Sacrifice"

The following chapter presents a limited synopsis and chronology from the student manual (SM) titled "the Life & teachings of Jesus and His Apostles" as taught by The Church of Jesus Christ of Latter Day Saints. These teachings are only a representation of the same understandings found in most Christian churches, and there are almost as many interpretations about the Passover as there are denominations. It's interesting to note, most all of the different denominations enter into what's called a "conversation in scholarship" and begin to share their understandings as well as their true or false logic with each other. As early as 200 AD, these scholarly conversations laid the foundation for the Council of Nicaea and the formation of the Universal Church. While the truth of the gospel is there, it's the precepts of men that ushered in the dark ages.

Untold volumes have been written and claim to be, the only true and correct chronology regarding the precepts of the Passover. The basically accepted Passover chronology is said to have occurred in a 7-day logic or time frame. Passover Palm Sunday, as the 1st day of the week, and at the end of the week a Friday Crucifixion, Saturday entombment & Sunday resurrection, this has been handed down since the 3rd century by the then emerging Catholic Church. As been pointed out in the previous chapter, and as you will see in the 4 gospels, the Passover is a 12-day time frame. Men of today claim you cannot attempt to harmonize the Matthew, Mark, Luke & John, because they cannot be placed into the 7-day time frame and as a result these writers must be in error. However, we will see that the 4 gospels synchronize perfectly in the proper Passover time frame of 12 days.

In the following synopsis the writers claim the Apostles were <u>dormant</u> through the trial and the crucifixion. (SM pg.135) However, this really wasn't the case:

<u>"Then saith Jesus unto them, all ye shall be offended because of me this night: for it is written, I will smite the shepherd, and the sheep of the flock shall be scattered abroad."[60]</u>

So, while it's true the Apostles were scattered and were only able to each observe the activities to which they were present, they still were inspired to write important revelations that God wanted included in their record. As evidenced by the final chapters of the four gospels, the Apostles recorded important information and events as they actually occurred. Most writers, in their synopsis of the four gospels, selectively leave out vital information in their writings, as they choose to ignore or disparage some parts of revelation that does not fit into the chosen 7-day chronology.

Let us preview, as is suggested in (SM)<u>section 5-pg.135</u>, some of the major events which led to the crucifixion.

(INSERT) from Life and Teachings[61]

The week of the atoning sacrifice and resurrection and the Three-Year Ministry Was About to End
The public ministry of Jesus was soon to come to an end. He had pursued his ministry by two bold thrusts. His first thrust was the clear, bold announcement of his messiahship. **He left no doubt of who he was when in Bethany he restored the dead Lazarus to mortal life.** *That miracle, more than anything else, had led the Jewish rulers to plot that "Jesus should die for the nation." (John 11:51) They could not refute the evidence-to stop his mission, they would have to destroy Jesus. Second, Jesus had trained leadership in his apostles, who*

---
[60] Matt 26:31
[61] SM p 135

would carry on the torch of his cause after his ascension. This leadership surfaced when they saw that Jesus was resurrected.

Although dormant through the trial and crucifixion, later the apostles were commissioned by Jesus to preach to all nations; *and after his ascension, they were endowed with the Holy Spirit. They had the keys; they had been called; and under the leadership of Peter, James, and John, they began their great task.*

Jesus Goes To Jerusalem

And so, Jesus turned to Jerusalem and to the people of that noble city whom he would have gathered "even as a hen would have gathered her chicks under wing, and ye would not!" (Matt 23:37.) He well knew that to go there was to face an inevitable, cruel death. But he went to the Holy City, for had he not himself said: "It cannot be that a prophet perish out of Jerusalem." (Luke13:33.) To go there was to fulfill the mission to which he had been sent by his Heavenly Father.

He planned to arrive in Jerusalem at a special time. **It was the season of the Passover, late March or early April. Jewish pilgrims from all over Jewry were present. The conditions were right. Jesus knew that in Jerusalem were "those who [were] the more wicked part of the world; and they [would] crucify him ...** *and there [was] none other nation on earth that would crucify their God." (2 Nephi 10:3)*

THE LAST DAYS _OF JESUS MORTAL_ MISSION

Let us now preview some of the major events which led to Jesus' crucifixion, death, and glorious resurrection.

FIRST DAY (Sunday)10th Nissan

Jesus arrived at Jerusalem, He secured a donkey and a colt, and rode through the city gates into Jerusalem. **A "very great multitude" who knew him to be "the Prophet of Nazareth of Galilee"** *placed palm branches in his way and greeted him with a hosanna shout: "Hosanna to the son of David: Blessed is he that cometh in the name of the Lord; Hosanna in the highest." (Matt 21:9)*

He went directly to the temple, and *according to Mark, took note of what he saw and retired to Bethany* **for the night** *(mark 11:11).*

SECOND DAY (Monday)11th Nissan

Early the next morning Jesus went again to the temple and made a decisive thrust calculated to challenge the Jewish religious leadership. He drove from the outer court area of the temple those who were trading and making money exchange from foreign currency. *The money exchange was apparently sanctioned by the Jewish leaders; and by preventing the merchandising, Jesus was in effect challenging their leadership. The issue was clear: Was the temple to be a place to worship god or of pursuit of gain? As he cleared the temple courts, he said, "It is written, my house shall be called a house of prayer; but ye have made it a den of thieves." (Matt 21:13)*

Again, that evening Jesus returned to Bethany.[62]

THIRD DAY (Tuesday) 12th Nissan

Jesus' wrath in the temple raised the issue of authority, and the priests were not about to let the incident pass. As Jesus came to the temple the next day, **the priests challenged him, "By what authority doest thou do these things? And who gave thee this authority?" (Matt 21:23) Jesus responded by relating a series of parables that offended the religious leaders of the Jews.** *The scribes and Pharisees challenged him again;* **Jesus openly denounced them and condemned them as hypocrites.**

---

[62] SM p 135

> *From this point on, Jesus did not teach the public, but only the twelve.*
>
> *Perceiving that Jesus had gained the upper hand in their confrontations,* **the Jewish leaders consulted again how they might bring about Jesus' death. They would have to move quickly before the Passover to avoid a riot,** *however, since Jesus had become very popular with the Jewish people. How to bring about and arrest without provoking crowd reaction was a problem. An unexpected turn of events that took place abetted their plot. One of Jesus' own disciples offered to betray him.*

In an effort to be fair and honest it should be pointed out; the LDS church has a harmonization of the four gospels which is more comprehensive than this overview.

> **FOURTH DAY (Wednesday) 13th Nissan**
>
> *Jesus well knew the plot. The fourth day was spent outside the city, perhaps in Bethany.* **The record of the gospel writers is silent on the proceedings of this day.**

The writers of this synopsis claim the record of the gospel writers is silent on the proceedings of this day. For good reason, however, this was a day of preparing the lamb before the Passover sacrifice on the next day. Most likely the Savior was preparing himself and his family for the impending ordeal & the apostles would be preparing for the Passover.

> **FIFTH DAY (Thursday)[63] 14th Nissan**
>
> **Jesus had arranged to commemorate the Passover meal in a home privately reserved for him and the Twelve. Following the Passover meal, Jesus introduced a new ordinance, the sacrament, which presaged his atoning sacrifice. He then prophesied of his death and indicated who would betray him.**
>
> *After some instructions,* **Jesus offered his great intercessory prayer.** *Then with the eleven (Judas had left), Jesus led them outside the walls to a familiar spot-Gethsemane.* **Then taking Peter, James, and John with him, he went further into the garden where he then left those three and went off by himself to pray.** *(Matt 26:36-39) There he pled with his Heavenly Father to* **"let this cup pass from me: nevertheless, not as I will, but as thou wilt".** *(Matt: 26:39) the cup did not pass and Jesus suffered "the pain of all men" (D&C 19:18).*
>
> *Sometime later he rejoined his apostles* **and indicated that his betrayer was at hand. While he spoke, an armed band led by Judas approached Jesus to seize him.** *Without resistance Jesus submitted.* **Jesus was brought to an illegal trial that night.**[64]

Chronologically speaking, the interpretation of the Final Christian Passover has followed the Exodus calendar reasonably well to this point.}

<u>Discussion of the 6th day</u>

> **SIXTH DAY (Friday) [65] 15th Nissan**

The Jewish leaders now faced another problem. They were not content that Jesus should be put to death; they also wanted to discredit him before his own people. To do this, the leaders arranged to have Jesus charged with two crimes. The first was blasphemy, a capital offense under Jewish law. He was unanimously convicted of this charge solely on the evidence that he said that he was the son of God. (Matt. 26; 57-66) Such a conviction would discredit Jesus before the Jews, but the rulers knew well that they could not carry out the

---

[63] SM
[64] SM p 136
[65] SM p 136

death penalty; only the Roman governor could pronounce this. Therefore, they had to find political indictment against Jesus. The surest means of securing this was to charge sedition against the state, for he had claimed to be a "king of the Jews".

Though Pilate's examination found Jesus guiltless of the charge, the Jewish leaders had incited the crowd to "destroy Jesus", (Matt. 27:20) Fearing a demonstration, Pilate gave into the clamor to crucify Jesus, and death sentence was pronounced.

And so, Jesus was executed by the brutal Roman practice of crucifixion. Later in the afternoon he voluntarily gave up the spirit. The next day, which began at sundown, was the Passover, and the Jewish leaders abhorred the idea that a man should remain on the cross on the Sabbath, particularly the paschal Sabbath. Before nightfall, Jesus' body was removed from the cross and buried in a sealed tomb, but in spirit he ministered in the realm of the departed spirits. (1 Pet. 3:18-20)

As we review the 6th and 7th days of this chronology, we must conclude its proponents either consider the logic of the Exodus Passover as being irrelevant or deliberately choose to ignore it.

If the Passover meal was consumed on the evening following the 5th day, which is correct, then the 6th day would have been the Passover feast day, also the 1st day of unleavened bread and the first "Convocation or High Day Sabbath". A Convocation Day is equivalent to a Solemn Assembly and as such is a very Holy Day. The seventh day would have been the regular Sabbath day and also the day of the "First Fruits" and as such, another Holy Day. The Jewish leaders would not have violated the law and crucified Jesus on either of these days. "Matt. 26:5 but they said, not on the feast day, lest there be an uproar among the people."

True, Jewish Leaders held "probable cause hearings" the night Jesus was arrested, so to bind him over for trial, but there are no scriptural references to night trials. It is only supposed there were night trials to try and accommodate all scripture into the 7-day logic.

We have previously discussed in Chapter One that the General Authority James E. Talmage, in his book "Jesus the Christ" concluded that, **The Day of the Passover Feast. -- Controversy has been rife for many centuries as to the day of the Passover feast in the week of our Lord's death. …..**

James E. Talmage, Jesus the Christ, Ch.33, p.618 - p.619

Much has been written by way of attempt to explain this seeming discrepancy. *No analysis of the divergent views of Biblical scholars on this subject will be attempted here; the matter is of incidental importance in connection with the fundamental facts of our Lord's betrayal and crucifixion; for brief summaries of opinions and concise arguments the student may be referred to Smith's Comprehensive Bible Dictionary, article "Passover"; Eldership's Life and Times of Jesus the Messiah, pp. 480-2, and 566-8; Farrar's Life of Christ, Appendix, Excursus 10; Andrews' Life of Our Lord, and Creswell's Dissertations.*

We now refer to a Map of Jerusalem

SECTION 5

AN APPRECIATION OF THE SORROW OF THE FINAL HOURS

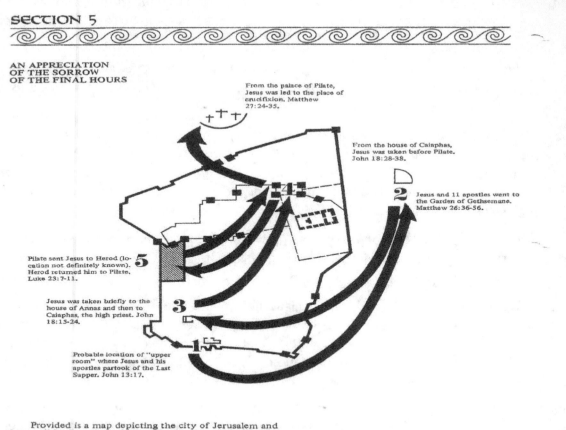

Provided is a map depicting the city of Jerusalem and the possible sites where the last days in the mortal life of Jesus Christ were spent. As you read the following narrative, picture in your mind the events that took place on that day of days and feel the sorrow of those final hours. Numbers on the map correspond to the numbers adjacent to the paragraphs.

The few scholars listed above, plus others, attempt to persuade us to accept the following happened on the 6th day:

1. Jesus was arrested early in the morning in Gethsemane (#2) and escorted by soldiers & and a mob to Caiaphas.
2. Night trials were held and Jesus was convicted. (#3)
3. When it was daylight *(after 6 am)*, and after a morning trial, Jesus was then escorted across the city to Pilate and tried. (#4)
4. Pilate determined Jesus to be under Herod's jurisdiction and sent Him to Herod. Herod (with many words) and more Jewish Leaders tried Jesus, the soldiers mocked & abused Jesus (#5) and returned Him to Pilate.
5. Pilate called the people and Jewish leaders together and held trial. Pilate attempted to release Jesus but the people cried for Barabbas. Pilate released Barabbas and turned Jesus over to the soldiers, **6th hr.** *(noon)* to be scourged and prepared for crucifixion. (#4)
6. Soldiers led Jesus away and crucified Him on the **3rd hour** *(9 am)* at Golgotha (#5)

7. Jesus was placed in the tomb Friday evening, remained there through Saturday and resurrected early Sunday morning.

There truly are many discrepancies which have created controversy over time and to this day have never been resolved. Here are just a few offhand:

1. Night trials are assumed, there are no scriptural references and totally against Jewish Law. Luke however, suggests a morning trial which would occur after 6 am sacrifices.
2. Items 3-6 above; **Shows a time frame of 3 hours, from 6 am to 9 am.** During that time frame there are 4 separate trials and the crucifixion occurring at 5 separate locations at approximately ¾ - mile to a mile apart. History shows as many as 3 million Jews could have been in or around the city of Jerusalem to celebrate the Passover. Jesus is escorted by a contingent of soldiers (perhaps 600) through these crowded conditions in three hours.
3. The scriptures show Jesus was crucified at 9 am and also say He was before Pilate at noon.
4. In the gospel of Matthew, Jesus states, He is to be in the heart of the earth 3 days and 3 nights, not just part of one night, one day and part of another night.

These are just a few obvious discrepancies which cannot be explained if the Friday crucifixion is to be accepted.

In the following chapters we will address these issues and many more. This is not an attempt to disparage the work of these many authors, in fact their work has been an inspiration and when properly applied, lends a great validation to the correct logic of the Passover.

Representing the Christian Passover as it is generally observed. Nissan days top-row

From the formal trial to the Crucifixion was 3 hrs.

10th	11th	12th	13th	14th	15th	16th	17th
1st day	2nd Day	3rd Day	4th Day	5th Day	6th Day	7th Day	1st Day
Jesus arrived in Jerusalem!	Jesus returned to the temple, threw out the money-changers!	Jesus return to Jerusalem and confronts Jew leaders about his authority!	Gospel writers are silent about Proceedings of this day.	Passover meal!	Betrayal by Judas -- Arrest Questioned by Annas- Examined by Caiaphas	Jewish Passover Sabbath day – Jesus in tomb	Resurrection
Hailed by a great multitude as a Prophet!	Returned to Bethany.	Answers in Parables!		Sacrament! Intercessory Prayer!	Peter denies Jesus **Formal Trial** (6am)		
Go to Temple- Took note of what he saw !		Returns to Bethany		Gethsemane!	Judas Iscariots death *Examined by Pilate Trial by Herod* & Priests		
Returned to Bethany.				Jesus seized & brought to illegal trial at night!	Mocked & derides by soldiers **Trial by Pilate** – Released Barabbas-		
Sunday					Pilate sentences Jesus-		Sunday

REV

Passover Calendar as taken from Exodus 12. Given by Jehovah to Moses and became the Law of Moses.
The days of Nissan is in the top row.
The days of the week of the Passover are in the second row.

*10	11	12	13	14	15	16	17	18	19	20	21
**1st	2nd	3rd	4th	5th	6th	7th	8th	9th	10th	11th	12
Select the lamb			Prepare the lamb	Sacrifice Day	Passover Day						
					1nd day unleavened bread	2rd day	3rd day	4th day	5th day prepare paschal lamb	6th meal	7th day of unleavened bread Convocation

Chapter 4
The Final Passover

The time is at hand, and "now it is expedient that there should be a great and last sacrifice made and it must be the infinite and eternal sacrifice,"[66] for the required atoning sacrifice, to fulfill the Passover part of the Law of Moses.[67]

President Taylor informs us:

> "*One of the first things that the Nephites did on their arrival at their new home, **was to build a temple**. They could not keep the judgments, the commandments, and the statues of the Lord in all things, according to the law of Moses, unless they did so; **and necessarily it was fashioned after the one at Jerusalem, for it was to be used for the same purposes; in it the same ordinances were to be performed, the same sacrifices were to be offered**.*"
>
> "*From the Bible we turn to the Book of Mormon, with a view to discover to what extent the law of sacrifice, **as a type of the offering up of the promised Messiah**, was observed among that branch of the house of Israel, which God planted on this continent. In perusing the pages of the sacred record, **we shall find several important facts and ideas**, in connection with this subject, presented very prominently by the ancient Nephite historians: among them --*
>
> *<u>First</u>, the Law of Moses, **with all its rites, ordinances, and sacrifices, was strictly observed** by the faithful Nephites, from the time of their arrival on the Promised Land, **until it was fulfilled in Christ**, and by his command, ceased to be observed.*
>
> *<u>Second</u>, that when **the Nephites brought any of the Lamanites to the knowledge and worship of the true God, they taught them to observe this law**.*
>
> *<u>Third</u>, that **those who apostatized** from the Nephites, as a general thing, **ceased to observe this law**.*
>
> *<u>Fourth,</u> that **the true import of the law of Moses, and of its ceremonies and sacrifices, as typical of the atonement yet to be made by our Lord and Savior, was thoroughly taught** by the Priesthood among that people, **and very generally understood by them**.*
>
> *<u>Fifth,</u> that associated with the **observance of this law**, they were continued admonitions given that salvation was in Christ and not in the law, **which was but the shadow and type of that of which he was the prototype and reality**.*
>
> *<u>Sixth</u>, that the temples were erected of the same pattern as that of Solomon at Jerusalem evidently **for the reason that they were to be used for the same purposes**.*
>
> *<u>Seventh</u>, that **the Gospel was preached in connection with the law, and churches were established and organized according to the Gospel requirements**, and that the higher Priesthood, although not fully organized in all its parts, ministered to the Nephites as well as the lesser.*
>
> *<u>Eighth</u>, it appears indubitable from the two records, that Bible and the Book of Mormon, that **the intent and true meaning of the law of Moses, of its sacrifices, etc., were far better understood and comprehended by the Nephites than by the Jews**. But in this connection, it **must not be forgotten, that a great many most plain and precious things**, as the Book of Mormon states, **have been taken from the Bible, through the ignorance of uninspired translators or the design and cunning of wicked men**.[68]"
>
> "The Nephites were not left by their Priesthood in ignorance of **the intent and symbolism of these ceremonies. They were not unmeaning, burdensome, spiritless performances to them**. Nephi and his successors were particularly careful in explaining, that these ordinances, like all other rites of the Church of God, **had their value in their association with or being directly typical of the great, infinite sacrifice of atonement to be offered up by the Lamb of God in His own person**."

> *Nephi informs us:*
>
> *"Behold, my soul delighteth **in proving unto my people the truth of the coming of Christ: for, for this end hath the law of Moses been given**; and all things which have been given of God from the beginning of the world, unto man, **are the typifying of him**.[69]"*

---

[66] Alma 34:10
[67] Ex 12:1-24
[68] Mediation & Atonement: Ch. 14
[69] 2 Nephi 11:4.

Josephus tells us:

In the **month of Xanthicus, which is by us called Nissan**, and is the beginning of our year, **on the fourteenth day of the lunar month**, when the sun is in Aries, (for in this month it was that **we were delivered from bondage under the Egyptians,)** the law ordained that we should every year slay that sacrifice which I before told you we slew when we came out of Egypt, and **which is called the Passover**; and so do we celebrate this Passover in companies, leaving nothing of what we sacrifice till the following day. **The feast of unleavened bread succeeds that of the Passover, and falls on the fifteenth day of the month and continues seven days, wherein they feed on unleavened bread; on every one of which days <u>two bulls are killed, and one ram, and seven lambs</u>.** Now these lambs are entirely burnt, beside the kid of the goats which are added to all of the rest, for sins; for it is intended as a feast for the priest on every one of those days. **But on the second day of unleavened bread, which is the sixteenth day of the month, they first partake of the fruits of the earth, for before that day they do not touch them.** And while they suppose it a proper honor to God, from which they obtain this plentiful provision, in the first place, they offer the first-fruits of their barley, and that in the manner following: They take a handful of the ears, and dry them, and then beat them small, and purge the barley from the bran; they then bring one tenth deal to the alter, to God; and, casting one handful of it upon the fire, they leave the rest for the use of the priest; and after this may publicly or privately reap their harvest. They also at this participation of the first fruits of the earth, sacrifice a lamb, as a burnt offering to God.[70]

President Taylor writes:

*"And notwithstanding **we believe in Christ, we keep the law of Moses, and look forward with steadfastness unto Christ, until the law shall be fulfilled; for, for this end was the law given;** wherefore the law hath become dead unto us, and **we are made alive in Christ, because of our faith; yet we keep the law because of the commandments; and we talk of Christ, we rejoice in Christ, we preach of Christ, we prophesy of Christ,** and we write according to our prophecies, that our children may know to what source they may look for a remission of their sins. Wherefore, **we speak concerning the law, that our children may know the deadness of the law; and they, by knowing the deadness of the law, may look forward to the like which is in Christ, and know for what end the law was given**. And after the law is fulfilled in Christ, that they need not harden their hearts against him, when the law ought to be done away."—2 Nephi 25:24-27.*

This agrees with the statement of Paul: "Wherefore, the law was our schoolmaster, to bring us unto Christ, that we might be justified by faith."[71]

Abinadi in the Book of Mormon taught:

> Mosiah 12:27 **Ye have not applied your hearts to understanding**; *therefore, ye have not been wise. Therefore, what teach ye this people?*
>
> *28 And they said:* **We teach the law of Moses.**
>
> *29 And again he said unto them:* **If ye teach the law of Moses why do ye not keep it ...**
>
> *...Mosiah 13:30 Therefore there was a law given them, yea,* **a law of performances and of ordinances, a law which they were to observe strictly from day to day, to keep them in remembrance of God and their duty towards him.**
>
> *31 But behold, I say unto you,* **that all these things were types of things to come.**

John Taylor in regards to this, quoted Alma:

> *"Alma 34:13 Therefore,* **it is expedient that there should be a great and last sacrifice,** *and then shall there be, or it is expedient there should be, a stop to the shedding of blood;* **then shall the law of Moses be fulfilled; yea, it shall be all fulfilled, every jot and tittle, and none shall have passed away.**
>
> *14 And behold, this is the whole meaning of the law,* **every whit pointing to that great and last sacrifice; and that great and last sacrifice will be the Son of God, yea, infinite and eternal"*.[72]

---

[70] Josephus antiq. 3-10-5
[71] mediation & atonement ch14
[72] ibid

Upon examining closely, the details involving the final Passover, it's informative to note President Taylor's narrative:

> As before stated, **these sacrifices**, which were offered up from the days of Adam until the time of our Savior's advent, **were typical of the great expiatory sacrifice which so many types, shadows and forms of which He was the great prototype—the substance, the reality prefigured and foreshadowed by the other sacrifices which had been offered up from the beginning.**
>
> When the law was given by Moses, all the forms pertaining to the **sacrificial ceremonies were revealed in detail, and the instructions in relation thereto, were not simply of a general nature, but they entered into minute particulars in relation to all things connected with those who officiated**, the form and pattern of the sacred utensils and of the vestments of the Priesthood, the creatures of all matters associated with the observance of these rites. Almost the whole of the book of Leviticus, and considerable of the book of Numbers, is occupied with these instructions and kindred matters. **This Mosaic law, with all its duties, observances, ceremonies and sacrifices, continued in force until Christ's death.**"[73]

Jesus was fully aware in going to Jerusalem He would be delivered into the hands of the chief priests and scribes, and they would condemn Him to death. Jesus is the one who gave the Law unto Moses and He was fully aware of the requirements to fulfill the law.[74]
He told his Apostles so:

> Mark 10:32 ¶ And they were in the way **going up to Jerusalem; and Jesus went before them:** and they were amazed; and as they followed, they were afraid. And he took again the twelve, and began to tell them what things should happen unto him,
>
> 33 [Saying], Behold, we go up to Jerusalem; and **the Son of man shall be delivered unto the chief priests, and unto the scribes; and they shall condemn him to death, and shall deliver him to the Gentiles:**
>
> 34 And they shall mock him, and shall scourge him, and shall spit upon him, and shall kill him: and the third day he shall rise again.

The miracle of raising Lazarus from the dead was a real turning point. A complete account of this can be read in John 11:1-46.
One of the important facts to be remembered in this miracle, is that Lazarus had been dead for over 4 days and the Savior had deliberately let it be so. Among the Jews the general belief was the spirit remained around the body for at least 3 days (24 hr. days) and by the 4th day decomposition had set in, and the spirit had finally and irrevocably departed from the area.[75] By raising Lazarus from the dead in this manner, there could be no mistake Jesus was the Son of God, and had power over life and death.

> John 11:43 And when he thus had spoken, **he cried with a loud voice, Lazarus, come forth.**
>
> 44 **And he that was dead came forth**, bound hand and foot with grave clothes: and his face was bound about with a napkin. Jesus saith unto them, Loose him, and let him go.
>
> 45 ¶ **Then many of the Jews** which came to Mary, and had seen the things which Jesus did, **believed on him.**
>
> 46 **But some of them went their ways to the Pharisees**, and told them what things Jesus had done.

Josephus Writes:

"Now, there was about this time **Jesus, a wise man, if it be lawful to call him a man,** for he was doer of wonderful works – a teacher of such men as receive the truth with pleasure. **He drew over to him both many of the Jews, and many of the Gentiles. He was the Christ**; and when **Pilate, at the suggestion of the principal men among us, had condemned him to the cross**, those that loved him a the first did not forsake him, **for he appeared to them alive again the third day, as the divine prophets had foretold these and ten thousand**

---

[73] Taylor-Mediation & Atonement: Ch. 16
[74] 3 Ne 15:5
[75] McConkie DNTC 533

other wonderful things concerning him; and **the tribe of Christians**, so named for him, **are not extinct at this day.**"[76]

Josephus confirms the fact many believed in Jesus, however some went back to Pharisees and told them what had happened. This created a schism among the population almost to the point of anarchy.

The Jewish hierarchy viewed the raising of Lazarus as the final serious threat:
John 11:47 Then gathered the chief priests and the Pharisees a council, and said, **What do we? for this man doeth many miracles.**

48 **If we let him thus alone,** *all [men] will believe on him: and the* **Romans shall come and take away both our place and nation.**

49 And one of them, [named] **Caiaphas***, being the high priest that same year,* **said unto them, Ye know nothing at all,**

50 Nor **consider that it is expedient for us, that one man should die for the people, and that the whole nation perish not.**

51 And this **spake he not of himself***: but being high priest that year,* **he prophesied that Jesus should die for that nation;**

52 And not for that nation only, but that **also he should gather together in one the children of God that were scattered abroad.**

53 Then from that day forth they took counsel together for to put him to death.

Bruce R. McConkie interprets these passages as follows:
<u>John 11:47-48</u>, what a testimony this is to the effect and verity of our Lord's miracles. None could explain them away. None could escape the very evident conclusion that they were performed by the power of God. None could justifiably attribute unrighteousness to him who performed them, for even the most spiritually untutored knew "that God heareth not sinners."[77]

The miracles proved Jesus' claim to divine Sonship. Either they must cease, or this Galilean must be accepted as the Messiah. To these sin-saturated souls who comprised the Sanhedrin, there was but one solution; Stop the miracles by slaying him who performed them. Such a course, they rationalized, was proper and justified, for it would avoid the tumult among the people which would bring on them further Roman restrictions.

<u>John 11:49-52.</u> Caiaphas began to speak, apparently intending to advocate the death of Jesus as a means of avoiding the supposed ruin that would come upon their nation through his teachings. The high priest's reasoning seemingly was, "It is better that one should perish" (1 Ne. 4:13) than that the Jewish nation with all its philosophies and beliefs should be restricted further by Rome through tumultuous conditions.

But Deity decreed that Caiaphus affirm his Son's divinity. Departing from his almost unvarying practice of using only righteous persons to give word to men, God sent the spirit of prophesy to Caiaphus, who was thereby led to say: 'Ye are ignorant of the divine will where this man is concerned. He has come to work out the infinite and eternal atonement, to be sacrificed for the sins of the world. He shall die for us and all the people of this nation, and not only for us and our nation, but for all men everywhere. Because of his death and by the preaching of his gospel, he shall gather together into one-fold all the obedient among the children of God in all nations, for salvation is only through Him'

Heedless of the high priest's prophetic utterance, setting forth the divine call resting on him who had called Lazarus forth, members of the Sanhedrin sought from that time forth to put him to death.
Is it any wonder Jesus went into seclusion till the Passover?

<u>John 11:54</u> **Jesus therefore walked no more openly among the Jews***; but went thence unto a country near to the wilderness, into a city called Ephraim, and there continued with his disciples.*

John 11:55 And the **Jews' Passover was nigh at hand***: and many went out of the country up to Jerusalem before the Passover, to purify themselves.*

56 Then **sought they for Jesus***, and spake among themselves, as they stood in the temple,* **What think ye, that he will not come to the feast?**

---

[76] Josephus Antiq. 18-3-3
[77] John 9:31

*57 Now both the **chief priests and the Pharisees had given a commandment, that, if any man knew where he were, he should shew [it], that they might take him.***

Untold numbers of books and interpretations have been written about the promised Messiah and the precise exactness in His fulfillment of the Passover and His Atonement. A comprehensive study would be impossible to attempt here, but the following by Bruce R. McConkie might give a small feeling of the scope and gravity concerning the events about to occur:

"Though the Twelve and others have been with him through his whole ministry, even they must be further conditioned to accept that which is about to be. Any remaining slivers of false Jewish tradition must be swept from their minds. Their Deliverer is to die; their God is to be crucified; their Messiah is to fail -- as far as the Jewish concept is concerned. Everything that is about to happen in his life will run counter to all that the scribes and Pharisees have supposed and believed and taught. Jesus, as we assume, has set apart this day to counsel and strengthen his chosen ones with reference to his coming demise and the glorious resurrection that will result therefrom.

That the Promised Messiah was appointed unto death, unto an agonizing death on a crucifier's cross, was something of which the prophets of old had spoken freely. They had said in plain words, and in many similitudes, that death and crucifixion awaited the mortal Son of the immortal Father. Of all this, fervent and extended witness is elsewhere borne. (The Promised Messiah, pp. 527-36.) For our present purposes we need only recount some of the numerous occasions of which we know, and there must have been many others, when the Mortal Messiah spoke of his coming crucifixion -- all preparatory to this day on which, we cannot doubt, he taught and explained the coming reality in fullness.

1. At the first Passover. Three years before, at the Passover, as he began his early Judean ministry, Jesus made the first such declaration of which we know. After the first cleansing of the temple, and in answer to the Jewish demands as to his authority for so doing, he said: "Destroy this temple" -- as John says, "he spake of the temple of his body" -- "and in three days I will raise it up." It was not, however, until after "he was risen from the dead" that the full significance of this pronouncement dawned upon his disciples. (John 2:13-22.) Yet it was the beginning; he was commencing the process of indoctrination that one day would leave them with a perfect knowledge of his death and resurrection.

2. To Nicodemus. In the great Born-Again Sermon, delivered, as we suppose, in the home of John in Jerusalem, Jesus told Nicodemus, a friendly Sanhedrinist: "As Moses lifted up the serpent in the wilderness, even so must the Son of man be lifted up." (John 3:14.) How apt are the figures and how plain the similitudes that bear record of Him!

3. To the disciples of John. When these worthies asked Jesus why his disciples did not fast often, as was the case with them and the Pharisees, our Lord replied: "Can the children of the bride-chamber mourn, as long as the bridegroom is with them? But the days will come, when the bridegroom shall be taken from them, and then shall they fast." (Matt. 9:14-15.) In keeping with the Jewish custom of pondering and discussing religious questions morning, noon, and night, seven days a week, how often thereafter must the disciples of John have thought and spoken of this reply.

4. To the Sign-seeking scribes and Pharisees. "For as Jonas was three days and three nights in the whale's belly; so, shall the Son of man be three days and three nights in the heart of the earth," he said as he excoriated them for their evil and adulterous lives. (Matt. 12:38-40.) Again, we are left to suppose that many people thereafter saw in the miraculous experience of Jonah a sign and a type of their Messiah.

5. To the Twelve. At the time of the sending forth of the Twelve, and as a part of a statement about losing one's life for Jesus' sake, our Lord said: "And he that taketh not his cross, and followeth after me, is not worthy of me." (Matt. 10:38-39.) The allusion is clear and the portent ominous.

6. In the sermon on the bread of life. All those whose hearts were open, familiar as they were with the usage of Jewish figures and symbolism, saw in his declarations that he was the Bread of Life who came down from heaven, a reaffirmation of his divine Sonship. When he said, "And the bread that I will give is my flesh, which I will give for the life of the world," they knew he meant he would be slain, so that, figuratively, all men might eat his flesh and drink his blood. (John 6:48-56.)

7. Following Peter's testimony near Caesarea Philippi. After Peter's solemn and Spirit-born confession, Matthew says: "From that time forth began Jesus to shew unto his disciples, how that he must go unto Jerusalem, and suffer many things of the elders and chief priests and scribes, and be killed, and be raised again the third day." (Matt.

16:21.) From this it appears that both then and on many subsequent occasions Jesus spoke in plainness to his chosen and favored ones of his death and resurrection.

8. On the Mount of Transfiguration. Though at the time the knowledge of such was reserved for Peter, James, and John only, Jesus discussed "his decease which he should accomplish at Jerusalem" with Moses and Elias, when those translated beings ministered to him on the Mount of Transfiguration.

(Luke 9:28-31.)

9. To the disciples in Galilee. After they came down from the Holy Mount -- hallowed forever because of the Transfiguration -- and returned to Galilee, the scripture says: "And while they abode in Galilee, Jesus said unto them, The Son of man shall be betrayed into the hands of men: And they shall kill him, and the third day he shall be raised again. And they were exceeding sorry." (Matt. 17:22-23.)

10. En route to Jerusalem. Again we but need to quote the scripture: "And Jesus going up to Jerusalem took the twelve disciples apart in the way, and said unto them, Behold, we go up to Jerusalem; and the Son of man shall be betrayed unto the chief priests and unto the scribes, and they shall condemn him to death, And shall deliver him to the Gentiles to mock, and to scourge, and to crucify him: and the third day he shall rise again." (Matt. 20:17-19.)

11. In the teachings about the good shepherd. How could he have spoken more plainly or with greater clarity than when he said: "I am the good shepherd: the good shepherd giveth his life for the sheep. . .. As the Father knoweth me, even so know I the Father: and I lay down my life for the sheep. . .. Therefore, doth my Father love me, because I lay down my life, that I might take it again. No man taketh it from me, but I lay it down of myself. I have power to lay it down, and I have power to take it again. This commandment have I received of my Father." (John 10:11-18.)

12. In the parable of the wicked husbandmen. "They will reverence my son," said the householder whose servants had been beaten, stoned, and killed. But instead, when the wicked "husbandmen saw the son, they said among themselves, This is the heir; come, let us kill him, and let us seize on his inheritance. And they caught him, and cast him out of the vineyard, and slew him." Jesus then announced himself as the Stone which the builders rejected, and the chief priests and Pharisees knew that "he spake of them" as the slayers of the Son. (Matt. 21:33-46.)

We cannot believe that all these sayings -- given as allusions, as similitudes, and in plain words -- constituted a tithe, or a hundredth, or a thousandth part of what the Blessed One said of his coming death and Crucifixion and of his resurrection on the third day. Nor can we think that the people generally were unaware of his teachings; friends and foes alike had fixed in their minds that such was his announced course. That few truly envisioned the import and glory of it all, there is no doubt. Even the Twelve needed yet added teachings about his atoning sacrifice. And we conclude that on this day, alone with them and others of like spiritual stature, he taught them all that they were then able to receive about his coming ordeal and the glory and exaltation -- for himself and for the faithful -- which would result therefrom."[78]

There can be little doubt that any representation other than a complete fulfillment of the Passover down to the last jot and tittle, could be construed as presenting false credentials as a representative of the Savior.

Event	Location	Matt.	Mark	Luke	John
To Jerusalem for Passover					11:55-57
7th day Sabbath (Saturday}	Bethany				
The Sixth day before Passover	Bethany, Bethphage				12:1
A supper at Martha & Mary's	Bethany				12:2
Jesus anointed by Mary	Bethany	(26:6-13}	(14:3-9)		12:3
Judas Protest	Bethany				12:4-8
Conspiracy against Lazarus	Bethany & Jerusalem				12:9-11

---
[78] Mortal Messiah vol. 4, pgs. 8-10

The day and night before the Passover began:

> *John 12:1 ¶ THEN Jesus six days before the Passover came to Bethany, where Lazarus was which had been dead, whom he raised from the dead.*

This clearly establishes on the Passover calendar the 15th of Nissan as the 6th day and the feast day of the Passover. It is no coincidence that the forgoing verses of John, clearly establish the fact that Jesus was in Bethany 6 days before feast day, which would place that on the 9th of Nissan, and that He entered Jerusalem the next day, which would have been the 10th of Nissan. Therefore, He entered the city on the 1st day of the Passover, when the lamb is selected for sacrifice, and He was hailed, unknowingly by the multitude, as the Lamb of God for that sacrifice.[79] The 6th day is the Passover Feast day and of course they would have eaten the Passover meal the night before. The 6th day is also the first day of unleavened bread.[80] (Consult the Exodus calendar.)

Continuing in John:

> *John 12:2 There they made him a supper; and Martha served: but **Lazarus was one of them that sat at the table with him.***
> *3 Then took **Mary** a pound of ointment of spikenard, very costly, and **anointed the feet of Jesus, and wiped his feet with her hair:** and the house was filled with the odour of the ointment.*
> *4 **Then saith** one of his disciples, **Judas Iscariot**, Simon's [son], which should betray him,*
> *5 **Why was not this ointment sold for three hundred pence, and given to the poor?***
> *6 This he said, not that he cared for the poor; but because he was a thief, and had the bag, and bare what was put therein.*
> *7 Then **said Jesus, Let her alone: against the day of my burying hath she kept this.***
> *8 For the poor always ye have with you; but me ye have not always.*
> *9 Much people of the Jews therefore knew that he was there: and they came not for Jesus' sake only, but that they might see Lazarus also, whom he had raised from the dead.*

The night before His entry into Jerusalem, Jesus had supper that Martha served and Lazarus sat at the table with Him. Mary anointed Jesus with expensive spikenard ointment in spite of the objections of Judas Iscariot, but Jesus told him, "leave her alone for she hath preserved this ointment until now, that she might anoint me in token of my burial." JST.[81] Many of the Jewish people had heard Jesus had come out of seclusion and was in Bethany. Not only did they want to see the Savior, but it was exciting to see also Lazarus as well having been raised from the dead.

John goes on to inform us of the response of the Sanhedrin:

> *John 12:10 But **the chief priests consulted that they might put Lazarus also to death;***
> *11 Because that by reason of him **many of the Jews went away, and believed on Jesus.***

Upon seeing more of their congregation of fellow Jews converting to Jesus, and particularly since they had witnessed Lazarus once again alive, these Sanhedrin wanted not only Jesus dead but Lazarus as well. This was a perplexing problem for this hierarchy, because

tomorrow was the beginning of the Passover!

REV

---

[79] John 12:13-14
[80] Matt 26:17-20
[81] John 12:1-9

Chapter 5
Triumphal Entry

1st day, - *10 Nissan*, - (Sunday)		Matthew	Mark	Luke	John
Prophecy fulfilled	Mount of Olives	21:1-7	11:1-7	19:28-34	
Triumphal Entry	Jerusalem	21:8-11	11:8-10	19:35-38	12:12-18
Pharisees Disapprove	Jerusalem			19:39-40	12:19
Visits Temple	Jerusalem		11:11		
Greeks desired to see Jesus	Out-side Temple				12:20-22
Jesus declare His mission & Then hid himself	Out-side Temple				12:23-36
Returned to Bethany			11:11		
2nd day, -*11 Nissan*, - (Monday)					
Returns to Jerusalem &wept	Mount			19:41-44	
Curses fig tree	Mount		11:12-14		
Moneychangers cast out	Temple	21:12-14	11:15-17	19:45-46	
Priests & scribes displeased	Temple	21:15-16	11:18	19:47-48	
Returns to Bethany		21:17	11:19		

FIRST DAY: 10th Nissan

When morning came, Jesus and the disciples departed Bethany to Jerusalem, a short distance away. As they approached Bethphage, a small intermediate village situated just outside the walls of Jerusalem, at the foot of Mount of Olivet;

Matthew 21:1 ¶ AND when they drew nigh unto Jerusalem, and were come to Bethphage, unto the mount of Olives, then sent Jesus two disciples,
*2 Saying unto them, Go into the village over against you, and **straightway ye shall find an ass tied, and a colt with her: loose [them], and bring [them] unto me.***
*3 And if any [man] say ought unto you, ye shall say, **The Lord hath need of them; and straightway he will send them.***
4 All this was done, that it might be fulfilled which was spoken by the prophet, saying,
*5 **Tell ye the daughter of Sion, Behold, thy King cometh unto thee, meek, and sitting upon an ass, and a colt the foal of an ass.***
6 And the disciples went, and did as Jesus commanded them,
7 And brought the ass, and the colt, and put on them their clothes, and they set [him] thereon.

Jesus demonstrates His seer ship by describing in detail the upcoming events before they have transpired, and in so doing, fulfills the known and understood prophecy:

Zechariah 9:9 Rejoice greatly, O daughter of Zion; shout, O daughter of Jerusalem: behold, thy King cometh unto thee: he [is [just, and having salvation; lowly, and riding upon an ass, and upon a colt the foal of an ass.

As we have earlier discovered in the writings of Josephus, many of the Jews and Gentiles have accepted Jesus as the Christ, perhaps thousands and even tens of thousands.[82]

---
[82] Josephus Antiq. 18-3-3

So much so John writes:

> *John 12:12 ¶ On the next day, much people that were come to the feast, when they heard that Jesus was coming to Jerusalem,*
>
> *13* ***Took branches of palm trees, and went forth to meet him,*** *and cried, Hosanna: Blessed [is] the King of Israel that cometh in the name of the Lord....*
>
> *...John 12:17 The people therefore, that was with him when he called Lazarus out of his grave, and raised him from the dead, bare record.*
>
> *18 For this cause* ***the people also met him, for that they heard that he had done this miracle.***

Matthew also writes

> *Matthew 21:8 And a* ***very great multitude spread their garments in the way; others cut down branches from the trees, and strawed [them] in the way.***
>
> *9 And* ***the multitudes that went before, and that followed, cried, saying, Hosanna to the Son of David:*** *Blessed [is] he that cometh in the name of the Lord; Hosanna in the highest.*
>
> *10 And when he was come into Jerusalem, all the city was moved, saying, Who is this?*
>
> *11 And the multitude said, This is Jesus the prophet of Nazareth of Galilee.*

The disciples at first did not understand the meaning of this until Jesus was glorified, but none-the-less they did as He bade them and placed their clothes on the colt and seated Him thereon.

Now, a great numbers of people had come to the city days before the Passover in order to be purified and attend to their sacrifices, and these are they who are the great multitude that went out to meet Him at the decent of Mount of Olivet, and carefully placing their clothing before Him and strewing the ground with palm branches.[83]

This royal treatment was only used for Kings and conquerors and was quite disconcerting to the Jewish clergy. However, the people having heard of his miracles and the raising of Lazarus from the dead were crying out, *"Hosanna to the son of David: Blessed is he that cometh in the name of the Lord; Hosanna in the highest".*[84]

Hosanna literally means, save now, or save we pray or save us we beseech thee, and is taken from the Messianic prophecy which foretold such would be the entreaty of Israel to their Lord at the day of His coming. For more than a thousand years the Jewish people had studied and considered the inspired utterance that the promised Lord of Israel would be "the stone which the builders refused", he would "become the head stone of the corner," and the cries of the people to him would include expressions, "Save now, I beseech thee, O Lord: O Lord, I beseech thee, send now prosperity. Blessed be he that cometh in the name of the Lord." (Psalm 118:22-26.) What more could the people have said to testify of their belief that Jesus was the Christ than to go back to this famous Messianic utterance and announce it was fulfilled in him![85]

As the procession moved through the city to the Temple, many people would ask the multitude what all the commotion was about, they would respond, *"This is Jesus the Prophet of Nazareth of Galilee".*[86] The resentful Pharisees, who had long plotted to destroy Jesus, were further upset and said, *"Perceive ye how ye prevail nothing? Behold, the world is gone after him."*[87] And some of the Pharisees said unto Him, *"Master, rebuke thy disciples."* And Jesus answered them saying, *"I tell you that, if these should hold their peace, the stones would immediately cry out."*[88]

Jesus, dismounting and to the response of the adulation that greeted Him, entered into the Temple looked round about on all things.[89] The purpose of Christ in thus, yielding Himself for the day to the desires of the people and accepting their homage with kingly grace may not be fully comprehended by us of finite mind. That the occasion was no accidental or fortuitous happening, of which He took advantage without preconceived intention, is evident. He knew beforehand what would be, and what He would do. It was no meaningless pageantry; but the actual advent of the King into His royal city, and His entry into the temple, the house of the King of kings. He came riding on an ass, in token of peace, acclaimed by the Hosanna shouts of multitudes; not on a caparisoned steed with the panoply of combat and the accompaniment of bugle blasts and fanfare of trumpets. That the joyous occasion was in no sense suggestive of physical hostility or of seditious disturbance is sufficiently demonstrated by the indulgent unconcern with which it was viewed by the Roman officials, who

---

[83] Matt 21:8
[84] Matt 21:9
[85] DNTC 579
[86] Matt 21:11
[87] John 12:19
[88] Luke 19:40
[89] Mark 11:11

were usually prompt to send their legionnaires swooping down from the fortress of Antonia at the first evidence of an outbreak; and they were particularly vigilant in suppressing all Messianic pretenders, for false Messiahs had arisen already, and much blood had been shed in the forcible dispelling of their delusive claims. But the Romans saw nothing to fear, perhaps much to smile at, in the spectacle of a King mounted upon an ass, and attended by subjects, who, though numerous, brandished no weapons but waved instead palm branches and myrtle sprigs. The ass has been designated in literature as "the ancient symbol of Jewish royalty," and one riding upon an ass as the type of peaceful progress.[90]

John is the only one who records the visiting Greeks who had come to the Passover, even though they could not participate in the ordinances and the sacrifices, he indicates the conversion of the Gentiles.

> *John 12:20* ¶ *And there were certain* **Greeks among them that came up to worship at the feast:**
> *21 The same* **came therefore to Philip**, *which was of Bethsaida of Galilee, and desired him, saying,* **Sir, we would see Jesus**.
> *22 Philip cometh and telleth Andrew: and again, Andrew and Philip tell Jesus.*

Subsequently they were granted an audience with Jesus:

> *John 12:23 And Jesus answered them, saying, The hour is come, that the Son of man should be glorified.*
> *24 Verily, verily, I say unto you,* **Except a corn of wheat fall into the ground and die, it abideth alone: but if it die, it bringeth forth much fruit.**
> *25* **He that loveth his life shall lose it**; *and* **he that hateth his life in this world shall keep it unto life eternal.**
> *26* **If any man serve me, let him follow me**; *and where I am, there shall also my servant be: if any man serve me,* **him will [my] Father honour**.

Jesus tells them in parable form He is the Christ and He must die, so all people may come forth and live. He tells all present, if they love the world and the things of the world more than Him, they will lose their eternal life. In order to gain eternal life, a person must set aside the things of the world, and if a person follows His teachings, and be of service to their fellow man, in so doing the Father will honor this person by being with Him in the Celestial world.

> *John 12:27* ¶ *Now is my soul troubled; and what shall I say? Father, save me from this hour:* **but for this cause came I unto this hour.**
> *28 Father, glorify thy name.* **Then came there a voice from heaven, [saying],** *I have both glorified [it], and will glorify [it] again.*
> *29 The people therefore, that stood by, and heard [it], said that it thundered: others said, An angel spake to him.*
> *30 Jesus answered and said, This voice came not because of me, but for your sakes.*

A special witness of Jesus in this dispensation worded the above scripture in these words: "Jesus came to die; his mission was to give his life for the world. Miraculous was his birth; incomparable as were his teachings, inspiring as were his miracles; and as perfect as was his life – yet, with it all, he came into the world to die, to atone, to save, to redeem, to bring to pass the immortality and possible eternal life of man.

Suppose the voice of god should speak from heaven today; suppose that voice should say in the ears of all living: 'I have restored my gospel through Joseph Smith. I command all men everywhere to repent and join the Church of Jesus Christ of Latter Day Saints.' How would men respond? Would they differ from those who heard the Almighty proclaim the divine Son ship of Jesus? Would they say it was a new type of radio broadcast? Or would they say it thundered, or an angle spoke? Whatever their response, we may rest assured that people are now as they were then, and that the voice of God himself, thundered from the heavens, would no more convince them of divine truth now than that very voice did then."[91]

> *John 12:31 Now is the judgment of this world:* **now shall the prince of this world be cast out.**

---

[90] JTC p 516
[91] DNTC 630

> *32 **And I**, if I be lifted up from the earth, **will draw all [men] unto me**.*
> *33 This he said, **signifying what death he should die**.*

Jesus explained, in the Book of Mormon, to people of the new world, the same thoughts to the Nephites in these words:

> *3 Nephi 27:14   And my **Father sent me that I might be lifted up upon the cross;** and after that I had been lifted up upon the cross, **that I might draw all men unto me**, that **as I have been lifted up by men even so should men be lifted up by the Father**, to stand before me, to be judged of their works, whether they be good or whether they be evil--*
>
> *15 And for this cause have I been lifted up; therefore, according to the power of the **Father I will draw all men unto me, that they may be judged according to their works.***
>
> *16 And it shall come to pass, that **whoso repenteth and is baptized in my name** shall be filled; and **if he endureth to the end**, behold, him **will I hold guiltless** before my Father at that day when I shall stand to judge the world.*
>
> *17 And **he that endureth not unto the end**, the same is **he that is also hewn down and cast into the fire**, from whence they can no more return, because of the justice of the Father.*

Prophets of old, from all dispensations, have prophesied of this event in very graphic detail:

> *1 Nephi 19:7 For the **things which some men esteem to be of great worth,** both to the body and soul**, others set at naught and trample under their feet. Yea, even the very God of Israel…**…. they set him at naught, and hearken not to the voice of his counsels.*
>
> *8 And **behold he cometh,** according to the words of the angel, in six hundred years from the time my father left Jerusalem.*
>
> *9 And **the world, because of their iniquity, shall judge him to be a thing of naught**; wherefore, **they scourge him**, and he suffereth it; and **they smite him**, and he suffereth it. Yea, **they spit upon him**, and he suffereth it, because of his loving kindness and his long-suffering towards the children of men.*
>
> *10 And **the God of our fathers**…… yea, the God of Abraham, and of Isaac, and the God of Jacob, **yieldeth himself…… as a man, into the hands of wicked men, to be lifted up**…….. and **to be crucified**, …… and **to be buried in a sepulcher**, ……, which he spake concerning **the three days of darkness, which should be a sign given of his death** unto those who should inhabit the isles of the sea, more **especially given unto those who are of the house of Israel**.*
>
> *11 For thus spake the prophet: The **Lord God surely shall visit all the house of Israel at that day, some with his voice……., and others with the thundering's and the lightnings of his power, by tempest, by fire, and by smoke, and vapor of darkness, and by the opening of the earth, and by mountains which shall be carried up.***
>
> *12………. And the rocks of the earth must rend; and because of the groanings of the earth, many of the kings of the isles of the sea shall be wrought upon by the Spirit of God, to exclaim: The **God of nature suffers**.*
>
> *13 And as **for those who are at Jerusalem**, saith the prophet, they **shall be scourged by all people**, because **they crucify the God of Israel**, and turn their hearts aside, rejecting signs and wonders, and the power and glory of the God of Israel.*
>
> *14 And **because they turn their hearts aside**, saith the prophet, **and have despised the Holy One of Israel,** they **shall wander in the flesh, and perish, and become a hiss and a byword, and be hated among all nations**.*
>
> *Isaiah 53: ¶ WHO hath believed our report?   ……**He is despised and rejected of men;** ……. and we esteemed him not……..he [was] wounded for our transgressions, [he was] bruised for our iniquities: …………...He was oppressed, and he was afflicted, yet he opened not his*

> *mouth: he is brought as a lamb to the slaughter, ………..for he was cut off out of the land of the living……………he made his grave with the wicked, and with the rich in his death;*

Jesus, our Lord God, knew precisely what would happen at the days of His sacrificial Passover.

The performances and ordinances and His fulfillment of them were laid out in full detail from the foundation of the world. To suppose Jesus did not fulfill all of the jots and tittles of the Law of Mose,s as He told his prophet to write and prepare us to understand, is nothing more than vain foolishness in the minds of self-serving and self-righteous men.

Jesus full well knew He would turn himself over to these men of the world who would judge even the God of Israel as a thing of naught and He would be lifted up, crucified and buried in a sepulcher. However, the Savior had given them a sign that after three day of darkness He would rise again and he will have visited the house of Israel in the Americas with judgments from the God of nature.

Those in Jerusalem who crucified Him and turned their hearts aside from love and truth and despised the Holy One of Israel shall wonder in the flesh, and perish and become a hiss and a by word and be hated among all nations.

Some of the people professing to have knowledge, Questioned Jesus more:

> *John 12:34 The people answered him,* **We have heard out of the law that Christ abideth for ever:** *and how sayest thou,* **The Son of man must be lifted up? who is this Son of man?**

….. the people on hand so understood, and they asked an explanation of what seemed to them an inconsistency, in that the scriptures, as they had been taught to interpret the same, declared that the Christ was to abide forever, and now He who claimed to be the Messiah, the Son of Man, averred that He must be lifted up. "Who is this Son of man?" they asked.[92]

Jesus answered:

> *John 12:35 Then Jesus said unto them,* **Yet a little while is the light with you.** *Walk while ye have the light, lest darkness come upon you:* **for he that walketh in darkness knoweth not whither he goeth.**
>
> *36* **While ye have light, believe in the light***, that ye may be the children of light. These things spake Jesus, and departed, and did hide himself from them.*
>
> *37 ¶ But though he had done so many miracles before them, yet they believed not on him:*

Mindful as ever not to cast pearls where they would not be appreciated, the Lord refrained from a direct avowal, but admonished them to walk in the light while the light was with them, for darkness would surely follow; and, as He reminded them, "he that walketh in darkness knoweth not whither he goeth." In conclusion the Lord admonished them thus: "While ye have light, believe in the light, that ye may be the children of light."[93]

Now eventide was come, He went out unto Bethany with the twelve.[94]

SECOND DAY: 11th Nissan

Jesus and the Apostles returned to Jerusalem the next morning and Jesus hungered and saw a fig tree in the way and found nothing thereon but leaves only, and said unto it, *"Let no fruit grow on thee henceforth now and forever."*[95]

Why would Jesus curse the fruitless fig tree? By exercising his power in this manner, He was showing He had power not only over creation but the very eternal power over life, death and the forces of nature itself. He had used these powers many times before in calming the tempest, walking on water, multiplying the loaves and fishes, healing the multitudes, and raising the dead. He was leaving an unmistakable witness of his divine Son ship and He had not only the power to bless but to curse as well.[96] The fig tree grows fruit first and then its leaves, and the fruitless fig tree was a representation of Judaism in that it had become a degenerated artificial religion.

> *Luke 19:41 ¶ And when he was come near,* **he beheld the city, and wept over it**,

---

[92] JTC p 520
[93] Ibid p 521
[94] Mark 11:11
[95] Matt 21:19
[96] D&C 132:47

42 Saying, **If thou hadst known, even thou, at least in this thy day***, the things [which belong] unto thy peace! but now they are hid from thine eyes.*

43 For the days shall come upon thee, **that thine enemies shall cast a trench about thee, and compass thee round, and keep thee in on every side,**

44 **And shall lay thee even with the ground, and thy children within thee***; and they shall not leave in thee one stone upon another;* **because thou knewest not the time of thy visitation.**

Whenever the legal administrators offer the gospel of temporal and spiritual salvation to the people, that is a day of visitation.

When Jesus beheld with his seeric vision, that the Roman legions would lay siege to Jerusalem, desecrate the Temple and not one stone upon another would be left, destroy and scatter the people, and spread unequaled terror and destruction, He wept! Why? This was the day of their visitation by legal administrators, offering temporal and spiritual salvation, and they would not hear.

Jesus and the twelve then entered into Jerusalem and went directly to the Temple:

Matthew 21:12 ¶ And **Jesus went into the temple of God, and cast out all them that sold and bought in the temple, and overthrew the tables of the money-changers, and the seats of them that sold doves,**

13 And said unto them, It is written, **My house shall be called the house of prayer***; but ye have made it a den of thieves.*

14 And the blind and the lame came to him in the temple; and he healed them.

15 And when the chief priests and scribes saw the wonderful things that he did, and the children crying in the temple*, and saying, Hosanna to the Son of David;* **they were sore displeased.**

At the last Passover of His ministry, Jesus went into the Temple as He had before, and using physical force drove out those who made merchandise in his Father's house. Declaring to all His divine Son ship by saying, "My house shall be called the house of prayer", the same as He told Isaiah.[97]

"Children crying in the Temple" were not infants or babies in that sense, but were the children of Israel, His disciples having been converted and baptized, crying out "Hosanna to the Son of David." Jesus remained in the Temple, healing the sick and working marvelous things.

The chief priests and scribes were sore displeased and said unto Him:

Matthew 21: "Hearest thou what these say?" And Jesus said unto them, Yea; have ye never read the scriptures which saith, **Out of the mouths of babes and sucklings, O Lord, thou hast perfected praise?**[98]

Mark and Luke also describe how Jesus taught daily in the Temple:

Luke 19:47 And he taught daily in the temple. **But the chief priests and the scribes and the chief of the people sought to destroy him,**

48 And **could not find what they might do: for all the people were very attentive to hear him.**

His wrath of indignation was followed by the calmness of gentle ministry; there in the cleared courts of His house, blind and lame folk came limping and groping about Him, and He healed them. The anger of the chief priests and scribes was raging against Him; but it was impotent. They had decreed His death, and had made repeated efforts to take Him, and there He sat within the very area over which they claimed supreme jurisdiction, and they were afraid to touch Him because of the common people, whom they professed to despise yet heartily feared -- "for all the people were very attentive to hear him."

The rage of the officials was further aggravated by a touching incident, which seems to have accompanied or to have immediately followed His merciful healing of the afflicted folk at the temple. Children saw what He did; with their innocent minds yet unsullied by the prejudice of tradition and their sight yet undarkened by sin, they perceived in Him the

---

[97] Isa. 56:7
[98] I.V. Matt 21:13-14

Christ, and burst forth into praise and worship in a hymn that was heard by the angels: "Hosanna to the Son of David." With ill-concealed anger the temple officials demanded of Him: "Hearest thou what these say?" They probably expected Him to disclaim the title, or possibly hoped that He would reassert His claim in a manner that would afford excuse for legal action against Him, for to most of them the Son of David was the Messiah, the promised King. Would He clear Himself of the blasphemy that attached to the unjustified acknowledgment of so awful a dignity? Jesus answered, with an implied rebuke for their ignorance of the scriptures: "Yea; have ye never read, Out of the mouth of babes and sucklings thou hast perfected praise?"[99]

As we can see, however, the Jewish leadership sought even more the opportunity to destroy Him because they feared Him. Why? because many of the people were believing what Jesus was teaching them.

Nevertheless, among the chief rulers also many believed on Him; but because of the Pharisees they did not confess Him.[100]

Jesus and the Apostles then returned to Bethany that even.

Mark 11:19 And when even was come, he went out of the city.

Matthew 21:17 ¶ And **he left them, and went out of the city into Bethany; and he lodged there.**

---

[99] JTC 529
[100] John 12:42

Chapter 6
A day of Authority

3rd day, -12 Nissan,- (Tuesday)	location	Matthew	Mark	Luke	John
Withered fig tree and discourse on faith	Road to Jerusalem	21:18-22	11:20-26		
Priests challenge Jesus' authority	Temple	21:23-27	11:27-33	20:1-8	
Parable of two sons	Temple	21:28-32			
Wicked husbandmen	Temple	21:33-41	12:1-9	20:9-16	
Rejected corner stone	Temple	21:42-46	12:10-12	20:17-18	
Royal Marriage	Temple	22:1-14			
Question on tribute to Caesar	Temple	22: -15-22	12:13-17	20:19-26	
Marriage after resurrection Sadducees	Temple	22:23-33	12:18-27	20:27-38	
Great commandment Pharisees	Temple	22:34-40	12:28-34		
Who is the Father of Christ	Temple	22:41-46	12:35-37	20:39-44	
Scribes & Pharisees condemned	Temple	23:1-36	12:38-40	20:45-47	
Jesus Lament over Jerusalem	Temple	23:37-39			12:37-41
Some rulers believed	Temple				12:42-50

On the morning of the third day Jesus, when traveling from Bethany back to Jerusalem, He and the Apostles passed by the fig tree which He cursed the day before.

> *Mark 11:20 And in the morning, as they passed by,* **they saw the fig tree dried up** *from the roots.*
> *21 And Peter calling to remembrance saith unto him, Master,* **behold, the fig tree which thou cursedst is withered away.**

"The leafy, fruitless tree was a symbol of Judaism, which loudly proclaimed itself as the only true religion of the age, and condescendingly invited all the world to come and partake of its rich ripe fruit; when in truth it was but an unnatural growth of leaves, with no fruit of the season, nor even an edible bulb held over from earlier years, for such as it had of former fruitage was dried to worthlessness and made repulsive in its worm-eaten decay. The religion of Israel had degenerated into an artificial religionism, which in pretentious show and empty profession outclassed the abominations of heathendom."[101]

> *Mark 11:22 And Jesus answering saith unto them,* **Have faith in God.**
> *23 For verily I say unto you, That* **whosoever shall say unto this mountain, Be thou removed, and be thou cast into the sea; and shall not doubt** *in his heart, but shall believe that* **those things which he saith shall come to pass; he shall have whatsoever he saith.**
> *24 Therefore I say unto you, What things so ever ye desire, when ye pray, believe that ye receive [them], and ye shall have [them].*

Matthew confirms:

> *Matthew 21:20 And when the disciples saw it, they* **marveled, saying, How soon is the fig tree withered away!**
> *21 Jesus answered and said unto them, Verily I say unto you,* **If ye have faith, and doubt not, ye shall not only do this which is done to the fig tree, but also if ye shall say unto this mountain, Be thou removed, and be thou cast into the sea; it shall be done.**
> *22 And all things,* **whatsoever ye shall ask in prayer, believing, ye shall receive.**

---
[101] JTC 527

Jesus displayed to the Apostles the power of faith in God, is the possibility of accomplishing miracles in the spiritual as well as the temporal realms. Faith, then, is the first governing principal which has power, dominion, and authority over all things; by it they exist, by it they are upheld, by it they are changed or by it they remain, agreeable to the will of God.

*Mark 11:25 And **when ye stand praying, forgive, if ye have ought against any**: that your Father also which is in heaven may forgive you your trespasses.*

*26 But **if ye do not forgive, neither will your Father which is in heaven forgive your trespasses.***

Forgiveness plays a major role in this process:

*D&C 64:8 My disciples, in days of old, **sought occasion against one another and forgave not one another in their hearts; and for this evil they were afflicted and sorely chastened.***

*9 Wherefore, I say unto you, that ye ought to forgive one another; **for he that forgiveth not his brother his trespasses standeth condemned before the Lord; for there remaineth in him the greater sin.***

*10 I, the Lord, will forgive whom I will forgive, **but of you it is required to forgive** all **men.***

In order for men to obtain the companionship of the Spirit, which is essential to the working of miracles, they have washed their garments in the blood of the Savior, because of their faith, and the repentance of all their sins, and their faithfulness to the end. Remember we must forgive even if our offender did not repent and ask for forgiveness, "…forgive them; for they know not what they do."

Question on Authority:

Then Jesus and the twelve Apostles then proceeded on into the city.

*Mark 11:27 ¶ And they come again to Jerusalem: and as he was walking in the temple, **there come to him the chief priests, and the scribes, and the elders**,*

*28 And say unto him, **By what authority doest thou these things? and who gave thee this authority to do these things?***

A group of chief priests and scribes had counseled together and derived a plan how they might entrap the Savior in a violation of their laws and traditions. They had been debating about him overnight and decided on a plan to challenge his authority, after all they were the guardians of the temple and the ecclesiastical authority. Just who was this Galilean upstart that allowed him-self to be called Christ and for the second time had ignored their authority? They came to Him saying: 'By what authority do ye preach and teach since you have not been trained and appointed a rabbi?' It was obvious in all Jesus demonstrated and miracles performed, he had authority. These ecclesiastical upstarts were attempting to show Jesus void of a rabbinical commission and He was in violation of their law and standards. This was the first step to try and suppress the activities of Jesus and discredit him in front of the people.

It was true in those days as it is now, a professing minister has authority or he does not.

"A man must be called of God, by prophecy, and by the laying on of hands, by those in authority to preach the Gospel and administer the ordinances thereof"[102]

It is quite disturbing to pay homage to so called ecclesiastical ministers that teach us about the particulars of the Passover, when their authority could be very questionable. Every individual exercising ministerial powers should ask himself: **"By what authority do I do these things?"**

These unclean zealots knew what authority the Lord claimed, their question was of sinister purpose. Jesus did not condescend to voice an answer in which they could possibly find further excuse for antagonizing Him, but He availed Himself of a method very common among themselves -- that of countering one question with another:

*Mark 11:29 And Jesus answered and said unto them, **I will also ask of you one question, and answer me, and I will tell you by what authority I do these things.***

---

[102] Fifth article of faith

*30 **The baptism of John, was [it] from heaven, or of men? answer me.***

*31 And they **reasoned with themselves, saying, If we shall say, From heaven; he will say, Why then did ye not believe him?***

*32 **But if we shall say, Of men; they feared the people**: for all [men] counted John, that he was a prophet indeed.*

*33 And they answered and said unto Jesus, **We cannot tell**. And Jesus answering saith unto them, **Neither do I tell you by what authority I do these things**.*

The trap they had set for the Master was neatly sprung on them. Should they answer John's baptism was of God, Jesus would probably demand of them why then they had not believed in the Baptist, and why they did not accept John's testimony concerning himself. On the other hand, should they aver John had no divine authority to preach and baptize, the people would turn against them, for the martyred Baptist was revered by the masses as a prophet. In spite of their boasted learning, they answered as puzzled schoolboys might do when they perceive hidden difficulties in what at first seemed but a simple problem. "We cannot tell" said they. Then Jesus replied, "Neither tell I you by what authority I do these things."

The Parable of the two Sons:

Now Jesus posed a question to His accusers:

*Matthew 21:28 ¶ But what think ye? **A [certain] man had two sons; and he came to the first, and said, Son, go work today in my vineyard.***

*29 He answered and said, **I will not: but afterward he repented, and went.***

*30 And he came **to the second, and said likewise**. And he answered and said, **I [go], sir: and went not**.*

*31 **Whether of them twain did the will of [his] father?** They say unto him, **The first**. Jesus saith unto them, Verily I say unto you, **That the publicans and the harlots go into the kingdom of God before you**.*

*32 For **John came unto you** in the way of righteousness, and ye believed him not: but **the publicans and the harlots believed him: and ye, when ye had seen [it], repented not afterward, that ye might believe him**.*

Jesus proceeded now to rebuke the Jewish leadership by saying the first son, who was symbolic of the publicans and harlots who refused to labor, but later repented and did so, was symbolic of those who flocked to the Baptist and asked: *"Master, what shall we do?"*[103]

The second son, while willing to work in the vineyard, did not do the appointed labor and consequently the vineyard degenerated into a fruitless wilderness. The second son was a representation of the Jewish leaders, and the publicans and harlots would enter into the kingdom heaven before them.

Parable of wicked husbandmen:

Jesus spoke to these miserable husbandmen further:

*Matthew 21:33 ¶ Hear another parable: **There was a certain householder, which planted a vineyard**, and hedged it round about, and digged a winepress in it, and built a tower, **and let it out to husbandmen, and went into a far country:***

*34 And when **the time of the fruit drew near, he sent his servants** to the husbandmen, **that they might receive the fruits of it**.*

*35 And **the husbandmen** took his servants, and **beat one, and killed another, and stoned another**.*

36 Again, he sent other servants more than the first: and they did unto them likewise.

*37 But last of all **he sent unto them his son, saying, They will reverence my son**.*

*38 But when **the husbandmen saw the son, they said** among themselves, **This is the heir; come, let us kill him, and let us seize on his inheritance**.*

*39 And **they caught him, and cast [him] out of the vineyard, and slew [him]**.*

*40 **When the lord therefore of the vineyard cometh, what will he do unto those husbandmen?***

---

[103] Luke 3:12

*41 They say unto him, **He will miserably destroy those wicked men**, and will let out [his] vineyard unto other husbandmen, which shall render him the fruits in their seasons.*

*42 Jesus saith unto them, Did ye never read in the scriptures, **The stone which the builders rejected, the same is become the head of the corner**: this is the Lord's doing, and it is marvelous in our eyes?*

*43 Therefore say I unto you, **The kingdom of God shall be taken from you, and given to a nation bringing forth the fruits thereof.***

44 And whosoever shall fall on this stone shall be broken: but on whomsoever it shall fall, it will grind him to powder.

This parable is a summary of God's dealings with men from the creation of Adam down to the Second Coming of the Son of Man. The householder is God himself and the earth and the people are His vineyard.

The husbandmen were those who were appointed as spiritual overseers of the people. These same husbandmen were those who persecuted, beat, stoned and killed the prophets, not only the prophets but also even the Son & Heir, Jesus Christ. As a result, of 2nd sons' actions, the church would be taken from the Jews and given to the Gentiles. Later the Gentiles would be in the same condition and the vineyard would have to be let out to other husbandmen preparatory to the Savior's final return to reign.

*Matthew 21:45 And when **the chief priests and Pharisees had heard his parables, they perceived that he spake of them.***

*46 But when they sought to lay hands on him, **they feared the multitude, because they took him for a prophet.***

Unquestionably, the chief priests and Pharisees wanted Jesus dead but, because so many of the people thought Him a prophet, feared to touch Him. However, these wicked husbandmen had a carefully crafted final plan to kill Him.

Parable of Royal Marriage:

Matthew 22:1 ¶ AND Jesus answered and spake unto them again by parables, and said,
*2 The kingdom of heaven is like unto a **certain king, which made a marriage for his son,***
*3 And sent forth **his servants to call them that were bidden to the wedding: and they would not come.***
*4 Again, he sent forth other servants, saying, Tell them which are bidden, Behold, I have prepared my dinner: my oxen and [my] fatlings [are] killed, and all things [are] ready: **come unto the marriage**.*
*5 But **they made light of [it], and went their ways**, one to his farm, another to his merchandise:*
6 And the remnant took his servants, and entreated [them] spitefully, and slew [them].
*7 But when **the king** heard [thereof], he was wroth: and **he sent forth his armies, and destroyed those murderers, and burned up their city.***

*8 Then saith he to his servants, **The wedding is ready, but they which were bidden were not worthy.***
*9 **Go ye therefore into the highways,** and as many as ye shall find, bid to the marriage.*
*10 So those **servants went out into the highways, and gathered together all as many as they found,** both bad and good: and the wedding was furnished with guests.*
*11 And when the **king came in to see the guests, he saw there a man which had not on a wedding garment:***
*12 And he saith unto him, **Friend, how camest thou in hither not having a wedding garment?** And he was speechless.*
*13 Then said the king to the servants, **Bind him hand and foot, and take him away, and cast [him] into outer darkness;** there shall be weeping and gnashing of teeth.*
*14 **For many are called, but few [are] chosen.***

One gospel writer put it this way: "Jesus teaches these truths: (1) His own divine Son ship; (2) The impending destruction of Jerusalem; (3) the rejection of the Jewish remnant of the covenant race; (4) The gospel call to the Gentiles; and (5) those who answer the gospel call, will not be chosen for salvation unless they put on the robes of righteousness.

Deity himself is the king in the parable; Jesus, his offspring and heir, is the king's son; and those first invited to the "marriage of the Lamb" are the chosen and favored hosts of Israel to whom the gospel had been offered in ages past. "The remnant" who rejected the later invitation with violence and murder were the Jewish descendants of ancient Israel; and it was their city, Jerusalem, which was violently destroyed.[104]

While this parable was a truth for the meridian of time, it is currently being played out in this dispensation right now. Are we going to the wedding? Have we put on the robes of righteousness?

Tribute to Caesar

The Pharisees and Herodians came next:

Matthew 22:15 ¶ *Then went the **Pharisees, and took counsel how they might entangle him in [his] talk.***

16 *And they sent out unto him their disciples with the Herodians, saying,* **Master, we know that thou art true,** *and teachest the way of God in truth, neither carest thou for any [man]: for thou regardest not the person of men.*

17 *Tell us therefore,* **What thinkest thou? Is it lawful to give tribute unto Caesar, or not?**

18 *But Jesus perceived their wickedness, and said,* **Why tempt ye me, [ye] hypocrites?**
19 **Shew me the tribute money.** *And they brought unto him a penny.*
20 *And he saith unto them,* **Whose [is] this image and superscription?**
21 **They say unto him, Caesar's.** *Then saith he unto them,* **Render therefore unto Caesar the things which are Caesar's; and unto God the things that are God's.**
22 *When they had heard [these words], they marveled, and left him, and went their way.*
23 *The Herodians tried to get Jesus to make a choice in* **the old argument – which is greater the church or the state?**

Knowing men of the world will not repent and come to the perfect order of the Lord's government, the Savior asked for a coin of the realm. He asked, *"Whose image and superscription hath it?"* They answered and said Caesar's. And He said unto them *"Render therefore unto Caesar the things which be Caesar's and unto God the things that be God's."*[105] Thus the Savior told them in this world there are two powers, one ecclesiastical and one civil. One has authority over spiritual matters and the other over civil matters and as such one cannot dictate to the other and man is subject to both. They marveled at His answer and held their peace. Whenever one system dominates the other, then men are denied their agency and subsequently are denied the opportunity to work out their salvation.

Marriage after Resurrection:

Then came the Sadducees who believed in no resurrection, and knowing it was commonly accepted by Jesus and within the Jewish population there was marriage in heaven, wanted to ridicule and belittle the situation by asserting everyone knows a woman who has had seven husbands, could not have them all at once in the life to come.

Matthew 22:23 ¶ *The same day* **came to him the Sadducees, which say that there is no resurrection,** *and asked him,*

24 *Saying, Master,* **Moses said, If a man die, having no children, his brother shall marry his wife, and raise up seed unto his brother.**

25 **Now there were with us seven brethren**: *and the first, when he had married a wife, deceased, and, having no issue, left his wife unto his brother:*

26 *Likewise the second also, and the third, unto the seventh.*

27 *And last of all the woman died also.*

---

[104] DNTC 597
[105] Luke 20 24-25

*28 Therefore **in the resurrection whose wife shall she be of the seven**? for they all had her.*

Mosaic Law required and authorized like circumstances for the purpose of rearing up children to the name of the dead, to perpetuate the family lineage.

*29 Jesus answered and said unto them, **Ye do err, not knowing the scriptures, nor the power of God.***

*30 For **in the resurrection they neither marry, nor are given in marriage**, but are as the angels of God in heaven.*

*31 But **as touching the resurrection of the dead**, have ye not read that which was spoken unto you by God, saying,*

*32 I am the God of Abraham, and the God of Isaac, and the God of Jacob? **God is not the God of the dead, but of the living.***

33 And when the multitude heard [this], they were astonished at his doctrine.

Jesus answered by telling them they were in error because they didn't know the scriptures or the power of God. The Savior did not go into the principles of eternal marriage, as it would have been of little understanding to those who didn't believe in a resurrection. So, he explained in the resurrection they neither marry, nor are they given in marriage, which is true, because it is an earthly sealing ordinance to be performed by worthy couples.

Then Jesus told them there could be no God if there is not a resurrection. There are no dead. God raises the dead up out of their graves and all are alive because of Him, and thus the dead fulfill the reason for their creation. When the multitude heard this, they were astonished at His doctrine and durst not ask Him any question at all.[106]

Great commandment in the Law?

The Pharisees, now seeing their rivals being put down, called upon one of their lawyers, a scribe, apparently a well taught professor of ecclesiastical law, to go forward and ask:

*Mark 12:28 ¶ And **one of the scribes came**, and having heard them reasoning together, and perceiving that he had answered them well, **asked him, which is the first commandment of all?***

*29 And **Jesus answered him, The first of all the commandments [is]**, Hear, O Israel; The Lord our God is one Lord:*

*30 And **thou shalt love the Lord thy God with all thy heart, and with all thy soul, and with all thy mind, and with all thy strength: this [is] the first commandment.***

*31 And **the second [is] like, [namely] this, Thou shalt love thy neighbour as thyself.** There is none other commandment greater than these.*

Without hesitation Jesus called to attention the first and second commandments given to Moses, and the very words were written on the phylacteries, which was worn as frontlets between their eyes. To which the scribe answered:

*32 And **the scribe said unto him, Well, Master, thou hast said the truth: for there is one God; and there is none other but He:***

*33 And **to love Him with all the heart**, and with all the understanding, and with all the soul, and with all the strength, and to love [his] neighbour as himself, **is more than all whole burnt offerings and sacrifices.***

*34 And when Jesus saw that he answered discreetly, he said unto him, **Thou art not far from the kingdom of God.** And no man after that durst ask him [any question].*

The scribe was honest enough to admit the truth of the Master, and Jesus seeing the scribe was sincere, gave an encouraging assurance he was not far from the kingdom of God...

---

[106] Mark 12:18-27, Luke 20:27-36

Who is Christ's Father:

Seeing the Sadducees, Herodians, Pharisees, lawyers and scribes, had all been silenced and dare not ask Him any more questions, Jesus now becomes the questioner.

Matthew 22:41 ¶ While the Pharisees were gathered together, **Jesus asked them,**

42 Saying, **What think ye of Christ? Whose son is he? They say unto him, [The Son] of David.**

43 He saith unto them, How then doth **David in spirit call him Lord, saying,**

44 The LORD said unto my Lord, Sit thou on my right hand, till I make thine enemies thy footstool?

45 If David then call him Lord, how is he his son?

46 And no man was able to answer him a word, neither durst any [man] from that day forth ask him any more [questions].

When the Pharisees answered that Christ was the son of David, Jesus directs them to Psalm 110, wherein, by the power of the spirit (Holy Ghost) David calls Him Lord. Then how could He be David's son. They had no answer!

Scribes and Pharisees condemned:

After the humiliating defeat of the Pharisees, Jesus turns to His disciples and the multitude, and launches a final denunciation of the system and condemnation of the unworthy Jewish leadership.

Matthew 23:1 ¶ **THEN spake Jesus** *to the multitude, and to his disciples,*

2 Saying, **The scribes and the Pharisees sit in Moses' seat:**

3 All **therefore whatsoever they bid you observe,** *[that] observe and do;* **but do not ye after their works: for they say, and do not.**

Jesus points out that scribes & Pharisees are the doctrinal expounders and official administrators of the law, and who were to be obeyed in their authoritative rule. Disobedience to the law was not excusable because of the corruption among the law's representatives. However, the people should not conduct themselves in like manner as these officials because individual wickedness could not be condoned or palliated because of another's villainy.

Matthew 23: **4 For they bind heavy burdens and grievous to be borne, and lay [them] on men's shoulders; but they [themselves] will not move them with one of their fingers.**

Rabbinism, in many cases had superseded the laws and substituted multitudinous rules and extractions, with conditional penalties for the general population, yet these hypocritical leaders could find personal exemption for themselves.

Matthew 23: 5 But **all their works they do for to be seen of men**: *they make broad their phylacteries, and enlarge the borders of their garments,*

6 **And love the uppermost rooms at feasts**, *and the chief seats in the synagogues,*

7 And **greetings in the markets, and to be called of men, Rabbi, Rabbi**.

8 But **be not ye called Rabbi**: *for one is your Master, [even] Christ; and all ye are brethren.*

9 And **call no [man] your father upon the earth**: *for one is your Father, which is in heaven.*

10 **Neither be ye called masters**: *for one is your Master, [even] Christ.*

11 But he that is **greatest among you shall be your servant.**

12 And **whosoever shall exalt himself shall be abased; and he that shall humble himself shall be exalted.**

Jesus pointed out the divine sanctity of the priesthood had been replaced by the desire to have high-sounding titles such as, Rabbi, signifying Master, Teacher or Doctor. Those having the responsibility of building His church should not aspire to the honors of men, but are brethren, and should be imbued with the sole purpose of rendering the greatest possible service to their one and only Master, Christ.

Jesus now turns from His audience of disciples and unbelievers, who are listening eagerly to learn, and directly addresses the unabashed, angry rulers, which He unleashes a torrent of righteous indignation of scorching invective and divine anathema.

*Matthew 23:13 ¶ But **woe unto you, scribes and Pharisees, hypocrites! for ye shut up the kingdom of heaven against men**: for ye neither go in [yourselves], neither suffer ye them that are entering to go in.*

As it is today, the hypocrites establish schools, in which religious titles are conferred on men who explain and teach the scriptures in such a confusing and perverted way as to mislead their congregations. Thus, standing as obstacles at the entrance to the kingdom of God, refusing to go in themselves and barring the way for others.

*Matthew 23:14 Woe unto you, scribes and Pharisees, **hypocrites! for ye devour widows' houses, and for a pretense make long prayer**: therefore, ye shall receive the greater damnation.*

Under the cover of religious duty and long prayers the Jewish hierarchy, had by extortion and exaction amassed a great wealth. Many people cast in much to the treasury, even to the point scribes were able to confiscate widows' homes.

*Matthew 23:15 Woe unto you, scribes and Pharisees, hypocrites! for ye compass sea and land to **make one proselyte**, and when he is made, **ye make him twofold more the child of hell than yourselves.***

*16 Woe unto you, [ye] **blind guides**, which say, Whosoever shall **swear by the temple**, it is nothing; but whosoever shall **swear by the gold of the temple**, he is a debtor!*

17 [Ye] fools and blind: for whether is greater, the gold, or the temple that sanctifieth the gold?

*18 And, whosoever shall **swear by the altar**, it is nothing; but whosoever sweareth by the gift that is upon it, he is guilty.*

*19 [Ye] fools and blind: **for whether [is] greater, the gift, or the altar that sanctifieth the gift?***

20 Whoso therefore shall swear by the altar, sweareth by it, and by all things thereon.

*21 And whoso shall **swear by the temple, sweareth by it, and by him that dwelleth therein**.*

*22 And he that shall **swear by heaven, sweareth by the throne of God, and by him that sitteth thereon.***

Thus, did the Lord condemn the infamous enactments of the schools and the Sanhedrin concerning oaths and vows; for they had established or endorsed a code of rules, inconsistent and unjust, as to technical trifles by which a vow could be enforced or validated. If a man swore by the temple, the House of Jehovah, he could obtain an indulgence for breaking his oath; but if he vowed by the gold and treasure of the Holy House, he was bound by the unbreakable bonds of priestly dictum. Though one should swear by the altar of God, his oath could be annulled; but if he vowed by the corban gift or by the gold upon the altar; his obligation was imperative. To what depths of unreason and hopeless depravity had men fallen, how sinfully foolish and how willfully blind were they, who saw not that the temple was greater than its gold, and the altar than the gift that lay upon it! In the Sermon on the Mount the Lord had said, "Swear not at all"; but upon such as would not live according to that higher law, upon those who persisted in the use of oaths and vows, the lesser and evidently just requirement of strict fidelity to the terms of self-assumed obligations was to be enforced, without unrighteous quibble or inequitable discrimination.[107]

---
[107] JTC pg.556

> *Matthew 23:***23** ***Woe unto you, scribes and Pharisees, hypocrites! for ye pay tithe of mint and anise and cumin, and have omitted the weightier [matters] of the law,*** *judgment, mercy, and faith: these ought ye to have done, and not to leave the other undone.*
> **24** *[Ye]* ***blind guides, which strain at a gnat, and swallow a camel.***

Jesus recognizes the tithing law, even down to tithing of herb and grains. However, to observe the rabbinical classifications of "light" and "heavy" organic and physical requirements under the law, and disregard the spiritual and covenant blessings as a child of God, is unacceptable.

> *Matthew 23:25 Woe unto you, scribes and Pharisees,* ***hypocrites! for ye make clean the outside of the cup and of the platter, but within they are full of extortion and excess.***
> **26** *[Thou] blind Pharisee,* ***cleanse first that [which is] within the cup and platter,*** *that the outside of them may be clean also.*

The Pharisees would meticulously clean the cups and platters of offering but, as the Lord points out in all of His chastisement so far, their offerings are full of extortion and excess.

> *Matthew 23:27 Woe unto you, scribes and Pharisees,* ***hypocrites! for ye are like unto whited sepulchers,*** *which indeed* ***appear beautiful outward****, but are* ***within full of dead [men's] bones, and of all uncleanness****.*
> **28** *Even so* ***ye also outwardly appear righteous unto men, but within ye are full of hypocrisy and iniquity****.*

The rabbis made even the slightest contact with a dead body or its cerements, or the bier, or the grave in which it had been laid, as cause for personal defilement. Ceremonial washings and the offering of sacrifices could remove this filthy pollution. They went to great lengths to make the tombs brilliantly white so a person could not accidentally find them in proximity the dead. Jesus compared the Pharisees to the tombs and, no matter how white and nice they appeared on the outside, the putrescence was still on the inside. No matter how righteous the Pharisees & scribes tried to appear they were still full of corruption.

> *Matthew 23:29 Woe unto you, scribes and Pharisees, hypocrites!* ***because ye build the tombs of the prophets,*** *and garnish the sepulchers of the righteous,*
> **30** *And say, If we had been in the days of our fathers,* ***we would not have been partakers with them in the blood of the prophets****.*
> **31** ***Wherefore ye be witnesses unto yourselves, that ye are the children of them which killed the prophets****.*
> **32** ***Fill ye up then the measure of your fathers****.*
> **33** *[Ye] serpents, [ye] generation of vipers,* ***how can ye escape the damnation of hell?***

Jesus went on further to say: 'You honor the prophets of old and say if you had been there you wouldn't have taken part in these murderous deeds.' By making this claim, however, they are admitting they are the offspring of those who had shed innocent blood. 'You hypocrites, you will measure up to your father's deeds and not escape the damnation of hell.'

> *Matthew 23:4 ¶ Wherefore, behold,* ***I send unto you prophets, and wise men, and scribes:*** *and [some] of* ***them ye shall kill and crucify;*** *and [some] of* ***them shall ye scourge*** *in your synagogues, and* ***persecute [them] from city to city:***
> **35** *That upon you may come all the righteous blood shed upon the earth, from the blood of righteous Abel unto the blood of Zacharias son of Barachias, whom ye slew between the temple and the altar.*
> **36** *Verily I say unto you,* ***All these things shall come upon this generation****.*

Jesus predicted, that like their fathers of old who had killed Jehovah's envoys, they too would likewise shed the blood of prophets, wise and righteous men who he would send among them. Righteous blood would rest upon them as a witness before God, that they were literal sons of murderers, and murderers themselves.

Jesus laments over Jerusalem

Jesus looked down from the temple heights and as His gazed over the city and, soon to be abandoned to destruction, He was filled with emotions of profound sorrow, as He broke forth in heart-felt lamentation.

Matthew 23:37 ***O Jerusalem, Jerusalem****, [thou] that killest the prophets, and stonest them which are sent unto thee,* **how often would I have gathered thy children** *together, even as a hen gathereth her chickens under [her] wings, and ye would not!*

38 Behold, ***your house is left unto you desolate.***

39 For I say unto you, ***Ye shall not see me henceforth, till ye shall say, Blessed [is] he that cometh in the name of the Lord****.*

Jesus was about to leave the temple, which He had called "His house" the day before, and said; "your house is now left desolate". Jesus was about to leave them as a nation and, they would see Him no more, until through the centuries of suffering, in the end days, they raise up in faith and proclaim; "Blessed is he that come in the name of the Lord." Now the disciples understood of His glorification and of His coming to earth again.

Chapter 7
Afternoon of 3rd day

Afternoon 3rd Day, 12 Nissan, (Tuesday)	Location	Matthew	Mark	Luke	John
The widows mite	Against the treasury		12:41-44	21:1-4	
Destruction of Temple		24:1-2	13:1-2		
Olivet Discourse		JST 24 I.V.			
False Christs & False Prophets & Great calamities	Mount of Olives	24:3-31	13:3-31	21:5-28	
Parable Fig Tree (watch)	Mount of Olives	24:32-41	13:32-37	21:29-33	
Watch Therefore	Mount of Olives	24:42-51	13:38	21:34-38	
Parable of Ten Virgins	Mount of Olives	25:1-13			
Parable of entrusted Talents	Mount of Olives	25:14-30			
Final and inevitable Judgment	Mount of Olives	25:31-46			

The Widows Mite

Jesus moved from the open courts and sat resting against the treasury, seemingly absorbed in a reverie of sorrow. As He watched the people depositing their donations into the various chests marked for specific purposed.

*Mark 12:41 ¶ And **Jesus sat over against the treasury**, and beheld how the people cast money into the treasury: and **many that were rich cast in much.***

*42 And there came **a certain poor widow, and she threw in two mites**, which make a farthing.*

*43 And **he called [unto him] his disciples**, and saith unto them, Verily I say unto you, That **this poor widow hath cast more in, than all they which have cast** into the treasury:*

44 For all [they] did cast in of their abundance; but she of her want did cast in all that she had, [even] all her living.

Even though her offering was probably less than half a cent in American money, in the books in heaven the value is recorded in quality not quantity, it's the spirit of sacrifice and devout intent with which she gave that counts most.

2 Corinthians 8:2 For if there be first a willing mind, [it is] accepted according to that a man hath, [and] not according to that he hath not.

Olivet discourse:

As Jesus was departing from the enclosure wherein stood what once had been the House of the Lord, (An extract from the translation of the Bible as revealed to Joseph Smith the Prophet in 1831: Matthew 23:39 and chapter 24.)

*Matthew 24:1 FOR I say unto you, **that ye shall not see me henceforth** and know that I am he of whom it is written by the prophets, **until ye shall say: Blessed is he who cometh in the name of the Lord, in the clouds of heaven, and all the holy angels with him**. Then understood his disciples that he should come again on the earth, **after that he was glorified and crowned on the right hand of God.***

How many times would Jesus have gathered His people, but now they would be left desolate. However, there will be a time when He will return to His house after receiving the glory he rightly deserves.

> *Matthew 24:2 And **Jesus went out, and departed from the temple**; and his **disciples came to him**, for to hear him, saying: Master, **show us concerning the buildings of the temple, as thou hast said**--They shall be thrown down, and left unto you desolate.*
>
> *3 And Jesus said unto them: **See ye not all these things, and do ye not understand them?** Verily I say unto you, **there shall not be left here, upon this temple, one stone upon another that shall not be thrown down.***"

One or more of the disciples called His attention to the magnificent structures, the massive stones, the colossal columns, and the lavish and costly adornment of the several buildings. The Lord's answering comment was an unqualified prophecy of the utter destruction of the temple and everything pertaining to it. "Verily I say unto you, there shall not be left here one stone upon another, that shall not be thrown down." Such was the definite and dire prediction. Those who heard were dumbfounded; neither by question nor other response did they attempt to elicit more. The literal fulfillment of that awful portent was but an incident in the annihilation of the city less than forty years later.[108]

Having said that, Jesus started on His last walk from Jerusalem to His home in Bethany and, stopped to rest at a convenient spot on the Mount of Olives.

> *Matthew 24:4 And Jesus left them, and went upon the Mount of Olives. And as he sat upon the Mount of Olives, the disciples came unto him privately, saying: **Tell us when shall these things be which thou hast said concerning the destruction of the temple, and the Jews; and what is the sign of thy coming, and of the end of the world, or the destruction of the wicked, which is the end of the world?***"

As Jesus was sitting in thoughtful reverie, The Apostles came to Him and asked a compound question, 'when would the destruction of the temple and the Jews take place and, what would be the sign of thy coming at the end of the world, being the destruction of the wicked, not the earth itself.

> *Matt I.V.5 And Jesus answered, and said unto them: **Take heed that no man deceive you**;*
>
> *6 For **many shall come in my name**, saying--I am Christ--**and shall deceive many**;*
>
> *7 Then **shall they deliver you up to be afflicted**, and shall kill you, and ye shall be hated of all nations, **for my name's sake**;*

"Take heed that no man deceive you" was the first and all-important caution; for within the lives of most of those apostles, many blaspheming imposters would arise, each claiming to be the Messiah. The return of Christ to earth as Lord and Judge was more remote than any of the Twelve realized.

They, the apostles, were told to expect persecution, not only at the hands of irresponsible individuals, but at the instance of the officials such as they who were at that moment intent on taking the life of the Lord Himself, and who would scourge them in the Synagogues, deliver them up to hostile tribunals, cite them before rulers and kings, and even put some of them to death -- all because of their testimony of the Christ.

> *Mark 13:11 But when **they shall lead [you], and deliver you up, take no thought beforehand what ye shall speak**, neither do ye premeditate: but **whatsoever shall be given you in that hour, that speak ye: for it is not ye that speak, but the Holy Ghost**.*

As they had been promised before, so again were they assured, when they would stand before councils, magistrates, or kings, the words they should speak would be given them in the hour of their trial, and therefore they were told to take no premeditative thought as to what they should say or how they should meet the issues confronting them; "for," said the Master, "it is not ye that speak, but the Holy Ghost."

> *Matt I.V. 8 And **then shall many be offended**, and shall betray one another, and shall hate one another;*
>
> *9 And many **false prophets shall arise, and shall deceive many**;*

---

[108] JTC Pg. 563

> *10 And because **iniquity shall abound, the love of many shall wax cold**;*
> *11 But **he that remaineth steadfast and is not overcome, the same shall be saved.***

Their labors would be complicated and opposed by the revolutionary propaganda of many false prophets, and differences of creed would disrupt families, and engender such bitterness that brothers would betray one another, and children would rise against their parents, accusing them of heresies and delivering them up to death. Even among those who had professed discipleship to Christ many would be offended and hatred would abound; love for the gospel would wax cold, and iniquity would be rampant among men; and only those who would endure to the end of their lives could be saved.

> *Matt I.V. 12 When **you, therefore, shall see the abomination of desolation**, spoken of by Daniel the prophet, **concerning the destruction of Jerusalem, then you shall stand in the holy place**; whoso readeth let him understand.*

This was a specific sign none could misunderstand. Daniel the prophet had foreseen the desolation and the abominations thereof, which comprised the forcible cessation of temple rites, and the desecration of Israel's shrine by pagan conquerors. A brief summary of notable events that transpired between His ascension and the destruction of Jerusalem.

Josephus and other historians record the constant war between the Jews and Roman emperors, other nations also entered in. The assault of the Greeks and the Syrians upon the Jews, in the course of which 50,000 Jews were slain at Seleucia, and 20,000 at Caesarea, 13,000 at Scythopolis, and 2,500 at Ascalon. Famine and earthquakes were of alarming frequency and of unusual severity including violent seismic disturbances at Rome. Josephus records a particularly severe earthquake that disrupted parts of Judea, and was accompanied by "amazing concussions and bellowing's of the earth—a manifest indication that some destruction was coming upon men."

As to the unprecedented horrors of the siege, which culminated in the utter destruction of Jerusalem and the Temple, Josephus estimates the number slain in Jerusalem alone as 1,100,000 and in other cities and rural parts a third as many more. Many tens of thousands were taken captive, to be afterward sold into slavery, or to be slain by wild beasts, or gladiatorial combat in the arena for the amusement of Roman spectators.

In the course of the siege, a wall was constructed about the entire city, thus fulfilling the Lords prediction (Luke 19:43), "thine enemies shall cast a trench about thee." In September A.D. 70 the city fell into the hands of the Romans; and afterwards the destruction was so thorough that its site was plowed up. Jerusalem was "trodden down of the Gentiles," and ever since has been under Gentile dominion, and so shall continue to be "until the times of the Gentiles be fulfilled." (Luke 21:24)[109]

A warning for salvation:
> *Matt I.V. 13 Then **let them who are in Judea flee into the mountains;***
> *14 **Let him who is on the housetop flee, and not return to take anything out of his house;***
> *15 **Neither let him who is in the field return back to take his clothes**;*
> *16 **And WO unto them that are with child**, and unto them that give suck in those days;*
> *17 Therefore, **pray you the Lord that your flight be not in the winter, neither on the Sabbath day;***
> *18 **For then, in those days, shall be great tribulation on the Jews, and upon the inhabitants of Jerusalem,** such as was not before sent upon Israel, of God, since the beginning of their kingdom until this time; no, **nor ever shall be sent again upon Israel.***
> *19 All things which have befallen them are **only the beginning of the sorrows which shall come upon them.***
> *20 And **except those days should be shortened, there should none of their flesh be saved;** but for the elect's sake, **according to the covenant, those days shall be shortened.***

---
[109] JTC and Josephus

The warning to all to flee from Jerusalem and Judea to the mountains when the armies begin to surround the city was so generally heeded by members of the Church, according to early Church writers not one Christian perished in the awful siege. The first siege by Gallus was unexpectedly raised, and then before the armies of Vespasian arrived at the walls, all Jews who had faith in the warning given by Christ to the apostles, and by these to the people, fled beyond Jordan, and congregated mostly at Pella. While these prophesies were partially fulfilled in the meridian of time, they remain to be fulfilled in our day and are nearer than can be imagined.

>*Matt I.V.21 Behold, these things I have spoken unto you concerning the Jews; and again, **after the tribulation of those days which shall come upon Jerusalem**, if any man shall say unto you, Lo, here is Christ, or there, believe him not;*
>
>*22 For **in those days there shall also arise false Christ's, and false prophets**, and shall show great signs and wonders, insomuch, that, **if possible, they shall deceive the very elect, who are the elect according to the covenant.***
>
>*23 Behold, I speak these things unto you **for the elect's sake**; and **you also shall hear of wars, and rumors of wars; see that ye be not troubled**, for all I have told you must come to pass; **but the end is not yet**.*
>
>*24 Behold, I have told you before;*
>
>*25 Wherefore, if they shall say unto you: Behold, **he is in the desert**; go not forth: Behold, **he is in the secret chambers; believe it not**;*
>
>*26 For as **the light of the morning cometh out of the east**, and shined even unto the west, and **covered the whole earth, so shall also the coming of the Son of Man be.***
>
>*27 And now I show unto you **a parable**. Behold, **whosoever the carcass is, there will the eagles be gathered together; so likewise, shall mine elect be gathered from the four quarters of the earth.***

Great tribulation will be poured out upon Jerusalem and, for an unspecified amount of time, Satan will have the power to raise up false Christs and false prophets to deceive the very elect of the covenant. Deceiving prophets and emissaries of the devil, will be alluring people to go into deserts, into secret chambers and all kind of places trying to convince them there are the places Christ can be found.

Jesus assures them in the day of the his coming in glory and vengeance, there shall be no doubt nor a chance of conflicting claims by contending sects, His coming will be as the sun coming from the east and will light up the whole world. The gathering of Israel will be as the gathering of eagles flocking to the place where the body of the true church will be established and proclaiming the Lords covenants to four corners of the earth.

Jesus goes on to describe the conditions which will prevail and become increasingly more violent in these last days:

>*Matt I.V.28 And they shall hear of **wars, and rumors of wars**.*
>
>*29 Behold **I speak for mine elect's sake; for nation shall rise against nation, and kingdom against kingdom; there shall be famines, and pestilences, and earthquakes, in divers' places.***
>
>*30 And again, because **iniquity** shall abound, the **love of men shall wax cold**; but **he that shall not be overcome, the same shall be saved**.*
>
>*31 And again, this **Gospel of the Kingdom shall be preached in all the world, for a witness unto all nations**, and then shall the end come, or the destruction of the wicked;*

No attempt is made in this commentary to be all comprehensive but, we feel inclined to give modern prophetic utterance for a more inclusive for-sight of these present times. As the Lord stated above ", this **Gospel of the Kingdom shall be preached in all the world, for a witness unto all nations.**"

>*"Now here is the difference between Zion and old Jerusalem. The Jews, or many of them, will gather back to Jerusalem in a state of unbelief in the true Messiah, believing in the prophets but rejecting the New Testament, and looking for the Messiah to come, honest-hearted no doubt, many of them. And they will rebuild Jerusalem after the times of the Gentiles are fulfilled. While in that state of unbelief*

> *Gog and Magog, the inhabitants of Russia and all those nations in northern Europe and northern Asia, a great multitude, will gather against the Jews before Jesus comes, and they will fill up the great valley of Armageddon, the great valley of Jehoshaphat and all the surrounding valleys; they will be like a cloud covering the land. Horses and chariots and horsemen, a very great army, will gather up there to take a spoil. For you know when the Rothschilds and the great bankers among the Jewish nation shall return back to their own land to rebuild the city of Jerusalem, carrying their capital with them, it will almost ruin some of the nations, and the latter will go up against Jerusalem to take a spoil. And they will succeed in taking half the city captive; and when they are in the act of destroying that city, behold the Lord will come with all his Saints, and he shall stand his feet on the Mount of Olives, "And in that day" says the Prophet Zachariah "shall the Lord go forth and fight against all those nations that have fought against Jerusalem, and their flesh shall consume away upon their bones, their eyes in their sockets. This great calamity comes upon the Jewish nation in consequence of their unbelief in the true Messiah"*[110].

While the world has gone into a state of a great apostasy since the Atonement of Jesus, we have been promised a restoration will take place in the end days.

The proper harmonization of the gospels shows Jesus to be in complete control of the Passover Law and His fulfillment there-of, every jot and tittle. Our Savior is in total control and very much mindful of the end days by prophesying and for-warning us of events, including His ongoing participation.

> *Matt I.V 32 And **again shall the abomination of desolation**, spoken of by Daniel the prophet, be fulfilled.*

The destruction of Israel during the meridian of time was the prototype of the second fulfillment of the abomination of desolation, spoken by Daniel the prophet. The true gospel will be preached, the Church will be established, and then the destruction of the wicked will come.

> *Matt I.V.33 And **immediately after the tribulation of those days, the sun shall be darkened, and the moon shall not give her light, and the stars shall fall from heaven, and the powers of heaven shall be shaken.***
>
> *34 Verily, I say unto you, **this generation**, in which these things shall be shown forth, **shall not pass away until all I have told you shall be fulfilled**.*
>
> *35 Although, **the days will come**, that heaven and earth shall pass away; yet my words shall not pass away, but **all shall be fulfilled**.*
>
> *36 And, as I said before, **after the tribulation of those days, and the powers of the heavens shall be shaken**, then shall appear the **sign of the Son of Man in heaven, and then shall all the tribes of the earth mourn; and they shall see the Son of Man coming in the clouds of heaven, with power and great glory;***
>
> *37 And whoso **treasureth up my word**, shall not be deceived, for **the Son of Man shall come**, and **he shall send his angels** before him with the great sound of a trumpet, and **they shall gather together the remainder of his elect from the four winds**, from one end of heaven to the other.*

Jesus unfolded before the Apostles many of the signs and destructions which would happen at His second coming, however He does not reveal the time. The Apostles thought it might be soon but Jesus answered their curiosity with a parable.

> *Matt I.V.38 **Now learn a parable of the fig-tree**--When its branches are yet tender, and it begins to put forth leaves, **you know that summer is nigh at hand;***
>
> *39 So likewise, **mine elect**, when they shall see all these things, **they shall know that he is near, even at the doors;***

---

[110] Orson Pratt JD Vol. 14: pg352

*40 **But of that day, and hour, no one knoweth**; no, not the angels of God in heaven, but my Father only.*

The <u>parable of the fig tree</u> is given for our understanding; for as the fig tree puts on its fruit first, so has the gospel and the Church been established first. As leaves begin to burst forth and show strong growth, so as the Church begins to go forth into the world, by this we may know the time of His coming is nigh, even at the door.

The day or the hour is not known, however, we shall be able to judge the closeness of the time by the actions, among other things, of the people around us.

*Matt I.V. 41 **But as it was in the days of Noah, so it shall be also at the coming of the Son of Man;***

*42 For it shall be with them, as it was in the days which were before the flood; for until the day that Noah entered into the ark **they were eating and drinking, marrying and giving in marriage;***

43 And knew not until the flood came, and took them all away; so shall also the coming of the Son of Man be.

*44 **Then shall be fulfilled that which is written, that in the last days, two shall be in the field, the one shall be taken, and the other left;***

*45 **Two shall be grinding at the mill**, the one shall be taken, and the other left;*

*46 And what I say unto one, I say unto all men; **watch, therefore, for you know not at what hour your Lord doth come.***

*47 But know this, **if the good man of the house had known in what watch** the thief would come, **he would have watched, and would not have suffered his house to have been broken up**, but would have been ready.*

The condition of men in the lasts days, just like in the days of Noah men will be given over to temporal living without any thought of what is to come. The good man and the elect of God need to be preparing for not only the daily physical needs but for the spiritual growth as well. Otherwise, their homes and their loved ones may be separated, because, as in the field and as in the mill, the Lord will come as a thief in the night and the faithful will be taken up and the sinner will be left standing alone.

*Matt I.V. 48 **Therefore be ye also ready**, for in such an hour as ye think not, **the Son of Man cometh**.*

*49 **Who, then, is a faithful and wise servant**, whom his lord hath made ruler over his household, to give them meat in due season?*

*50 **Blessed is that servant whom his lord, when he cometh, shall find so doing**; and verily I say unto you, he shall make him ruler over all his goods.*

51 But if that evil servant shall say in his heart: My lord delayeth his coming,

52 And shall begin to smite his fellow-servants, and to eat and drink with the drunken,

*53 **The lord** of that servant **shall come in a day when he looketh not for him, and in an hour that he is not aware of,***

*54 And shall cut him asunder, and **shall appoint him his portion with the hypocrites; there shall be weeping and gnashing of teeth.***

*55 And **thus cometh the end of the wicked**, according to the prophecy of Moses, saying: **They shall be cut off from among the people**; but the end of the earth is not yet, but by and by.*

We can speculate about the Lord's coming but, whether based on assumption, deduction, or calculation of dates, we cannot know of the hour or the day of the Savior's return. The good servant, however, will be honoring God by taking care of his personal and worldly responsibilities to his fellow man, and looking forward to the return of the Son of man. On the other hand, the evil servant, who denies any possible near advent of the Lord, who begins to take advantage of his fellow man and joins in their gluttony and drunkenness, will be cut off and be appointed a miserable portion of salvation.

The Parable of the 10 virgins

After the Savior gave the Apostles a view of future times and events and them the warning to watch, pray and be ready, He gave the following parable as good advice to the elect:

*Matthew 25:1 ¶ THEN shall the kingdom of heaven be likened unto **ten virgins, which took their lamps, and went forth to meet the bridegroom.***

*2 And **five of them were wise, and five [were] foolish**.*

*3 **They that [were] foolish** took their lamps, **and took no oil with them**:*

*4 But **the wise took oil** in their vessels with their lamps.*

*5 While the bridegroom tarried, **they all slumbered and slept.***

*6 And **at midnight** there was a cry made, Behold, **the bridegroom cometh**; go ye out to meet him.*

*7 Then **all those virgins arose, and trimmed their lamps***

*8 And **the foolish said unto the wise, Give us of your oil**; for our lamps are gone out.*

*9 But **the wise answered, saying, [Not so]; lest there be not enough for us and you: but go** ye rather to them that sell, **and buy for yourselves**.*

*10 And **while they went to buy, the bridegroom came**; and they that were ready went in with him to the marriage: **and the door was shut**.*

*11 Afterward came also **the other virgins, saying, Lord, Lord, open to us.***

*12 But he answered and said, Verily I say unto you, **I know you not.***

*13 Watch therefore, **for ye know neither the day nor the hour wherein the Son of man cometh.***

Joseph Smith summed it up nicely in the Doctrine & Covenants:

D&C 45:56 And at that day, when I shall come in my glory, shall the parable be fulfilled which I spake concerning the ten virgins.

57 For they that are wise and have received the truth, and have taken the Holy Spirit for their guide, and have not been deceived--verily I say unto you, they shall not be hewn down and cast into the fire, but shall abide the day.

58 And the earth shall be given unto them for an inheritance; and they shall multiply and wax strong, and their children shall grow up without sin unto salvation.

59 For the Lord shall be in their midst, and his glory shall be upon them, and he will be their king and their lawgiver.

How do you get oil for your lamp?

Jesus answered that question when He followed right up with:

The Parable of the talents.

*Matthew 25:14 ¶ For [the kingdom of heaven is] **as a man travelling into a far country,** [who] called his own servants, and delivered unto them his goods.*

*15 And, **unto one he gave five talents, to another two, and to another one**; to **every man according to his several ability**; and straightway took his journey.*

*16 Then **he that had received the five talents went** and traded with the same, **and made [them] other five talents**.*

*17 And likewise **he that [had received] two, he also gained other two.***

*18 But **he that had received one went and digged in the earth, and hid his lord's money.***

*19 **After a long time the lord of those servants cometh**, and reckoneth with them.*

*20 And so **he that had received five talents came and brought other five talents**, saying, Lord, thou deliveredst unto me five talents: **behold, I have gained beside them five talents more.***

*21 **His lord said unto him, Well done, [thou] good and faithful servant**: thou hast been faithful over a few things, **I will make thee ruler over many things**: enter thou into the joy of thy lord.*

*22 **He also that had received two talents came and said,** Lord, thou deliveredst unto me two talents: behold, **I have gained two other talents beside them**.*

*23 **His lord said unto him, Well done**, good and faithful servant; thou hast been faithful over a few things, **I will make thee ruler over many things**: enter thou into the joy of thy lord.*

24 Then he which had received the one talent came and said, Lord, I knew thee that thou art an hard man, reaping where thou hast not sown, and gathering where thou hast not strawed:

25 And I was afraid, and went and hid thy talent in the earth: lo, [there] thou hast [that is] thine.

*26 **His lord answered and said unto him, [Thou] wicked and slothful servant, thou knewest that I reap where I sowed not, and gather where I have not strawed:***

27 Thou oughtest therefore to have put my money to the exchangers, and [then] at my coming I should have received mine own with usury.

*28 Take therefore the talent from him, and **give [it] unto him which hath ten talents**.*

29 For unto every one that hath shall be given, and he shall have abundance: but from him that hath not shall be taken away even that which he hath.

30 And cast ye the unprofitable servant into outer darkness: there shall be weeping and gnashing of teeth.

The story in this particular, as in the other features relating to human acts and tendencies, is psychologically true; in a peculiar sense man are prone to conceive of the attributes of God as comprising in augmented degree the dominant traits of their own nature.

Both the servant who had been entrusted with five talents and he who had received but two were equally commended, and, as far as we are told, were equally recompensed. The talents bestowed upon each were the gift of his Lord, who knew well whether that servant was capable of using it to better advantage one, two, or five. Let no one conclude that good work of relatively small scope is less necessary or acceptable than like service of wider range. Many a man who has succeeded well in business with small capital would have failed in the administration of vast sums; so also, in spiritual achievements "there are diversities of gifts, but the same Spirit." Of the man endowed with many talents greater returns were expected; of the one-talented man relatively little was required, yet in that little he failed. At the least he could have delivered the money to the bank, through which it would have been kept in circulation to the benefit of the community, and would have earned interest meanwhile. Likewise, in the spiritual application, a man possessed of any good gift, such as musical ability, eloquence, skill in handicraft, or the like, ought to use that gift to the full, that he or others may be profited thereby; but should he be too neglectful to exercise his powers in independent service, he may assist others to profitable effort, by encouragement if by nothing more.[111]

Jesus uttering his last parable, and in words of certainty, impresses upon His disciples the inevitable judgment that awaits the world when He comes in the last days.

Matthew 25:31 ¶ When the Son of man shall come in his glory, and all the holy angels with him, then shall he sit upon the throne of his glory:

32 And before him shall be gathered all nations: and he shall separate them one from another, as a shepherd divideth [his] sheep from the goats:

33 And he shall set the sheep on his right hand, but the goats on the left.

34 Then shall the King say unto them on his right hand, Come, ye blessed of my Father, inherit the kingdom prepared for you from the foundation of the world:

35 For I was an hungred, and ye gave me meat: I was thirsty, and ye gave me drink: I was a stranger, and ye took me in:

---

[111] JTC ch. 32

36 Naked, and ye clothed me: I was sick, and ye visited me: I was in prison, and ye came unto me.

37 Then shall the righteous answer him, saying, Lord, when saw we thee an hungred, and fed [thee]? or thirsty, and gave [thee] drink?

38 When saw we thee a stranger, and took [thee] in? or naked, and clothed [thee]?

39 Or when saw we thee sick, or in prison, and came unto thee?

40 And the King shall answer and say unto them, Verily I say unto you, Inasmuch as ye have done [it] unto one of the least of these my brethren, ye have done [it] unto me.

41 Then shall he say also unto them on the left hand, Depart from me, ye cursed, into everlasting fire, prepared for the devil and his angels:

42 For I was an hungered, and ye gave me no meat: I was thirsty, and ye gave me no drink:

43 I was a stranger, and ye took me not in: naked, and ye clothed me not: sick, and in prison, and ye visited me not.

44 Then shall they also answer him, saying, Lord, when saw we thee an hungered, or athirst, or a stranger, or naked, or sick, or in prison, and did not minister unto thee?

45 Then shall he answer them, saying, Verily I say unto you, Inasmuch as ye did [it] not to one of the least of these, ye did [it] not to me.

46 And these shall go away into everlasting punishment: but the righteous into life eternal.

Viewing as one discourse the two parables and the teaching that directly followed, we find in it such unity of subject and thoroughness of treatment as to give to the whole both beauty and worth beyond the sum of these qualities exhibited in the several parts. Vigilant waiting in the Lord's cause, and the dangers of not being ready are exemplified in the story of the virgins; diligence in work and the calamitous results of sloth are prominent features of the tale of the talents. These two phases of service are of reciprocal and complementary import; it is as necessary at times to wait and at others to work. The lapse of a long period, as while the Bridegroom tarried, and as during the Master's absence in "a far country," is made plain throughout as intervening between the Lord's departure and His return in glory. The absolute certainty of the Christ coming to execute judgment upon the earth, in the which every soul shall receive according to his deserts, is the sublime summary of this unparalleled discourse.[112]

Jesus expects His sheep, those saints who have known His law, to be charitable, benevolent, and cooperative toward their fellow man, with light of the gospel to guide them. If the heart is right then great shall be the reward.

After Jesus finished these sayings, and in the last rays of the afternoon sun they were returned home.
REV

---

[112] JTC chap. 32

Chapter 8
The Passover meal

Passover preparation & meal	Event	Matthew	Mark	Luke	John
4th day, - *13th Nissan*, - (Wednesday)					
Preparing the Lamb	Jerusalem	Exodus			
Feast day in Two days	Bethany	26:1-2			
Jesus betrayal foretold	Bethany	26:2			
Chief priests plot to kill Jesus- not on feast day		26:3-5	14:1-2	22:1-2	
Woman anoints Jesus	Bethany	26:5-13	14:3-9		
Judas-final arrangements to betray Jesus		26:14-16	14:10-11	22:3-6	
5th day, - *14th Nissan*, - (Thursday)					
Preparing the Passover	Jerusalem	26:17-19	14:12-16	22:7-13	
6th day, - *15th Nissan* – (Friday night)					
Sat down w/Apostles	Jerusalem			22:14-18	
Began Supper	Jerusalem	26:20-21		22:19-20	
One will betray me	Jerusalem	26:22-25	14:17-21	22:21-23	
Institute Sacrament	Jerusalem	26:26-29	14:22-25		
Jesus washes their feet	Jerusalem				13:1-11
Jesus explains service	Jerusalem				13:12-17
Jesus dismisses Judas from table	Jerusalem				13:18-30
Strife at table	Jerusalem			22:23-30	
Love one another	Jerusalem				13:31-35
Peters' denial prophesied	Jerusalem			22:31-34	13:36-38
Buy a Sword	Jerusalem			22:35-38	

Jesus and the disciples left the Mount of Olives and returned to Bethany for the night and, most probably on the way home, The Savior made another specific prediction concerning His impending betrayal and subsequent crucifixion.

He said to the disciples:
*Matthew 26: 2"Ye know that **after two days** is the feast of the Passover, and the Son of man is <u>betrayed</u> to be crucified".*[113]

Once again this identifies the 6th day, or the 15th of Nissan, as the feast day and the day of His betrayal and the mode His death by crucifixion.
Matthew 26:3 **Then assembled together the chief priests, and the scribes, and the elders of the people,** *unto the palace of the high priest, who was called Caiaphas,*
4 **And consulted that they might take Jesus by subtlety, and kill [him].**
5 But they said, **not on the feast [day], lest there be an uproar among the people.**

Two days before the Feast Day, members of the Sanhedrin in consultation at the palace of Caiaphas, were discussing how they might take Jesus and kill Him. However, these evil conspirators were adamant about accomplishing their deathly deed with subtlety on the feast day, and above all don't kill Him on this day for fear of the people. There were thousands, perhaps tens of thousands of His converts in town, and they feared an uprising.

---

[113] Matt 26:1-2, Mark 14:1-2

Jesus, knowing this was His last day of freedom with his family, and knowing the ordeal He was facing, He no doubt was giving them comfort and praying with them and preparing Himself. Understandably, little is written concerning this day, there are few words that can describe the emotions surrounding the feelings involved. Knowing that Jesus had been anointed to this end would no doubt be heart rending time.

John in his Gospel, fixes the day of the anointing as 6 days before the Passover:

> *John 12:1 ¶ THEN **Jesus six days before the Passover came to Bethany**, where Lazarus was which had been dead, whom he raised from the dead.*
>
> *2 There they made him a supper; and **Martha served: but Lazarus was one of them that sat at the table with him.***
>
> *3 Then took **Mary a pound of ointment of spikenard, very costly, and anointed the feet of Jesus, and wiped his feet with her hair**: and the house was filled with the odour of the ointment.*

A careful reading and understanding of this event, places the actual anointing on the evening before the 1st day of the Passover or on the 9th of Nisan.

> *Matthew 26:6 ¶ Now when **Jesus was in Bethany**, in the house of Simon the leper,*
>
> *7 **There came unto him a woman having an alabaster box of very precious ointment, and poured it on his head, as he sat [at meat].***
>
> *8 But when **his disciples saw [it], they had indignation, saying, To what purpose [is] this waste?***
>
> *9 For this **ointment might have been sold for much**, and given to the poor.*
>
> *10 When Jesus understood [it], he said unto them, **Why trouble ye the woman?** for she hath wrought a good work upon me.*
>
> *11 For ye have the poor always with you; but me ye have not always.*
>
> *12 For in that **she hath poured this ointment on my body, she did [it] for my burial.***
>
> *13 Verily I say unto you, Wheresoever this gospel shall be preached in the whole world, [there] shall also this, that this woman hath done, be told for a memorial of her.*

Mark 14: 3-9 gives us a supportive account of the same incident.

Matthew and Mark felt it necessary to share their testimony at this place in the gospel, to remind us that while at the supper in Bethany Jesus had been anointed by Mary. Why? "She did <u>for my burial</u>." What great faith and understanding Mary must have had, as she recognized Jesus was soon to die for the sins of all mankind. While these testimonies at this time seems to break the harmony of the gospels, it must be remembered, the apostles felt it necessary to remind us the anointing was of significance for His burial and not for the commemorative lamb they were preparing for the Passover meal. The Lord desires us to study out the gospels by the spirit and gain our own testimony.

However, Exodus tells us this 4th day, is when the chosen commemorative lamb of the Passover meal is brought forth and other preparations are being placed into motion and readied for sacrifice on the 5th day. Matthew, in speaking with Jesus, identifies the 15th of Nissan as the feast day, as well as reaffirming His betrayal.[114]

> *Matthew 26: 14 ¶ Then one of the twelve, called **Judas Iscariot, went unto the chief priests**,*
>
> *15 And said unto them, **What will ye give me, and I will deliver him unto you? And they covenanted with him for thirty pieces of silver.***
>
> *16 And from that time he sought opportunity to betray him.*

Mark 14:10-11 gives us virtually the same report as does Luke 22: 3-6. Readings of these three gospel writers does not actually fix this day, but their place in the harmony of the gospels unmistakably establishes this event on the 4th day.

Joseph Smith said,

> ***"Who is it that writes these Scriptures? Not the men of the world or mere casual observers, but Apostles**—men who knew one gift from another, and of course were capable of writing about it; ---*
> *---**No man knows the things of God but by the Spirit of God."***

---

[114] Mat 26:1-2

He further stated, *"Now taking it for granted that the scriptures say what they mean, and mean what they say, we have sufficient grounds to go on and prove from the bible that the gospel has always been the same; ...."*

Trying to speculate why God inspired the apostles to record events in this manner, only He knows. Without doubt God knew the great apostasy was about to take place and inspired the apostles in writing exactly what He wanted us to have. We have previously stated in chapter 4 that a great many of the most plain and precious truths have been taken from the bible.[115] However, what has been retained in the four gospels, and if studied closely and placed in the proper chronology, will give us a clear picture and a proper understanding of what transpired in those last days of the Savior's life.

However, the 4th day was indeed busy.

Try to imagine what anguish the family members, and especially Mary his mother, were feeling at this time. Mary knew her Son was the Christ, she had repeatedly heard Him prophecy of His own death, and the death of a child exceeds almost all sorrow and the heart aches in pain. Jesus was no doubt, trying to comfort Mary and the family and with prayer, preparing them for what was about to unfold.

The time of the Lord had now come for the last official Passover. The Great and Eternal Sacrifice, in order to fulfill the Law of Moses, is about to be ushered by the Last Meal. In order to understand more clearly what the Savior went through in our behalf and for our salvation, we will examine the details more thoroughly in the ensuing chapters.

*Mosiah 13:29 And now I say unto you that it was expedient that **there should be a law given to the children of Israel, yea, even a very strict law**; for they were a stiff-necked people, quick to do iniquity, and slow to remember the Lord their God;*

*30 Therefore there was a law given them, yea, **a law of performances and of ordinances, a law which they were to observe strictly from day to day**, to keep them in remembrance of God and their duty towards him.*

*31 But behold, **I say unto you, that all these things were types of things to come.***

Many people ask what difference it makes how strictly we observe the different laws as they proceed to act in accordance with their own understanding. These are a stiff-necked people who are slow to remember their God and without the Law of Moses, a very strict law of performances and ordinances, they will not remember their God and their duty towards Him. The law of the Passover and its accompanying strictness of detail down to the last jot and tittle, is about to be fulfilled by our Savior. This Law is a similitude of what the Savior must fulfill to accomplish our atonement.

5th Day, 14th Nissan

*Luke 22:7 ¶ Then came the **day of unleavened bread, when the Passover must be killed.***

*8 And **he sent Peter and John, saying, Go and prepare us the Passover**, that we may eat.*

*9 And they said unto him, **Where wilt thou that we prepare**?*

*10 And he said unto them, Behold, **when ye are entered into the city, there shall a man meet you, bearing a pitcher of water;** follow him into the house where he entereth in.*

*11 And ye shall **say unto the Goodman of the house, The Master saith unto thee, Where is the guest chamber, where I shall eat the Passover with my disciples?***

12 And he shall shew you a large upper room furnished: there make ready.

*13 **And they went, and found as he had said unto them: and they made ready the Passover.***

How do they make ready the Passover? Josephus, the historian during Christ's time, gave us these accounts of explanation of the Passover:

---

[115] 1 Nephi 13:28

> "In the month of Xanthicus, which by us called Nissan, and is the beginning of our year, *on the fourteenth day* of the lunar month, when the sun is in Aries, (for this month it was that we were delivered from bondage under the Egyptians) the law ordained that we should every year slay that sacrifice which I before told you we slew when we came out of Egypt, and which is called the Passover; and so do we celebrate this Passover in companies, leaving nothing of what we sacrifice till the following day.
>
> *The feast of unleavened bread succeeds that of the Passover, and falls on the fifteenth day of the month and continues seven days, wherein they feed on unleavened bread; on every one of which days two bulls are killed, and one ram, and seven lambs.* Now these lambs are entirely burnt, besides the kid of the goats which is added to all of the rest, for sins; for it is intended as a feast for the priest on every one of those days.
>
> But on the second day of unleavened bread, which is the sixteenth day of the month, they first partake of the fruits of the earth, for before that day they do not touch them. And while they suppose it proper to honor God, from whom they obtain this plentiful provision, in the first place, they offer the first fruits of their barley, and that in the following manner. They take a handful of the ears, and dry them, then beat them small, and purge the barely from the bran; they then bring one tenth deal to the alter, to God; and, casting one handful of it upon the fire, they leave the rest of it for the use of the priest; and after this it is that they may publicly or privately reap their harvest. They also at this participation of the first fruits of the earth, sacrifice a lamb, as a burnt offering to God."[116]

> "So these high priests, upon the coming of their feast which is called the Passover, when *they slay their sacrifices, from the ninth hour till the eleventh, but so that a company not less than ten belong to every sacrifice (for it is not lawful for them to feast singly by themselves), and many of us are twenty in a company.* The **count of the number of sacrifices was two hundred and fifty-six thousand five hundred**; which, upon allowance of no more than ten that feast together, **amounts to** *two million seven hundred thousand and two hundred persons* that were pure and holy; for those that have the leprosy, or the gonorrhea, or women that have their monthly courses, or such as are otherwise polluted, it is not lawful for them to be partakers of this sacrifice; nor indeed for any foreigners either, who come to worship."[117]

This recordation makes it abundantly clear the Passover Lamb is slain on the 14th day of Nisan, (5th day of the Passover), between the hours of 3pm and 6pm. The Passover is eaten on the evening of the 5th day and the next day, 15th of Nissan (6th day of the Passover), is the feast day, or Holy Convocation, and the 1st day of unleavened bread.

The 16th day of Nissan, (7th day of the Passover), is the 2nd day of unleavened bread and a special feast day of celebration, in partaking of the first fruits to honor God. As planned by the Savior, this 7th day was also the regular 7th day (Saturday) Sabbath.

This history has confirmed in Leviticus:
Leviticus 23:1 ¶ *AND the LORD spake unto Moses, saying,*
2 Speak unto the children of Israel, and say unto them, **[Concerning] the feasts of the LORD, which ye shall proclaim [to be] holy convocations, [even] these [are] my feasts.**
3 Six days shall work be done: **but the seventh day [is] the sabbath of rest, an holy convocation;** *ye shall do no work [therein]: it [is] the sabbath of the LORD in all your dwellings.*

4 ¶ **These [are] the feasts of the LORD, [even] holy convocations, which ye shall proclaim in their seasons***.*
5 In **the fourteenth [day] of the first month** *at even [is] the LORD'S Passover.*
6 And on the **fifteenth day of the same month [is] the feast of unleavened bread** *unto the LORD: seven days ye must eat unleavened bread.*
7 In the **first day ye shall have an holy convocation**: *ye shall do no servile work therein.*
8 But ye shall offer an offering made by fire unto the LORD seven days: in the seventh day [is] **an holy convocation:** *ye shall do no servile work [therein].*

---
[116] Josephus antiq. 3-10-5
[117] Josephus: Wars 6-9-3

Leviticus also confirms the 1st and 7th days of unleavened bread are holy convocations, much like modern day solemn assemblies, and are special days of worship that were preceded by a day of preparation with sacrifices. The preparation day was commonly called butcher day, because the sacrifices are to be slain for the Passover meal and the convocation day.

Now it was evening of the 5th day, the evening between the 14th and 15th day of Nissan. Jesus joined His Apostles in the large upper room in which Peter and John[118] had prepared the Passover meal, the final approved Passover to be known ever after to the Church as the Last Supper.

> *Luke 22:14 And **when the hour was come, he sat down, and the twelve apostles with him.***
>
> *15 And he said unto them with desire, **I have desired to eat this Passover with you before I suffer:***
>
> *16 **For I say unto you, I will not any more eat thereof, until it be fulfilled in the kingdom of God.***

Just as in the days of Egypt, when the great "I AM" provided a way for the obedient to escape the plague of death of the "first born", Jesus is now preparing the way for those who are willing to be obedient in following the doctrines of Christ, to be able to escape the snares of this world and obtain immortality and eternal life in His kingdoms.

After payer:

> *Matthew 26:21 And as they did eat, **he said, Verily I say unto you, that one of you shall betray me.***
>
> *22 And they were exceeding sorrowful, and **began every one of them to say unto him, Lord, is it I?***
>
> *23 And he answered and said, **He that dippeth [his] hand with me in the dish**, the same shall betray me.*
>
> *24 The Son of man goeth as it is written of him: **but woe unto that man by whom the Son of man is betrayed!** it had been good for that man if he had not been born".*
>
> *25 Then **Judas, which betrayed him, answered and said, Master, is it I?** He said unto him, Thou hast said.*

The Savior made a very grievous statement to the Apostles, one of them would betray Him, upon which they were exceedingly sorrowful. Each of them slowly began to ask the question, *"is it I?"* Even Judas who had betrayed Him asked as well, so his silence would not give him away, to which Jesus must have given a general answer *"Thou hast said."* There was deep concern among them because the Savior had stated, *"it had been good for that man if he had not been born".*

There are many discussions regarding Judas's betrayal; is he the king of traitors? Is he a son of perdition? Did he partake of all knowledge through the Holy Ghost? Many questions can be raised, but for now we will let the Book of Mormon give us a possible answer:

> *3 Nephi 28:34 **And wo be unto him that will not hearken unto the words of Jesus,** and also to them whom he hath chosen and sent among them; for whoso receiveth not the words of Jesus and the words of those whom he hath sent receiveth not him; **and therefore he will not receive them at the last day;***
>
> *35 And it would be **better for them if they had not been born. For do ye suppose that ye can get rid of the justice of an offended God,** who hath been trampled under feet of men, that thereby salvation might come?*

As Jesus and the Apostles began to eat:

> *Matthew 26:26 ¶ And as they were eating, Jesus took bread, and blessed [it], and brake [it], and gave [it] to the disciples, and said, **Take, eat; this is my body.***

---

[118] Matt. 22:8

>   *JST: Matt 26:22 And as they were eating, Jesus took bread and brake it, and blessed it, and gave to his disciples, and said,* **Take, eat; this is in remembrance of my body which I give a ransom for you.**
>
>   *Luke 22:20 Likewise also the* **cup after supper,** *saying,* **This cup [is] the <u>new testament</u> in my blood, which is shed for you.**
>
>   *JST Mark 14:23 And he said unto them,* **This is in remembrance of my blood which is shed for many, and the new testament which I give unto you;** *for of me ye shall bear record unto all the world.*
>   *24 And* **as oft as ye do this ordinance, ye will remember me in this hour that I was with you and drank with you of this cup,** *even the last time in my ministry.*
>   *25 Verily I say unto you,* **Of this ye shall bear record;** *for I will no more drink of the fruit of the vine with you, until that day that I drink it new in the kingdom of God.*
>   *26 And now they were grieved, and wept over him.*

The God of Heaven, beginning with Adam and for four thousand years, had directed his people to offer sacrifices, sacrifices that were in the similitude of the future atonement of the Son of God. In explaining the rituals and performances followed in celebrating the Passover, McConkie quotes Dummelow as follows:

"(1) the first cup was blessed and drunk. (2) the hands were washed while a blessing was said. (3) Bitter herbs, emblematic of the sojourn in Egypt, were partaken of, dipped in sour broth made of vinegar and bruised fruit. (4) The son of the house asked his father to explain the origin of the observance. (5) The lamb and the flesh of the thank offerings (*chagigah*) were placed on the table, and the first part of the Hallel sung (Psalms 113,114). (6) The second cup was blessed and drunk. (7) Unleavened bread was blessed and broken, a fragment of it eaten, then a fragment of the thank offerings, then a fragment of the lamb. (8) **Preliminaries being ended, the feast proceeded at leisure till all was consumed**. (9) The lamb being quite finished, the third cup, the cup of blessing, was blessed and drunk. (10) The fourth cup was drunk, and meanwhile the second part of the Hallel (Psalms 115-118 was sung." …

"The Jewish ritual of breaking the Passover bread was as follows: 'Then washing his hands, and taking two loaves, he breaks one, and lays the broken loaf upon the whole one, saying '"Blessed be he who causeth bread to grow out of the earth." Then, putting a piece of bread and some bitter herbs together, he dips them in sour broth, saying this blessing: 'Blessed be thou, O Lord God, our eternal King, he who hath sanctified us by his precepts, and commanded us to eat.'" Then he eats the unleavened bread and the bitter herbs together. But is unlikely that Jesus, who was founding a new rite, followed the Jewish ritual in every detail."

Of "the cup" which Jesus blessed and passed among them, Dummelow comments: "Since it was taken after supper (Luke and Paul), and is expressly called the latter the 'cup of blessing' (1 Cor. 10:16), it was clearly the third cup of the paschal supper, called the 'cup of blessing' (no.9). the ritual was as follows; (1) It was washed and cleansed; (2) the wine it was mingled with water, and blessed; (3) it was crowned, i.e. the worshippers stood around it in a ring; (4) the householder veiled his head and sat down; (5) he drank it, holding it with both hands.

"That **the cup of the Christian sacrament was also mingled with water,** was indicated by Jesus himself, when he called it 'this fruit of the vine,'" The Talmud says, "The rabbis have a tradition. **Over wine which hath not water mingled with it they do not say the blessing**, '"Blessed be he that created the fruit of the vine,'" but. "Blessed be he that created the fruit of the tree." And it is added, 'The wise agree with Rabbi Eleazar, that one ought not to bless the cup of the blessing till water is mingled with it.'"[119]

We include this information in order to point out just how extensive the jots and tittles of the gospel really are.

Now as Jesus and his apostles celebrated the feast of the Passover, the time had come for the last and great Eternal sacrifice to be made that would do away with the ordinances and performances of the Law of Moses.

Amulek explained:

>   *Alma 34:8 And now, behold, I will testify unto you of myself that these things are true. Behold,* **I say unto you, that I do know that Christ shall come among the children of men, to take upon him**

---
[119] Dummelow, p. 710

the transgressions of his people, and that he shall atone for the sins of the world; for the Lord God hath spoken it.

*9 **For it is expedient that an atonement should be made; for according to the great plan of the Eternal God there must be an atonement made, or else all mankind must unavoidably perish;** yea, all are hardened; yea, all are fallen and are lost, and must perish except it be through the atonement which it is expedient should be made.*

*10 For it is expedient that there should be a great and last sacrifice; yea, not a sacrifice of man, neither of beast, neither of any manner of fowl; for it shall not be a human sacrifice; **but it must be an infinite and eternal sacrifice.***

*11 Now **there is not any man that can sacrifice his own blood which will atone for the sins of another.** Now, if a man murdereth, behold will our law, which is just, take the life of his brother? I say unto you, Nay.*

12 But the law requireth the life of him who hath murdered; therefore, there can be nothing which is short of an infinite atonement which will suffice for the sins of the world.

*13 Therefore, it is expedient that **there should be a great and last sacrifice, and then shall there be, or it is expedient there should be, a stop to the shedding of blood; then shall the law of Moses be fulfilled; yea, it shall be all fulfilled, every jot and tittle and none shall have passed away.***

*14 And behold, this is the whole meaning of the law**, every whit pointing to that great and last sacrifice**; and that great and last sacrifice will be the Son of God, yea, infinite and eternal.*

When Jesus appeared to the Nephites right after His resurrection, He affirmed that animal sacrifice was no more and He had fulfilled the Law of Moses:

*3 Nephi 9:17 And as many as have received me, to them have I given to become the sons of God; and even so will I to as many as shall believe on my name, **for behold, by me redemption cometh, and in me is the law of Moses fulfilled.***

18 I am the light and the life of the world. I am Alpha and Omega, the beginning and the end.

*19 And **ye shall offer up unto me no more the shedding of blood;** yea, your sacrifices and your burnt offerings shall be done away, **for I will accept none of your sacrifices and your burnt offerings.***

*20 **And ye shall offer for a sacrifice unto me a broken heart and a contrite spirit.** And whoso cometh unto me with a broken heart and a contrite spirit, **him will I baptize with fire and with the Holy Ghost,** even as the Lamanites, because of their faith in me at the time of their conversion, were baptized with fire and with the Holy Ghost, and they knew it not.*

21 Behold, I have come unto the world to bring redemption unto the world, to save the world from sin.

Washing of the feet;
*John 13:2 **And supper being ended, the devil having now put into the heart of Judas Iscariot, Simon's [son], to betray him;***

3 Jesus knowing that the Father had given all things into his hands, and that he was come from God, and went to God;

*4 **He riseth from supper, and laid aside his garments; and took a towel, and girded himself.***

*5 After that he poureth water into a bason, and **began to wash the disciples' feet,** and to wipe [them] with the towel wherewith he was girded.*

*6 Then cometh he to Simon Peter: and **Peter saith unto him, Lord, dost thou wash my feet?***

*7 Jesus answered and said unto him, **What I do thou knowest not now;** but thou shalt know hereafter.*

8 Peter saith unto him, Thou shalt never wash my feet. Jesus answered him, If I wash thee not, thou hast no part with me.

9 Simon Peter saith unto him, Lord, not my feet only, but also [my] hands and [my] head.

10 Jesus saith to him, **He that is washed needeth not save to wash [his] feet, but is clean every whit: and ye are clean, <u>but not all</u>.**

11 For he knew who should betray him; therefore, said he, Ye are not all clean.

12 So after he had washed their feet, and had taken his garments, and was set down again, he said unto them, Know ye what I have done to you?

Washing is a custom under the Jewish law, and Jesus performed this ordinance and thus fulfilled another part of the Law of Moses. In washing his apostles' feet, He instituted a sacred ordinance that will be found with the legal administrators in the true Church, wherever it may be found. Seek and ye shall find.

When Jesus had finished he pronounced them clean "every whit", except one, the one who would betray Him.

...Know ye what I have done to you?

John 13:14 If I then, [your] Lord and Master, have washed your feet; ye also ought to wash one another's feet.

15 For **I have given you an example**, that ye should do as I have done to you.

16 Verily, verily, I say unto you, **The servant is not greater than his lord; neither he that is sent greater than he that sent him**.

17 If ye know these things, happy are ye if ye do them.

Jesus had just given them the perfect example of what it meant to serve. If He as Master served them by washing their feet and sent them into the world, then how could they be greater than the Master and do anything but be a servant to each other and the world? If they could know this principle, then they should be happy to follow His example.

As Jesus reseated Himself at the table with the apostles He said:

Luke 22:21 ¶ But, **behold, the hand of him that betrayeth me [is] with me on the table.**

22 And truly the Son of man goeth, as it was determined: **but woe unto that man by whom he is betrayed!**

Jesus has referenced Psalm 41, *9 Yea, mine own familiar friend, in whom I trusted, which did eat of my bread, hath lifted up [his] heel against me.*

John 13:18 ¶ **I speak not of you all: I know whom I have chosen: but that the scripture may be fulfilled, He that eateth bread with me hath lifted up his heel against me**

19 **Now I tell you before it come, that, when it is come to pass, ye may believe that I am [he].**

20 Verily, verily, I say unto you, He that receiveth whomsoever I send receiveth me; and he that receiveth me receiveth him that sent me.

21 When Jesus had thus said, he was troubled in spirit, and testified, and said, Verily, verily, **I say unto you, that one of you shall betray me.**

22 Then the **disciples looked one on another**, doubting of whom he spake.

23 Now there was leaning on Jesus' bosom one of his disciples, whom Jesus loved.

24 Simon Peter therefore beckoned to him, that he should ask who it should be of whom he spake.

25 He then lying on Jesus' breast saith unto him, Lord, who is it?

John looked up quietly and said, *"Lord, who is it?"*
Jesus softly answered him, *"to whom I give the sop when I dipped it"*.

26 Jesus answered, He it is, to whom I shall give a sop, when I have dipped [it]. And **when he had dipped the sop, he gave [it] to Judas Iscariot**, [the son] of Simon.

27 And after the sop Satan entered into him. Then said Jesus unto him**, That thou doest, do quickly**

Jesus then handed the sop to Judas Iscariot and Satan entered into him. The savior then looked at Judas and said, *"that thou doest, do quickly."* No one at the table knew why Jesus told Judas to do that, except they thought probably He was sending him on an errand. Judas went out immediately into the night.

> *28 Now **no man at the table knew for what intent he spake** this unto him.*
>
> *29 For some [of them] thought, because Judas had the bag, that Jesus had said unto him, Buy [those things] that we have need of against the feast; or, that he should give something to the poor.*
>
> *30 He then having received the sop went immediately out: and it was night.*

Judas, already the possessor of 30 pieces of silver, had Satan entered into his heart and was only waiting for the opportunity to accomplish his deed. The rest of the apostles wonder at these proclamations and ask questions and also created some contention in their hearts:

> *Luke 22:23 And **they began to enquire among themselves**, which of them it was that should do this thing.*
>
> *24 And **there was also a strife among them, which of them should be accounted the greatest.***
>
> *25 And he said unto them, **The kings of the Gentiles exercise lordship over them**; and they that exercise authority upon them are called benefactors.*
>
> *26 **But ye [shall] not [be] so: but he that is greatest among you, let him be as the younger; and he that is chief, as he that do***
>
> *27 For **whether [is] greater, he that sitteth at meat, or he that serveth? [is] not he that sitteth at meat**? but I am among you as he that serveth.*
>
> *28 Ye are they which have continued with me in my temptations.*
>
> *29 And **I appoint unto you a kingdom**, as my Father hath appointed unto me;*
>
> *30 **That ye may eat and drink at my table in my kingdom, and sit on thrones judging the twelve tribes of Israel.***

The Apostles began to discuss the situation between themselves, as to which of them would do such a thing. Then they began to contend one with another, as to which among them would be the greatest? Jesus had explained this question to them before and restated; you have been with me from the beginning and you are not of the worldly kingdoms; I appoint unto you kingdoms, as the father has appointed unto me; you eat and drink at my table and will be judges over the twelve tribes of Israel.

> *John 13:31 ¶ Therefore, when he was gone out, Jesus said, **Now is the Son of man glorified, and God is glorified in him.***
>
> *32 If God be glorified in him, God shall also glorify him in himself, and shall straightway glorify him.*
>
> *33 Little children, yet a little while I am with you. Ye shall seek me: and as I said unto the Jews, **Whither I go, ye cannot come; so now I say to you.***
>
> *34 A new commandment I give unto you, **That ye love one another**; as I have loved you, that ye also love one another.*
>
> *35 **By this shall all [men] know that ye are my disciples, if ye have love one to another.***

Jesus adds glory to the Father! Jesus speaks as though the atonement was complete, and so the final stages are in motion.
"What did Jesus do? Why; I do the things I saw my Father do when worlds came rolling into existence. My Father worked out His kingdom with fear and trembling, and I must do the same; when I get my kingdom, I shall present it to the Father, so that He may obtain kingdom upon kingdom, and it will exalt him in glory. He will obtain a higher exaltation, and I will take his place, and thereby become exalted myself. So that Jesus treads the tracks of his Father, and inherits what God did before; and God is thus glorified and exalted in the salvation and exaltation of all his children."[120] In a little while He goes

---

[120] Joseph Fielding Smith, Teachings pp.374-378

to be with His Father, and at this time the apostles could not go, but the work was not done and so a new commandment He gave them, "Love one another."

> *John 13:36 Simon **Peter said unto him, Lord, whither goest thou?** Jesus answered him, **Whither I go, thou canst not follow me now; but thou shalt follow me afterwards**.*
>
> *37 Peter said unto him, Lord, **why cannot I follow thee now? I will lay down my life for thy sake**.*
>
> **38 Jesus answered him, Wilt thou lay down thy life for my sake?**
>
> *Luke 22:31 And the Lord said, Simon, **Simon, behold, Satan hath desired [to have] you, that he may sift [you] as wheat:***
>
> *32 But **I have prayed for thee, that thy faith fail not**: and **when thou art converted, strengthen thy brethren**.*

Peter was still insistent:
> *Luke 22:33 And he said unto him, Lord, I am ready to go with thee, both into prison, and to death.*

When Peter stoutly declared again his readiness to go with Jesus, even into prison or to death, the <u>Lord silenced him with the remark</u>:

> **Luke 22:34 And he said, I tell thee, Peter, the cock shall not crow this day, before that thou shalt thrice deny that thou knowest me.**
>
> **Luke 22:35 And he said unto them, When I sent you without purse, and scrip, and shoes, lacked ye anything? And they said, Nothing.**

> *36 Then said he unto them, But now, he that hath a purse, let him take it, and likewise his scrip: and he that hath no sword, let him sell his garment, and buy one.*
> *37 For I say unto you, that this that is written must yet be accomplished in me, and he was reckoned among the transgressors: for the things concerning me have an end.*

The Lord was soon to be numbered among the transgressors, as had been foreseen; and His disciples would be regarded as the devotees of an executed criminal. Jesus reminded them when He sent them out to declare the gospel without purse, scrip or shoes they lacked nothing because He had provided for them. Jesus tells them He is about to fulfill prophecy concerning Him and will be no longer in their midst. When they as the Lords ministers are faced with persecution, do they turn the other cheek or defend themselves? Will their daily needs be supplied by others or do they fend for themselves? When the Lord is no longer in their midst providing the way, what will be their choices?

> *Luke22: 38 And they said, Lord, behold, here [are] two swords. And He said unto them ,It is enough.*

"Jesus had authorized the disciples to defend themselves in the days of turmoil ahead. Not fully understanding they here offer two swords to defend Him. He, however, has made the election to die and so dismisses their offer with an, 'Enough-of-this-kind-of-talk' statement."[121]

---
[121] DNTC 772

Chapter 9
Mount of Olives & Intercessory Prayer

Night 6th day, 15th Nissan, (Thursday)	Location	Matthew	Mark	Luke	John
Went to Mount of Olives	Mount	26:30	14:26	22:39	
Let not your Heart be troubled-mansions	Mount				14:1-4
Doubting Thomas	Mount				14:5-7
Shew us the Father -Keep my commandments	Mount				14:8-15
Second comforter	Mount				14:16-18
Soon ye will not see me	Mount				14:19-26
I go to the Father	Mount				14:27-31
Jesus the vine	Mount				15:1-9
Keep the commandments & Love one another	Mount				15:10-17
World will hate you	Mount				15:18-25
Send the comforter	Mount				15:26-27
All ye shall be offended		26:31-32	14:27-28		16:1-6
Whither thou goest Peter, I will not be offended		26:33-35	14:29-31		
Jesus to Leave & send the Holy Ghost	Mount				16:7
Mission of the Holy Ghost	Mount				16:8-15
Sorrow of His death & Joy in His Resurrection	Mount				16:16-22
Relationship between the Father & Son	Mount				16:23-30
Apostles to be scattered	Mount				16:31-33
Intercessory Prayer (Eternal Life, prays for Apostles & saints, all to be one)	Gethsemane			22:39	17:1-5, 6-19, 20-26

"And **when they had sung an hymn**, they went out into the mount of Olives." ……

"¶ And **he came out, and went, as he was wont, to the mount of Olives; and his disciples also followed him**."[122]

We are indebted to the gospel of John for information on the discourse of this night, such as we have, as he alone gave us chapters 14-17. We will only briefly discuss the contents of these chapters in order to obtain a general understanding of what transpired that fateful night. The purpose of this work is to have a clearer understanding of what happened in the fulfillment of the Law of Moses, not to explore the deeper meaning of all the doctrinal revelations involved.

Seeing the sorrowful state of the Eleven, Jesus bid them to be of good cheer:
John 14:1 ¶ **LET not your heart be troubled**: ye believe in God, believe also in me.
   2 **In my Father's house are many mansions**: if [it were] not [so], I would have told you. **I go to prepare a place for you**.
   3 And if I go and prepare a place for you, **I will come again, and receive you unto myself; that where I am, [there] ye may be also**.

---
[122] Matt 26:30, , Mark 14:26

4 ¶ And whither I go ye know, and the way ye know.

The Savior tries to calm the disciples' anxiety by explaining to them there are many degrees of life and salvation in the kingdom of heaven. The idea that after death there is only Heaven or Hell is a false concept. On the contrary, a place is prepared for every man where he shall be rewarded according to his works. Jesus tells the disciples, since they believe in God, to believe in Him also He will be returning home to prepare a place of exaltation for them in His Fathers' world. Jesus assures them of His eventual return and that He will personally receive them so they too may live with Him in the celestial glory. He tells them they know where He is going and how to get there.

Doubting Thomas, the skeptical one, desired to have a little more clarity:

John 14:5 Thomas saith unto him, Lord, **we know not whither thou goest; and how can we know the way?**

6 Jesus saith unto him, **I am the way,** *the truth, and the life:* **no man cometh unto the Father, but by me.**

7 **If ye had known me, ye should have known my Father also***: and from henceforth ye know him, and have seen him*
.

Christ tells them He is the one who charts the course, and entrance into the kingdoms of heaven are gained only by walking in the paths He has established. "Ye shall be even as I am, and I am even as my Father."[123] There is no other way.

At this point Philip had a request:

John 14:8 Philip saith unto him, **Lord, shew us the Father, and it sufficeth us***.*

Jesus answered with sympathetic and mild reproof:

John 14:9 Jesus saith unto him, **Have I been so long time with you, and yet hast thou not known me, Philip?** *he that hath seen me hath seen the Father; and* **how sayest thou [then], Shew us the Father?**

10 Believest thou not that I am in the Father, and the Father in me? **the words that I speak unto you I speak not of myself: but the Father that dwelleth in me***, he doeth the works.*

11 Believe me that I [am] in the Father, and the Father in me: or else **believe me for the very works' sake.**

Jesus said unto Philip, 'after all the time we have been together, don't you know I am the Son of God and that my Father shows himself to the world through me? You should know by now I am so entirely like my Father and by seeing me you have seen Him.' The Savior tells Philip further, 'if nothing else believe me for the sake of the work we are trying to accomplish.'

John 14:12 ¶ Verily, verily, I say unto you, **He that believeth on me, the works that I do shall he do also; and greater [works] than these shall he do; because I go unto my Father.**

13 **And whatsoever ye shall ask in my name, that will I do, that the Father may be glorified in the Son***.*

14 **If ye shall ask any thing in my name, I will do [it].**

Belief is synonymous with faith, and if you do His works, then by faith even greater works may be obtained. "And whatsoever ye shall ask the Father in my name, which is right, believing ye shall receive, behold it shall be given you,"[124] The Father has given the name of Jesus Christ whereby all things of faith may be granted, and thus the Father is glorified in the Son.

Jesus then discourses on the first and second comforters:

¶ John 14:15 If ye love me, keep my commandments.

John 14:16 And I will pray the Father, and **he shall give you another Comforter***, that he may abide with you forever;*

---

[123] 3 Ne. 28:10
[124] 3 Ne. 18:20

*17 [Even] the Spirit of truth; whom the world cannot receive, because it seeth him not, neither knoweth him: **but ye know him; for he dwelleth with you, and shall be in you.***

*18 ¶ I will not leave you comfortless: **I will come to you.***
*19 **Yet a little while, and the world seeth me no more; but ye see me: because I live, ye shall live also.***
20 At that day ye shall know that I am in my Father, and ye in me, and I in you.
*21 **He that hath my commandments, and keepeth them, he it is that loveth me:** and he that loveth me shall be loved of my Father, **and I will love him, and will manifest myself to him.***

*22 **Judas saith unto him,** not Iscariot, **Lord, how is it that thou wilt manifest thyself unto us, and not unto the world?***
*23 Jesus answered and said unto him, **If a man love me, he will keep my words:** and my Father will love him, and **we will come unto him, and make our abode with him.***
*24 He that loveth me not keepeth not my sayings: **and the word which ye hear is not mine, but the Father's which sent me.***
*25 These things have I spoken unto you, **being yet present with you.***
*26 But **the Comforter, which is the Holy Ghost, whom the Father will send in my name**, he shall teach you all things, and bring all things to your remembrance, whatsoever I have said unto you.*

Jesus promises the saints, if they keep the commandments based on love and obedience, they may have the gift constant companionship of the Holy Ghost. The Holy Spirit will bring them comfort and peace as well as sanctifying power and revelation, which will prepare men for the companionship with the angels and gods in the hereafter. The world will not receive him because they cannot see him. Jesus explains to the disciples, He is the second comforter, and after His death will appear to them as a resurrected being and as He lives so shall they. Jesus further explains He is the Son, and will come down from His Father's mansions and make personal visitations and shall visit man, take up abode with him, as it were, and reveal to him all the mysteries of his kingdom.[125]

The world does not keep the commandments and keep His words and therefore will not be privileged to be blessed in this manner...

*John 14:27 **Peace I leave with you, my peace I give unto you: not as the world giveth,** give I unto you. Let not your heart be troubled, neither let it be afraid.*

*28 ¶ Ye have heard how **I said unto you, I go away, and come [again] unto you.** If ye loved me, ye would rejoice, because I said, **I go unto the Father: for my Father is greater than I.***
*29 And now **I have told you before it come to pass, that, when it is come to pass, ye might believe.***
*30 Hereafter, I will not talk much with you: **for the prince of this world cometh, and hath nothing in me.***
31 But that the world may know that I love the Father; and as the Father gave me commandment, even so I do. Arise, let us go hence.

Christ is "The Prince of Peace,"[126] the revealer and dispenser of inner spiritual peace, that "peace of God, which passeth all understanding,"[127] that peace which is the gift of God to the obedient. Those who gain this peace in this life shall die in peace, continue in peace in the paradise of God, and then rise in peace in the resurrection to inherit eternal peace in the kingdom of God.[128]

---

[125] John 14:16-27
[126] Isa. 9:6
[127] Philip. 4:7
[128] MD p508

Are they not one? Do they not both possess all power, all wisdom, all knowledge, and all truth? Have they not both gained all godly attributes in their fullness and perfection? Verily, yes for the revelations so announce and the Prophet so taught.[129] And yet our Lord's Father is greater than he.

Once again, the Savior reminds the disciples of His death, so they may understand and believe all He has taught and instructed them. Why? Satan, the prince of darkness, who is of this world, will still try to exercise power over them, for they have not yet overcome this world.

"*Arise, let us go hence.*"

As they moved a little closer to Gethsemane, the Lord gave them the allegory of the fruit of the vine to illustrate the vital relationship between the apostles and Himself, and between Himself and the Father, using the figure of a vine-grower, a vine, and its branches:

John 15:1 ¶ **I am the true vine, and my Father is the husbandman**.
　2 Every branch in me that beareth not fruit he taketh away: and every [branch] that beareth fruit, he purgeth it, that it may bring forth more fruit.
　3 Now ye are clean through the word which I have spoken unto you.
　　4 **Abide in me, and I in you.** *As the* **branch cannot bear fruit of itself, except it abide in the vine;** *no more can ye, except ye abide in me.*
　5 **I am the vine, ye [are] the branches:** *He that abideth in me, and I in him, the same bringeth forth much fruit:* **for without me ye can do nothing**.
　6 **If a man abide not in me, he is cast forth as a branch, and is withered;** *and men gather them, and cast [them] into the fire, and they are burned.*
　7 **If ye abide in me,** *and my words abide in you,* **ye shall ask what ye will, and it shall be done unto you.**
　8 **Herein is my Father glorified**, *that ye bear much fruit; so, shall ye be my disciples*

In this allegory, Jesus is the vine and the Father is the husbandman, and the disciples are the branches. Unfruitful branches will be cast into the fire, and fruitful branches will be pruned so as to be more productive. The words of Christ has pronounced the disciples clean and productive so long as they abide in Him, for by themselves they can do nothing, and are nothing more than unschooled Galileans. As long as they abide in Christ and his words then they may ask what they will and it will be granted, thus glorifying the Father and becoming one with Jesus and the Father.

John 15:9 ¶ *As the Father hath loved me, so have I loved you:* **continue ye in my love.**
　10 **If ye keep my commandments, ye shall abide in my love**; *even as I have kept my Father's commandments, and abide in his love.*
　11 These things have I spoken unto you, **that my joy might remain in you, and [that] your joy might be full.**
　12 This is my commandment, **That ye love one another, as I have loved you**.
　13 **Greater love hath no man than this, that a man lay down his life for his friends.**
　14 **Ye are my friends**, *if ye do whatsoever I command you.*
　15 **Henceforth I call you not servants**; *for the servant knoweth not what his lord doeth: but I have called you friends; for all things that I have heard of my Father I have made known unto you.*
　16 **Ye have not chosen me, but I have chosen you, and ordained you**, *that ye should go and* **bring forth fruit**, *and [that] your fruit should remain:* **that whatsoever ye shall ask of the Father in my name, he may give it you.**
　17 These things I command you, that ye **love one another.**

This promise, in principle, is available to all saints, for "Men are, that they might have joy" and that God who is no respecter of persons, desires to reward all his children with the choicest of blessings of time and eternity. "Obtaining exaltation consists in gaining a fullness of joy; it is to enter into the joy of the Lord. The saints are to 'reap [eternal joy' for

---

[129] DNTC 738-740

all their sufferings, though their joy is not to be in this life. A fullness of joy is found only among resurrected, exalted beings 'those who have died in Jesus Christ may expect to enter into all fruition of joy when they come forth, which they possessed or anticipated here.'[130]

Jesus laid down his life for his friends; isn't it a great anticipation to realize if we can overcome all things, keep his commandments, having made our callings and elections sure, he will call us and we can dwell with him in glorious exaltation.

This close relationship with the apostles in no way lessens the position of Christ as their Lord and Master, quite the contrary, for He purposely chose them and ordained them; and it was His will they should go forth and bear fruit, and whatever they asked in His name the Father would grant them.

Jesus went on to warn them if they were of the world they would be loved, but since Jesus had chosen them out of the world they would be hated as He was.

*John 15:18 ¶ **If the world hate you, ye know that it hated me before [it hated] you.***

*19 If ye were of the world, the world would love his own: but because ye are not of the world, **but I have chosen you out of the world, therefore the world hateth you.***

*20 Remember the word that I said unto you, **The servant is not greater than his lord. If they have persecuted me, they will also persecute you**; if they have kept my saying, they will keep yours also.*

*21 But **all these things will they do unto you for my name's sake, because they know not him that sent me.***

*22 If I had not come and spoken unto them, they had not had sin: **but now they have no cloke for their sin.***

*23 **He that hateth me hateth my Father also.***

*24 If I had not done among them the works which none other man did, they had not had sin: **but now have they both seen and hated both me and my Father.***

*25 But [this cometh to pass], that the word might be fulfilled that is written in their law, **They hated me without a cause. The world, or worldly people, have hated the truth from the beginning to the present time;***

Joseph Smith for example:

D&C 122:5 If thou art called to pass through tribulation; if thou art in perils among false brethren; if thou art in perils among robbers; if thou art in perils by land or by sea;

6 If thou art accused with all manner of false accusations; if thine enemies fall upon thee; if they tear thee from the society of thy father and mother and brethren and sisters; and if with a drawn sword thine enemies tear thee from the bosom of thy wife, and of thine offspring, and thine elder son, although but six years of age, shall cling to thy garments, and shall say, My father, my father, why can't you stay with us? O, my father, what are the men going to do with you? And if then he shall be thrust from thee by the sword, and thou be dragged to prison, and thine enemies prowl around thee like wolves for the blood of the lamb;

7 And if thou shouldst be cast into the pit, or into the hands of murderers, and the sentence of death passed upon thee; if thou be cast into the deep; if the billowing surge conspire against thee; if fierce winds become thine enemy; if the heavens gather blackness, and all the elements combine to hedge up the way; and above all, if the very jaws of hell shall gape open the mouth wide after thee, know thou, my son, that all these things shall give thee experience, and shall be for thy good.

8 The Son of Man hath descended below them all. Art thou greater than he?

Because of the influence of Satan in the world, we find that the servants and friends of the Lord will have to endure much persecution. Jesus promises however, he will send the Holy Ghost and the spirit of truth from the Father.

*John 15:26 ¶ **But when the Comforter is come**, whom I will send unto you from the Father, [even] the Spirit of truth, which proceedeth from the Father, **he shall testify of me:***

*27 **And ye also shall bear witness, because ye have been with me from the beginning.***

---

[130] J. Fielding Smith teachings

Jesus went on to be a little more specific as He and the disciples were wending their way down the Mount of Olives and towards the Garden of Gethsemane, where they were accustomed to go, the eleven gathered around Him and continued to listen to His preparatory teachings:

*Matthew 26:31 ¶ Then saith Jesus unto them, **All ye shall be offended** because of me this night: for it is written, **I will smite the shepherd,** and the sheep of the flock shall be scattered abroad.*

*32 But **after I am risen again**, I will go before you into Galilee.*[131]

The Savior purposely referred to Zechariah's message of His death so the disciples might know they would be scattered, but they must know they would need to gather themselves back together and He would come forth and lead them.[132]

Peter spoke out strongly:

*Matthew 26:33 Peter answered and said unto him, **Though all [men] shall be offended because of thee, [yet] will I never be offended.***

*34 **Jesus said unto him, Verily I say unto thee, that this night, before the cock crow, thou shalt deny me thrice.***[133]

In spite of the Saviors answer, Peter and all the disciples spoke out:

*Matthew 26:35 Peter said unto him, **Though I should die with thee, yet will I not deny thee. Likewise, also said all the disciples.***

The Lord's reference to His impending separation was indeed troubling to Peter and the other disciples, to the point they all greed they would die with Him. These valiant disciples felt they could stand in defense of their Master, but they had not yet been endowed with the Holy Ghost and weakness of the flesh would spell out failure to do so.

Peter seems to have realized his Master was going to His death; yet, undeterred, he asserted his readiness to follow even that dark way rather than be separated from his Lord. We cannot doubt the earnestness of Peter's purpose, or the sincerity of his desire at that moment. In his bold avowal, however, he had reckoned with the willingness of his spirit only, and had failed to take into full account the weakness of his flesh. However, the Savior had earlier prophetically pronounced the way He would die, and Peter would sometime afterwards would follow and die in like manner. Jesus, who knew Peter better than the man knew himself, thus tenderly reproved his excess of self-confidence:

The first of the apostles, the Man of Rock, yet had to be converted, or as more precisely rendered, "turned again"; for as the Lord foresaw, Peter would soon be overcome, even to the extent of denying his acquaintanceship with Christ. Jesus knew Satan wanted to harvest the earth and it would be easier for him to do so if Peter was not there. Jesus informed Peter He had been praying for him to be converted and for him to strengthen his fellow saints.

*John 16:1 ¶ THESE things have **I spoken unto you, that ye should not be offended.***

*2 They shall put you out of the synagogues: yea, the time cometh, **that whosoever killeth you will think that he doeth God service.***

*3 And these things will they do unto you, **because they have not known the Father, nor me.***

*4 But these things have **I told you, that when the time shall come, ye may remember that I told you of them**. And these things **I said not unto you at the beginning, because I was with you.***

Jesus began to tell them things that he had not previously told them, because He had always been with them. The Apostles were now soon to be on their own, and Jesus wanted to prepare them so they wouldn't become angry or discouraged. They were about to come into confrontation with… "men who drink damnation to their own souls except they humble themselves and become as little children, and believe that salvation was, and is, is to come, in and through the atoning blood of Christ, the Lord Omnipotent. For the natural man is an enemy to God, and has been from the fall of Adam, and will be, forever and ever, unless he yields to the enticing of the Holy Spirit, and puteth off the natural man and become a saint through the atonement of Christ the Lord…"[134]

---

[131] Mark 14:27-28
[132] Zech 13:7
[133] Mark 14:29-30
[134] Mosiah 3:18-19

These natural men were so depraved that they thought they would be doing a service to God by killing the disciples of Jesus.

> *John 16:5 But now I go my way to him that sent me; and none of you asketh me, Whither goest thou?*
> *6 But because I have said these things unto you, sorrow hath filled your heart.*

The disciples had earlier asked Jesus, 'whither goest thou?' and He was saying to them, 'instead of feeling sorrow in your hearts why don't you ask me questions and find out more about the gospel truths involved.'

> *John 16:7 ¶ Nevertheless I tell you the truth;* ***It is expedient for you that I go away: for if I go not away, the Comforter will not come unto you;*** *but if I depart, I will send him unto you.*
> *8 And **when he is come, he will reprove the world of sin, and of righteousness, and of judgment:***
> *9 Of sin, because **they believe not on me;***
> *10 Of righteousness, because I go to my Father, and **ye see me no more**;*
> *11 **Of judgment**, because the prince of this world is judged.*
> *12 I have yet many things to say unto you, but ye cannot bear them now.*
> *13 Howbeit when **he, the Spirit of truth, is come, he will guide you into all truth:** for he shall not speak of himself; but whatsoever he shall hear, [that] shall he speak: and **he will shew you things to come.***
> *14 He shall glorify me: **for he shall receive of mine, and shall shew [it] unto you**.*
> *15 All things that the Father hath are mine: therefore, said I, that he shall take of mine, and shall shew [it] unto you.*

Jesus informs the disciples that He must go away to be able to send them the Holy Ghost, and through them the comforter will rebuke and censure the world and those of the natural man. The world will be convicted of sin for rejecting the disciples' Spirit inspired testimony that Jesus is the Son of God, through whom salvation comes. They will be convicted for rejecting their testimony of the Savior's righteousness, for supposing that He was a blasphemer, a deceiver, and an imposter. They will also be convicted of false judgment for rejecting the disciples' testimony against the religions of the day, and for choosing to follow Satan, the prince of this world, who himself, with all his religious philosophies, will be judged and found wanting.

Jesus told the disciples they would receive, "[Even] the Spirit of truth; whom the world cannot receive, because it seeth him not, neither knoweth him: but ye know him; for he dwelleth with you, and shall be in you."[135] This would be the "Gift of the Holy Ghost" which is a constant companionship, "And by the power of the Holy Ghost ye may know the truth of all things."[136]

Joseph smith said: "No man can receive the Holy Ghost without receiving revelations. The Holy Ghost is a revelator"…Also; "a person may profit by noticing the first intimation of the spirit of revelation; for instance, when you feel pure intelligence flowing into you, it may give you sudden strokes of ideas, so that by noticing it, you may find it fulfilled the same day or soon; that is, those things that were presented unto your minds by the Spirit of God, will come to pass; and thus by learning [to recognize] the spirit of god and understanding it, you may grow in the principle of revelation, until you become perfect in Christ."[137]

> *16 A little while, and ye shall not see me: and again, a little while, and ye shall see me, because I go to the Father.*
> *17 Then said some of his disciples among themselves, What is this that he saith unto us, A little while, and ye shall not see me: and again, a little while, and ye shall see me: and, Because I go to the Father?*
> *18 They said therefore, What is this that he saith, A little while? we cannot tell what he saith.*
> *19 Now Jesus knew that they were desirous to ask him, and said unto them, Do ye inquire among yourselves of that I said, A little while, and ye shall not see me: and again, a little while, and ye shall see me?*
> *20 Verily, verily, I say unto you, That ye shall weep and lament, but the world shall rejoice: and ye shall be sorrowful, but your sorrow shall be turned into joy.*

---

[135] John 14:10
[136] Moro. 10: 4-5
[137] Teachings p 328 & 151

21 A woman when she is in travail hath sorrow, because her hour is come: but as soon as she is delivered of the child, she remembereth no more the anguish, for joy that a man is born into the world.

22 And ye now therefore have sorrow: but I will see you again, and your heart shall rejoice, and your joy no man taketh from you.

Turning again to the matter of His departure, then so near as to be reckoned by hours, the Lord said, in amplified form of what He had before affirmed. The apostles pondered and some questioned among themselves as to the Lord's meaning of *a little while*, yet so deep was the solemnity of the occasion that they ventured no open inquiry. Jesus knew of their perplexity and graciously explained that they would soon weep and lament while the world would rejoice at His death. However, He promised that their sorrow should be turned into joy and this was based on His resurrection to which they should be witnesses. He compared their then present and prospective state to that of a woman in travail, who in the after joy of blessed motherhood forgets her anguish.

John:23 And in that day ye shall ask me nothing. Verily, verily, I say unto you, Whatsoever ye shall ask the Father in my name, he will give it you.

24 Hitherto have ye asked nothing in my name: ask, and ye shall receive, that your joy may be full.

25 These things have I spoken unto you in proverbs: but the time cometh, when I shall no more speak unto you in proverbs, but I shall shew you plainly of the Father.

26 At that day ye shall ask in my name: and I say not unto you, that I will pray the Father for you:

27 For the Father himself loveth you, because ye have loved me, and have believed that I came out from God.

28 I came forth from the Father, and am come into the world: again, I leave the world, and go to the Father.

29 His disciples said unto him, Lo, now speakest thou plainly, and speakest no proverb.

30 Now are we sure that thou knowest all things, and needest not that any man should ask thee: by this we believe that thou camest forth from God.

31 Jesus answered them, Do ye now believe?

In the day that He dies, Jesus tells them they will no longer pray to Him and so He can pray to the Father for them, but they were to be advanced to such honor and exalted recognition, that they should approach the Father in prayer direct, but in the name of the Son. For they were beloved of the Father because they had loved Jesus, the Son, and had accepted Him as One sent by the Father.

The Lord again solemnly averred, I will no longer speak to you in proverbs and I will state it clear and simple, *"I came forth from the Father, and am come into the world: again, I leave the world, and go to the Father."* The disciples were gratified at this plain avouchment, and exclaimed: *"Lo, now speaks thou plainly, and speaks no proverb. Now are we sure that thou knowest all things, and needest not that any man should ask thee: by this we believe that thou camest forth from God."*[138]

Their satisfaction threatened danger through over-confidence; and the Lord cautioned them:

John 16:32 **Behold, the hour cometh, yea, is now come, that ye shall be scattered,** *every man to his own, and shall leave me alone: and yet I am not alone, because the Father is with me.*

33 These things **I have spoken unto you, that in me ye might have peace.** *In the world ye shall have tribulation: but* **be of good cheer; I have overcome the world.**

Saying, that in an hour, then close, they should all be scattered, every man to his own, leaving Jesus alone, except for the Father's presence. In the same connection, He told them that before the night had passed every one of them would be offended because of Him, even as it had been written: *"I will smite the shepherd, and the sheep of the flock shall be scattered abroad."* Peter, the most vehement of all in his protestations, had been told, as we have seen, that by cock-crow that night he would have thrice denied his Lord; but all of them had declared they would be faithful whatever the trial. In further affirmation of the material actuality of His resurrection, Jesus promised the apostles that after He had risen from the grave He would go before them into Galilee.[139]

---

[138] John 16:28-31
[139] JTC p 608-609

LORD'S HIGH PRIESTLY PRAYER Or INTERCESSORY PRAYER

John 17:1 ¶ THESE words spake Jesus, and lifted up his eyes to heaven, and said, **Father, the hour is come; glorify thy Son, that thy Son also may glorify thee:**

2 As thou hast given him power over all flesh, that he should **give eternal life to as many as thou hast given him.**

3 And **this is life eternal, that they might know thee the only true God, and Jesus Christ, whom thou hast sent.**

4 **I have glorified thee on the earth: I have finished the work which thou gavest me to do.**

5 And now, O Father, glorify thou me with thine own self with the glory **which I had with thee before the world was.**

Jesus now lifts His eyes to heaven and His Father, as He knows the time is come for Him to make the final sin sacrifice in fulfilling the Law of Moses. Jesus now addresses none but the Eternal Father, and acknowledges the Father as his source of power and authority over all flesh. Jesus declares to the Father the knowledge to everlasting life, is to understand the true nature of God and His son whom He sent, and this He has declared and shown to mankind and those who are worthy how they may obtain eternal life. "Eternal life is God's life; it is the name of the kind of life he lives, The Father has eternal life for two reasons: (1) He has all the power in heaven and on earth; he is omnipotent, omniscient, and, by the power of his Spirit, omnipresent; all things are subject to him; he possesses what, in summary, is called the fullness of the Father, or the fullness of the glory of the Father. (2) He lives in the family unit; he has an eternal increase; he has a continuation of the seeds and of the lives forever and ever."[140]

Jesus then asks our Father to glorify Him, so He may in turn glorify the Father and be glorified by the Father and return to the glory He had in the preexistence. Thereby I have finished the work on earth that thou has sent me to do.

John 17:6 ¶ **I have manifested thy name unto the men** *which thou gavest me out of the world: thine they were, and thou gavest them me; and they have kept thy word*

7 Now they have known that all things whatsoever thou hast given me are of thee.

8 **For I have given unto them the words which thou gavest me; and they have received [them], and have known surely that I came out from thee, and they have believed that thou didst send me.**

9 **I pray for them**: *I pray not for the world, but for them which thou hast given me;* **for they are thine**.

10 And **all mine are thine, and thine are mine; and I am glorified in them.**

11 ¶ And now I am no more in the world, but these are in the world, and **I come to thee. Holy Father,** *keep through thine own name* **those whom thou hast given me, that they may be one, as we [are]**.

12 While I was with them in the world, I kept them in thy name: **those that thou gavest me I have kept, and none of them is lost, but the son of perdition; that the scripture might be fulfilled.**

13 And now come I to thee; and **these things I speak in the world, that they might have my joy fulfilled in themselves.**

14 I have given them thy word; and the **world hath hated them, because they are not of the world,** *even as I am not of the world.*

15 **I pray not that thou shouldest take them out of the world, but that thou shouldest keep them from the evil.**

16 **They are not of the world,** *even as I am not of the world.*

17 ¶ **Sanctify them through thy truth:** *thy word is truth.*

18 As thou hast sent me into the world, even so have **I also sent them into the world.**

19 And **for their sakes I sanctify myself, that they also might be sanctified through the truth.**

Jesus now gives a final report to the Father, for us to see that while He was on earth He glorified the Father as instructed. In the Father's name, the Savior taught the gospel to all that the Father had given Him, and Jesus testifies that the apostles know that all things are from the Father and that it was the Father that sent Jesus. With unfathomable love, the

---

[140] MM 69

Lord pleaded for those whom the Father had given Him, the apostles then present, who had been called out from the world, and who had been true to their testimony of Himself as the Son of God. Of them but one, the son of perdition, had been lost. As Jesus was about to return to his Father, He declared these things openly before the world, so the Apostles might openly find joy in fulfilling their Priesthood calling of declaring the plan of salvation to the world. However, Jesus knew they would be hated by the worldly people just He was, but He did not pray for them to be removed from the world of evil but protected from it, for they had yet to work out their sanctification even as He had. As the Father had sent Jesus out into the world to declare the truth of God's word, He now sends out the Apostles into the world so they may also be sanctified by declaring the truths of God's word.

In the fervor of devoted supplication, the Lord pleaded:
John
20 ¶ ***Neither pray I for these alone***, *but for them also which shall believe on me through their word;*
21 *That* <u>***they all may be one***</u>; *as thou, Father, [art] in me, and I in thee, that they also may be one in us: that the world may believe that thou hast sent me.*

22 *And **the glory which thou gavest me** I have given them; **that they may be one, even as we are one:***
23 ***I in them, and thou in me, that they may be made perfect in one***; *and that the world may know that thou hast sent me, and hast loved them, as thou hast loved me.*

Now Jesus turns his attention and concerns to people in general and in particular to those who believe on Him as they have received the words of salvation taught to them by those having true authority to do so.

'Be one!' To keep this command ever before the people, the Lord thunders it into their ears by using himself and the eternal Godhead as the illustration of what unity is and how it operates. Be one, even as the Father and I are one; unite together as the Gods of heaven unite. Do not go your separate ways; rally round one standard. Believe the same doctrines; teach the same truths; testify of the same God; walk the same paths; live the same laws; hold the same priesthood; marry in the same celestial order; become one with me. Be one!'

To pretend to believe that the Father and Son are one in some mysterious and incomprehensible way so that the designations are simply different manifestations of the same thing, is to wrest the scriptures and mangle the plain and simple language they contain, and do away with some of the best similitudes and most perfect teaching known to man. Three Gods are one as endless millions should be one – and in no other sense.

Jesus further prays that the Eternal life that has been granted Him by the Father, may also be obtained by those who will become one with them, in order that the world may know the truth about the Father and the Son.

*John 17:24 ¶ Father, **I will that they also, whom thou hast given me, be with me where I am**; that they may behold my glory, which thou hast given me: for thou lovedst me before the foundation of the world.*
*25 O righteous Father, the **world hath not known thee: but I have known thee, and these have known that thou hast sent me.***
*26 And **I have declared unto them thy name, and will declare [it]**: that the love wherewith thou hast loved me may be in them, and I in them.*

Jesus declares His existence with Father in heaven before the foundation of the world, and it's His sincere desire that the ones whom He has been given will be able to behold the glories of salvation that has been given to Him by the Father and that it has been so, since the very beginning of the world. 'The world has not known thee but I have and these have known thou has sent me, therefor I love them with the same love Thou has shown Me.' Let us become one.

The purpose of this work is to establish the logic and fulfillment of the Passover and not an in depth doctrinal study. Simplicity has been the goal.

Chapter 10

Gethsemane & Arrest

AM 6th day, *15th Nissan*, (Thursday)	Location	Matthew	Mark	Luke	John
Enter Gethsemane	Gethsemane	26:36	14:32	22:40	18:1
Sit ye here, while I pray	Gethsemane	26:37-44	14:32-41	22:41-46	
Judas Betrayal	Gethsemane	26:45-50	14:42-46	22:47-48	18:2-3
Whom seek ye? They fell backwards	Gethsemane				18:4-7
Let these go	Gethsemane				18:8-9
Peter defend Jesus w/sword	Gethsemane	26:51-54	14:47	22:49-51	18:10-11
Jesus arrested & disciples flee	Gethsemane	26:55-56	14:48-52	22:51-53	18:12
Jesus before Annas &Caiaphas	Jerusalem	26:57-68	14:53-65	22:54-55	18:13-24
Denial by Peter	Jerusalem	26:69-75	14:66-72	22:56-62	18:15-18 18:25-27

John 18:1 ¶ **WHEN Jesus had finished praying the Intercessory Prayer, he went forth with his disciples over the brook Cedron, where was a garden into which he entered, and his disciples.**

Matthew 26: 36 ¶ **Then cometh Jesus with them unto a place called Gethsemane**, *and saith unto the disciples,* **Sit ye here, while I go and pray yonder.**

37 And he took with him Peter and the two sons of Zebedee, and began to be sorrowful and very heavy.

38 Then saith he unto them, **My soul is exceeding sorrowful**, *even unto death:* **tarry ye here, and watch with me.**

39 And he went a little further, and fell on his face, and prayed, saying, **O my Father, if it be possible, let this cup pass from me: nevertheless not as I will, but as thou wilt.**

40 And he **cometh unto the disciples, and findeth them asleep**, *and saith unto Peter, What, could ye not watch with me one hour?*

41 Watch and **pray, that ye enter not into temptation:** *the spirit indeed is willing,* **but the flesh is weak.**

42 **He went away again the second time**, *and prayed, saying,* **O my Father,** *if this cup may not pass away from me, except I drink it,* **thy will be done.**

43 **And he came and found them asleep again:** *for their eyes were heavy.*

44 And he left them, **and went away again, and prayed the third time,** *saying the same words.*

45 Then cometh he to his disciples, and saith unto them, **Sleep on now,** *and take your rest: behold,* **the hour is at hand, and the Son of man is betrayed into the hands of sinners.**[141]

"Jesus and the eleven apostles went forth from the house in which they had eaten, passed through the city gate, which was usually left open at night during a public festival, crossed the ravine of the brook Cedron, or more accurately Kidron, brook. After a night of instruction and the great Intercessory Prayer, they entered an olive orchard known as Gethsemane, on the slope of Mount Olivet. Eight of the apostles He left at or near the entrance, with the instruction: "Sit ye here, while I go and pray yonder"; and with the earnest injunction: "Pray that ye enter not into temptation." Accompanied by Peter, James and John, He went farther; and was soon enveloped by deep

---

[141] Mark 14: 32-41, Luke 22:41-46

Sorrow, which appears to have been, in a measure, surprising to Himself, for we read that He "began to be sore amazed, and to be very heavy." He was impelled to deny Himself the companionship of even the chosen three; and, "Saith he unto them, My Soul is exceeding Sorrowful, even unto death: tarry ye here, and watch with me. And he went a little farther, and fell on his face, and prayed, saying, O my Father, if it be possible, let this cup pass from me: nevertheless, not as I will, but as thou wilt." Mark's Version of the prayer is: "Abba, Father, all things are possible unto thee; take away this cup from me; nevertheless, not what I will, but what thou wilt."

This part of His impassioned supplication was heard by at least one of the waiting three; but all of them soon yielded to weariness and ceased to watch. As on the Mount of Transfiguration, when the Lord appeared in glory, so now in the hour of His deepest humiliation, these three Slumbered. Returning to them in an agony of soul Jesus found them sleeping; and addressing Peter, who so short a time before had loudly proclaimed his readiness to follow the Lord even to prison and death, Jesus exclaimed: "What, could ye not watch with me one hour? Watch and pray, that ye enter not into temptation"; but in tenderness added, "the spirit indeed is willing, but the flesh is weak." The admonition to the apostles to pray at that time lest they be led into temptation may have been prompted by the exigencies of the hour, under which, if left to themselves, they would be tempted to prematurely desert their Lord.

Aroused from slumber the three apostles saw the Lord again retire, and heard Him pleading in agony: "O my Father, if this cup may not pass away from me, except I drink it, thy will be done." Returning a second time He found those whom He had so sorrowfully requested to watch with Him sleeping again, "for their eyes were heavy"; and when awakened they were embarrassed or ashamed so that they whist not what to say. A third time He went to His lonely vigil and individual struggle, and was heard to implore the Father with the same words of yearning entreaty. Luke tells us that "there appeared an angel unto him from heaven, strengthening him"; but not even the presence of this super-earthly visitant could dispel the awful anguish of His Soul. "And being in an agony he prayed more earnestly: and his sweat was as it were great drops of blood falling down to the ground."

Peter had had a glimpse of the darksome road which he had professed himself so ready to tread; and the brothers James and John knew now better than before how unprepared they were to drink of the cup which the Lord would drain to its dregs.

When for the last time, Jesus came back to the disciples left on guard, He Said: "Sleep on now, and take your rest: behold, the hour is at hand, and the Son of man is betrayed into the hands of sinners." There was no use of further watching; already the torches of the approaching band conducted by Judas were observable in the distance. Jesus exclaimed: "Rise, let us be going: behold, he is at hand that doth betray me." Standing with the Eleven, the Lord calmly awaited the traitor's coming.[142]

In the accounts of the betrayal, arrest, and trial of Jesus we see the value of the four gospels recording the same events. Each recitation is inspired, but each tells only part of the happenings; …. Taken together they recount in a better way than one author alone could do, the series of events that took Jesus to the death out of which came life.[143]

*Matthew 26:46 **Rise, let us be going: behold, he is at hand that doth betray me.**

47 ¶ *And while he yet spake, lo,* **Judas,** *one of the twelve,* **came, and with him a great multitude with swords and staves, from the chief priests and elders of the people.**

*John 18:2 And **Judas** also, which betrayed him,* knew the place*: for Jesus ofttimes resorted thither with his disciples.*

John 18:3 3 *Judas then, having received* **a band [of men] and officers** *from the chief priests and Pharisees,* **cometh thither with lanterns and torches and weapons.**

Judas guided a small army well supplied with weapons. A band consisted of some six hundred Roman soldiers with a tribune at their head. The roman overlords were taking no chance on an uproar during the week of the Passover. Accompanying the soldiers was a "great multitude", perhaps thousands in number. This was no secret arrest, no private kidnapping; all Jerusalem was aware of the taking into custody of the cities most noted inhabitant. Probably Judas would have led the entire "army" to the site of the upper room and not finding Jesus and the disciples would have guided them to Gethsemane, for "Judas…knew the place: for Jesus off-times restored thither with his disciples."[144]

---

[142] JTC p 611-p 612
[143] DNTC p 779
[144] DNTC p 781

Luke 22:47 ¶ *And **while he yet spake**, behold a multitude, and he that was called **Judas**, one of the twelve, went before them, and **drew near unto Jesus to kiss him**.*
*48 But **Jesus said unto him, Judas, betrayest thou the Son of man with a kiss?***

Matthew 26:48 **Now he that betrayed him gave them a sign, saying, **Whomsoever I shall kiss, that same is he**: hold him fast.*
*49 And forthwith he came to Jesus, and said, **Hail, master; and kissed him**.*

A more traitorous token could not have been chosen. Among the prophets of old, among saints of that day, and even among the Jews, a kiss was the symbol of that love and fellowship which existed where pure religion was or should have been found. … Judas, thus, could have chosen no baser means of identifying Jesus than to plant on His face a traitor's kiss. Such act, not only singled out his intended victim but, by the means chosen, desecrated every principle of true fellowship and brotherhood.

Jesus stepped forward boldly:
John 18:4 Jesus therefore, <u>knowing all things that should come upon him**</u>, went forth, and said unto them, **Whom seek ye?***
*5 They answered him, **Jesus of Nazareth**. Jesus saith unto them, **I am [he]**. And Judas also, which betrayed him, stood with them.*
*6 As soon then as he had said unto them, I am [he], **they went backward, and fell to the ground**.*
*7 **Then asked he them again**, Whom seek ye? And they said, Jesus of Nazareth.*
*8 Jesus answered, I have told you that I am [he]: **if therefore ye seek me, let these go their way**:*
*9 **That the saying might be fulfilled, which he spake, Of them which thou gavest me have I lost none**.*

The armed band hesitated, though their guide had given the signal agreed upon. Jesus walked toward the officers, with whom Stood Judas, and asked, "*Whom Seek ye?*" To their reply, "*Jesus of Nazareth,*" the Lord rejoined: "*I am he.*" Instead of advancing to take Him, the crowd pressed backward, and many of them fell to the ground in fright. The simple dignity and gentle yet compelling force of Christ's presence, proved more potent than strong arms and weapons of violence. Again, He put the question, "*Whom seek ye?*" and again they answered, "*Jesus of Nazareth.*" *Then said Jesus: "I have told you that I am he; if therefore ye seek me, let these go their way."* The last remark had reference to the apostles, who were in danger of arrest; and in this evidence of Christ's solicitude for their personal safety, John saw a fulfillment of the Lord's then recent utterance in prayer, "Of them which thou gavest me have I lost none." It is possible that had any of the Eleven been apprehended with Jesus and made to share the cruel abuse and torturing humiliation of the next few hours, their faith might have failed them, relatively immature and untried as it then was; even as in succeeding years many who took upon themselves the name of Christ yielded to persecution and went into apostasy.[145]

Jesus spoke to Judas:
Matthew 26:50 And Jesus said unto him, Friend, wherefore art thou come? **Then came they, and laid hands on Jesus, and took him.*
51 And, behold, **one of them which were with Jesus stretched out [his] hand, and **drew his sword, and struck a servant of the high priest's, and smote off his ear**.*
*52 Then said Jesus unto him, **Put up again thy sword into his place: for all they that take the sword shall perish with the sword**.*
*53 **Thinkest thou that I cannot now pray to my Father**, and he shall presently give me more than twelve legions of angels?*
*54 But **how then shall the scriptures be fulfilled**, that thus it must be?*

Luke 22: 49 When they which were about him saw what would follow, **they said unto him, Lord, shall we smite with the sword?*

---
[145] JTC p 615

50 And **one of them smote the <u>servant of the high priest</u>**, and cut off his right ear.
51 And **Jesus** answered and said, **Suffer ye thus far. And he touched his ear, and healed him.**

*John 18:10 Then **Simon Peter having a sword drew it**, and smote the high priest's servant, and cut off his right ear. The **servant's name was Malchus**.

11 Then said Jesus unto Peter, Put up thy sword into the sheath: **the cup which my Father hath given me, shall I not drink it?**

When the officers approached, and seized Jesus, some of the apostles, ready to fight and die for their beloved Master, asked, "Lord, shall we smite with the sword?" Peter, waiting not for a reply, drew his sword and delivered a poorly aimed stroke at the head of one of the nearest of the crowd, whose ear was severed by the blade. The man thus wounded was Malchus, a servant of the high priest. Jesus, asking liberty of His captors by the simple request, "Suffer ye thus far," stepped forward and healed the injured man by a touch. Turning to Peter the Lord rebuked his rashness, and commanded him to return the sword to its scabbard, with the reminder that "all they that take the sword shall perish with the sword." Then, to show the needlessness of armed resistance, and to emphasize the fact that He was submitting voluntarily and in accordance with foreseen and predicted developments, the Lord continued: "Thinkest thou that I cannot now pray to my Father, and he shall presently give me more than twelve legions of angels? But how then shall the scriptures be fulfilled, that thus it must be?" And further, "the cup which my Father hath given me, shall I not drink it?"[146]

Luke 22:52 Then Jesus said unto **the chief priests, and captains of the temple, and the elders, which were come to him**, Be ye come out, as against a thief, with swords and staves?

53 When **I was daily with you in the temple, ye stretched forth no hands against me**: but this is your hour, and the power of darkness.

*Matthew 26:56 But all this was done, that the scriptures of the prophets might be fulfilled. **Then all the disciples forsook him, and fled.**

*John 18:12 Then **the band and the captain and officers of the Jews took Jesus**, and bound him,
13 ¶ And **led him away to Annas first**; for he was father in law to Caiaphas, **which was the high priest** that same year.
14 Now Caiaphas was he, which gave counsel to the Jews, that it was expedient that one man should die for the people.

John 18;19 The **high priest then asked Jesus of his disciples, and of his doctrine.**
20 Jesus answered him, **I spake openly to the world**; I ever taught in the synagogue, and in the temple, whither the Jews always resort; **and in secret have I said nothing**.
21 **Why askest thou me? ask them which heard me**, what I have said unto them: behold, they know what I said.
22 And when he had thus spoken, **one of the officers which stood by struck Jesus with the palm of his hand, saying, Answerest thou the high priest so?**
23 Jesus answered him, If I have spoken evil, bear witness of the evil: but if well, why smitest thou me?
24 Now **Annas had sent him bound unto Caiaphas** the high priest.

Matthew 26:57 ¶ And **they that had laid hold on Jesus led [him] away to Caiaphas** the high priest, where the scribes and the elders were assembled.

---

[146] JTC p 616

*58 But **Peter followed** him afar off unto the high priest's palace, **and went in, and sat with the servants, to see the end.***

*59 Now the **chief priests, and elders, and all the council, sought false witness** against Jesus, to put him to death;*

*60 But found none: yea, though many false witnesses came, [yet] found they none. **At the last came two false witnesses**,*

61 And said, This [fellow] said, I am able to destroy the temple of God, and to build it in three days.

*62 And the high priest arose, and said unto him, **Answerest thou nothing? what [is it which] these witness against thee?***

*63 **But Jesus held his peace.** And the high priest answered and said unto him, I adjure thee by the living God, that thou **tell us whether thou be the Christ, the Son of God.***

*64 Jesus saith unto him, Thou hast said: nevertheless I say unto you, **Hereafter shall ye see the Son of man sitting on the right hand of power, and coming in the clouds of heaven**.*

*65 Then the high priest rent his clothes, saying, **He hath spoken blasphemy**; what further need have we of witnesses? behold, now ye have heard his blasphemy.*

*66 **What think ye**? They answered and said, **He is guilty of death**.*

67 Then did they spit in his face, and buffeted him; and others smote [him] with the palms of their hands,

68 Saying, Prophesy unto us, thou Christ, Who is he that smote thee?

This is only the beginning of the controversy and confusion which surrounds the accepted logic of the Passover.

But, though surrendering Himself unresistingly, Jesus was not unmindful of His rights; and to the priestly officials, chief priests, captain of the temple guard, and elders of the people who were present, He voiced this interrogative protest against the illegal night seizure; *"Are ye come out as against a thief with swords and staves for to take me? I sat daily with you teaching in the temple, and ye laid no hold on me. But all this was done, that the scriptures of the prophets might be fulfilled."* Luke records the Lord's concluding words thus: *"but this is your hour, and the power of darkness."* Unheeding His question, and without deference to His submissive demeanor, the captain and the officers of the Jews bound Jesus with cords and led Him away, a Prisoner at the mercy of His deadliest enemies.

"John and he only, tells us that Jesus was taken before Annas, who then sent him to Caiaphas. Whether the questioning and smiting, of which John speaks, took place before the one or the other is not entirely clear. Elder James E. Talmage takes the view that the events occurred before Caiaphus and that "No details of the interview with Annas are of record," a conclusion he qualifies later by saying it "is matter of inference" as to which Jewish functionary was involved. Edersheim also concludes that Caiaphas was the high priest involved. (Talmage, pp. 621-622; 643-644.)

President J. Rueben Clark. Jr., on the other hand places the episode before Annas. (J. Rueben Clark, Jr., Our Lord of the Gospels, pp. 416-417), as does also Dummelow and Jamieson."[147]

For further consideration reference may be made to the following treatments: Edersheim, Life and Times of Jesus the Messiah; And Illegalities of the Jewish Trial of Jesus. -- Andrews, Life of Our Lord, -- Dupin, Jesus before Caiaphas and Pilate; Mendelsohn, C Criminal Jurisprudence of the Ancient Hebrews, -- Salvador, Institutions of Moses, -- Innes, The Trial of Jesus Christ, -- Maimonides, Sanhedrin; MM. Lemann, Jesus before the Sanhedrin, -- Benny, C Criminal Code of the Jews, -- and Walter M. Chandler, of the New York Bar, The Trial of Jesus from a Lawyer's Standpoint. The last named is a two-volume work treating respectively, "The Hebrew Trial" and "The Roman Trial," and contains citations from the foregoing and other works.[148]

We submit to you that these sources are presenting their own understanding of history and gospel for their conclusions, and they are all apologists for a particular modern day secular view point.

Edersheim, (vol. 2, pp. 556-58), contends that the night arraignment of Jesus in the house of Caiaphas was not a trial before the Sanhedrin and notes the irregularities and illegalities of the procedure as proof that the Sanhedrin could not have done what was done that night, with ample citations in corroboration of the legal requirements specified, the author says: "But besides, the trial and sentence of Jesus in the palace of Caiaphas would have outraged every principle of Jewish criminal law and procedure. Such causes could only be tried, and capital sentence pronounced, in the regular meeting-place

---

[147] DNTC p 783
[148] JTC p 645

of the Sanhedrin, not, as here, in the high priest's palace; no process, least of all such and one, might be begun in the night, nor even in the afternoon, although if the discussion had gone on all day, sentence might be pronounced at night. Again, no process could take place on Sabbaths or feast-days, or even on the eves of them, although this would not have nullified proceedings; and it might be argued on the other side, that a process against one who had seduced the people should preferably be carried on, and sentence executed, on public feast-days, for the warning of all. Lastly, in capital causes there was a very elaborate system of warning, and cautioning witnesses; while it may safely be affirmed that at a regular trial Jewish judges, however prejudiced, would not have acted as the Sanhedrists and Caiaphas did on this occasion.... But although Christ was not tried and sentenced in a formal meeting of the Sanhedrin, there can, alas! Be no question that His condemnation and death were the work, if not of the Sanhedrin, yet of the Sanhedrists -- of the whole body of them ("all the council") in the sense of expressing what was the judgment and purpose of all the supreme council and leaders of Israel, with only very few exceptions. We bear in mind that the resolution to sacrifice Christ had for some time been taken."[149]

The purpose in quoting the foregoing is to show that acknowledged and eminent authorities recognize some of the illegalities of the night trial of Jesus, which, as shown by the above, and by the scriptural record, was conducted by the high priests, scribes and elders, in admittedly an irregular and unlawful manner. If the Sanhedrists tried and condemned, yet were not in session as the Sanhedrin, the enormity of the proceeding is, if possible, deeper and blacker than ever.[150]

Much has been written about the illegalities of the night trial of Jesus. In *the Trial of Jesus from a Lawyer's Standpoint* by Walter M. Chandler this conclusion is reached: "The pages of human history present no stronger case of official murder than the trial and crucifixion of Jesus of Nazareth, for the simple reason that all forms of law were outraged and trampled under-foot in the proceedings instituted against him." Discussion on Chandlers brief will be in a following chapter. There are no scriptural references to a night trial and the scriptures above record only an arraignment hearing to bind Jesus over for trial. **There were no night trials!**

The apostles, seeing that resistance was useless, not only on account of disparity of numbers and supply of weapons, but chiefly because of Christ's determination to submit, turned and fled. Every one of them forsook Him, even as He had foretold. That they were really in jeopardy is shown by an incident preserved by Mark alone. An unnamed young man, aroused from sleep by the tumult of the marching band, had sallied forth with no outer covering but a linen sheet. His interest in the arrest of Jesus and his close approach caused some of the guardsmen or soldiers to seize him; but he broke loose and escaped leaving the sheet in their hands.[151]

*John 18:15 And **Simon Peter followed Jesus, and [so did] another disciple: that disciple was known unto the high priest, and went in with Jesus into the palace of the high priest**.*

16 But Peter stood at the door without. Then went out that other disciple, which was known unto the high priest, and spake unto her that kept the door, and brought in Peter.

*17 Then **saith the damsel** that kept the door unto Peter, **Art not thou also [one] of this man's disciples? He saith, I am not.***

18 And the servants and officers stood there, who had made a fire of coals; for it was cold: and they warmed themselves: and Peter stood with them, and warmed himself.

*John 18:25 And Simon Peter stood and warmed himself. They said therefore unto him, **Art not thou also [one] of his disciples? He denied [it], and said, I am not**.*

*26 **One of the servants of the high priest**, being [his] kinsman whose ear Peter cut off, saith, **Did not I see thee in the garden with him?***

*27 **Peter then denied again: and immediately the cock crew**.*

*Matthew 26:69 ¶ **Now Peter sat without in the palace**: and **a damsel came unto him, saying, Thou also wast with Jesus of Galilee**.*

*70 **But he denied before [them] all**, saying, I know not what thou sayest.*

---

[149] JTC p 645
[150] JCT p 645
[151] JTC p 616-617

71 And when he was gone out into the porch, **another [maid] saw him, and said** *unto them that were there,* **This [fellow] was also with Jesus of Nazareth.**

72 ***And again he denied with an oath, I do not know the man.***
73 And after a while came unto [him] they that stood by, and said to Peter, Surely thou also art [one] of them; for thy speech betrayeth thee.

74 ***Then began he to curse and to swear, [saying], I know not the man. And immediately the cock crew.***

75 And ***Peter remembered*** *the word of Jesus, which said unto him,* ***Before the cock crow, thou shalt deny me thrice. And he went out, and wept bitterly.***

As the disciples had all forsaken Him and fled, we can understand that they were in ignorance of what actually passed, till they had again rallied, at least so far, that Peter and `another disciple,' evidently John, `followed Him into the palace of the high priest' -- that is, into the palace of Caiaphas, not of Annas. For as, according to the three synoptic Gospels, the palace of the high priest Caiaphas was the scene of Peter's denial, the account of it in the fourth Gospel refers to the same locality, and not to the palace of Annas."
REV

Chapter 11

Establish the day of the Crucifixion

Days of the month (Nissan)														
10	11	12	13	14	15	16	17	18	19	20	21	22	23	24
Days of the Passover														
1	2	3	4	5	6	7	8	9	10	11	12	13	14	15
1. Select lamb				Sacrifice Preparation	Convocation 1st day of unleavened bread	2nd day of unleavened bread & first fruits				Preparation day & crucifixion	Convocation 7th day of unleavened bread			Resurrection
										½ nt	Day nt	Day & nt	Day & ½ nt	
Regular days of the week														
Sun	Mon	Tue	Wed	Thurs	Fri	Sat	Sun	Mon	Tue	Wed	Thurs	Fri	Sat	Sun

  At this point in the discussion it becomes necessary to identify the precise day of the crucifixion. With the Passover calendar unquestionably established in chapter 2, the passages of scripture concerning the day, circumstances, and time of the crucifixion are no longer hazy and unexplainable. Gospel synoptic writers, for a long time, have been claiming the scriptures to be misinterpreted or mistranslated, and errors have crept in and thus, confusion exists.

  In reading the scriptures it is not difficult to discover that apostasy would creep in and eventually lead the original church astray. By the time of the council of Nicaea the current logic of a 7-day Passover had been codified and accepted as the teachings of the founding fathers. Thus, apologists of different sects have been crunching the 15-day event into 7 days and gestating division and confusion.

  However, Joseph Smith said the scriptures say what they mean and mean what they say. Let's see what they say.

  Matthew 27:61 And there was Mary Magdalene, and the other Mary, sitting over against the sepulchre.

  62 Now the next day, that followed the day of preparation, the chief priests and Pharisees came together unto Pilate,

  63 Saying, Sir, we remember that that deceiver said, while he was yet alive, after three days I will rise again.

Mark 15:42 ¶ And now when the even was come, because it was the preparation, that is, the day before the Sabbath,

43 Joseph of Arimathaea, an honourable counsellor, which also waited for the kingdom of God, came, and went in boldly unto Pilate, and craved the body of Jesus.

Luke 23:52 This [man] went unto Pilate, and begged the body of Jesus.

53 And he took it down, and wrapped it in linen, and laid it in a sepulcher that was hewn in stone, wherein never man before was laid.

54 And that day was the preparation, and the Sabbath drew on.

John 19:31 ¶ The Jews therefore, because it was the preparation, that the bodies should not remain on the cross on the Sabbath day, (for that Sabbath day was an high day), besought Pilate that their legs might be broken, and [that] they might be taken away…….

38 ¶ And after this Joseph of Arimathaea, being a disciple of Jesus, but secretly for fear of the Jews, besought Pilate that he might take away the body of Jesus: and Pilate gave [him] leave. He came therefore, and took the body of Jesus. …..

42 There laid they Jesus therefore, because of the Jews' preparation [day], for the sepulcher was nigh at hand;

From these few passages, and there are others as well, we can learn many things.

1. The prophets were most certainly __not__ dormant in writing about the crucifixion, as some writers claim. In fact, they were very explicit but perhaps constrained by prophetic latitude.

2. All four Gospels, Matthew, Mark, Luke and John, establish the day of the crucifixion was most definitely on the preparation day prior to the Sabbath, and John establishes that the next day was a High Sabbath Day and not just a regular Sabbath. A High Day is the same a Solemn Assembly in our time, and the same was practiced by ancient Israel as part of their Mosaic worship. It was for this purpose the people had gathered to Jerusalem to sanctify and purify them-selves in order to participate in the Passover Sacrifices and the Convocations.

3. The Passover calendar is unmistakably clear there are two preparation days, each preceding the two Convocation or Holy High days. Generally speaking, all interpretations of the Gospels agree the Savior and the disciples partook of the Passover on the evening between the 5th ^{day} and morning of the 6th day. Therefore, this makes the 5th day the preparation day and therefore the 6th day is the Feast day (convocation) and the 1st day of Unleavened Bread. The 5th day is a preparation day when a Passover lamb is sacrificed between 3pm and 5pm and eaten that same evening. Jesus was obviously not crucified on the 5th day, then there is only one other day of preparation before a High day, and that is on the 11th day which is the final day of the Passover or the 20th of Nisan.

4. With this understanding we can clearly see that other scriptures, which have previously been claimed to be in question, now begin to be more understandable. The Jewish leadership was concerned about the Savior rising again after three days, as referenced in Matt 27. This was important, because according to Jewish beliefs a person could not be declared dead unless they had been interred for three days and three nights. Under those circumstances the 20th Nissan is the preparation day on which the Savior was crucified.

We find in:

Matthew 12:38 ¶ Then certain of the scribes and of the Pharisees answered, saying, Master, we would see a sign from thee.

39 But he answered and said unto them, an evil and adulterous generation seeketh after a sign; and there shall no sign be given to it, but the sign of the prophet Jonas:

40 For as Jonas was three days and three nights in the whale's belly; so shall the son of man be three days and three nights in the heart of the earth.

The book of Mormon gives us an account of what happened in the new world at the same time:

3 Nephi 8:19 And it came to pass that when the thunderings, and the lightnings, and the storm, and the tempest, and the quakings of the earth did cease--for behold, they did last for about the space of three hours; and it was said by some that the time was greater;

nevertheless, all these great and terrible things were done in about the space of three hours—then behold there was great darkness upon the face of the land.

20 And it came to pass that there was thick darkness upon all the face of the land, insomuch that the inhabitants thereof who had not fallen could feel the vapor of darkness;

21 And there could be no light, because of the darkness, neither candles, neither torches; neither could there be fire kindled with their fine and exceedingly dry wood, so that there could not be any light at all;

22 And there was not any light seen, neither fire, for so great were the mists of darkness which were upon the face of the land. nor glimmer, neither the sun, nor the moon, nor the stars,

23 And it came to pass that it did last for the space of three days that there was no light seen; and there was great mourning and howling and weeping among all the people continually; yea, great were the groanings of the people, because of the darkness and the great destruction which had come upon them.

1 Nephi:10 And the God of our fathers, who were led out of Egypt, out of bondage, and also were preserved in the wilderness by him, yea, the God of Abraham, and of Isaac, and the God of Jacob, yieldeth himself, according to the words of the angel, as a man, into the hands of wicked men, to be lifted up, according to the words of Zenock, and to be crucified, according to the words of Neum, and to be buried in a sepulchre, according to the words of Zenos, which he spake concerning the three days of darkness, <u>which should be a sign given of his death</u> unto those who should inhabit the isles of the sea, more especially given unto those who are of the house of Israel.

2 Nephi 25:13 Behold, they will crucify him; and after he is laid in a sepulchre for the space of three days he shall rise from the dead….

Helaman 14:20 But behold, as I said unto you concerning another sign, a sign of his death, behold, in that day that he shall suffer death the sun shall be darkened and refuse to give his light unto you; and also the moon and the stars; and <u>there shall be no light upon the face of this land, even from the time that he shall suffer death, for the space of three days, to the time that he shall rise again from the dead.</u>.

Jesus made it quite clear, the burial time before His resurrection would be at least 3 days and 3 nights, or at least 72 hours. The scriptures quoted above, as well as many in the New Testament, verify this time frame is exactly correct.

What is a day and night?

"1. In the bible one period of the earth's revolution on its axis (24 hours) is called a day.[152] Hebrew days were calculated "from even unto even"[153], meaning from sunset to sunset. The "Lord's" day is the first day of the week or Sunday,[154]

2. The period of time between dawn and dark is the day as distinguished from the night,[155] "Are there not 12 hours in a day?[156]"[157]

It becomes abundantly clear that Jesus could not have been placed in the tomb on Friday night and rose in the early morning hours of Sunday, and claim fulfillment of the scriptures concerning His burial.

If we refer to the comparison calendar presented above and place Jesus in the tomb, as described by the prophets, on the 11th day of Passover <u>(the preparation day)</u> and then move forward 3 days and 3 nights we

---

[152] Gen. 7:24,
[153] Lev. 23:32
[154] D&C 59:9-14
[155] Gen. 8:22, Ps 19:2
[156] John 11:9
[157] Mormon Doctrine p 180

find that the Savior rose from the tomb before daylight on the 15th day of the Passover, which was the 24th of Nissan. We know from D&C 59 that this was a Sunday and the 1st day of the week, and is generally accepted as such by most of Christianity.

Counting backward from there we find that the 6th day of the week, <u>(the 15th of Nissan)</u>, was the Passover and the 7th day of the week, <u>(16th of Nissan)</u> was the regular Saturday Sabbath. We therefore have a double Sabbath day, the 6th day being the Passover Convocation and the 7th day being a regular Sabbath and also the second day of unleavened bread, which is the day of the feast of the firstfruits. This is not unusual since feast days are fixed and the regular Sabbath is on different days of the week each year. It's like Christmas. Christmas is on a fixed day but never on the same day of the week from year to year. We should also remember in the days of the Passover there were no weekday appellations, it was simply 1st day and 7th day.

Therefore, the day of the crucifixion was on the 20th of Nisan or the 11th day of the Passover. The Gregorian calendar, a corrected form of the Julian calendar, introduced by Pope Gregory XIII in 1582 and is now used in most countries of the world. Thereby, we could say the crucifixion day would have been on Wednesday.

A prevailing but incorrect synopsis for the Passover celebration, however, is a Passion Week chronology, in which the Savior is crucified on Friday, in the tomb part of Friday night - all day Saturday day – part of Sunday night, and resurrected early Sunday morning. This chronology became codified somewhere between the Council at Nicaea and the 5th century and has been perpetuated ever since. This chronology was accepted by most Christianity, because the subject was highly controversial and not thought to be germane in the task of developing doctrinal issues, in the early formation of the church.

Talmage correctly accepted the evening of the 5th day as the Passover meal, which would have been Friday by the Hebrew calculation of the beginning of a day.[158] From that point forward he concentrates only on the doctrines of the gospel and not the time frame. However, in his endnote to the chapter he explains why.
"Notes to Chapter 33

James E. Talmage, Jesus the Christ, Ch.33, p.617 - p.618

1. The Day of the Passover Feast. -- Controversy has been rife for many centuries as to the day of the Passover feast in the week of our Lord's death. That He was crucified on Friday, the day before the Jewish Sabbath, and that He rose a resurrected Being on Sunday, the day following the Sabbath of the Jews, are facts attested by the four Gospel-writers. From the three synoptic, <u>we infer</u> that the last supper occurred on the evening of the first day of unleavened bread, and therefore at the beginning of the Jewish Friday……….,
….John also specifies that the day of the crucifixion was "the preparation of the Passover" (19:14), and that the next day, which was Saturday, the Sabbath, "was an high day" (verse 31), that is a Sabbath rendered doubly sacred because of its being also a feast day.

Much has been written by way of attempt to explain this seeming discrepancy. No analysis of the divergent views of Biblical scholars on this subject will be attempted here; the matter is of incidental importance in connection with the fundamental facts of our Lord's betrayal and crucifixion; for brief summaries of opinions and concise arguments the student may be referred to Smith's Comprehensive Bible Dictionary, article "Passover"; Edersheim's Life and Times of Jesus the Messiah, pp. 480-2, and 566-8; Farrar's Life of Christ, Appendix, Excursus 10; Andrews' Life of Our Lord, and Gresswell's Dissertations. Suffice it here to say that the apparent inconsistency may be explained by any of several assumptions………, …...it is interesting to note that Josephus (wars, vi, Ch. 9:3) records the number of lambs slain at a single Passover as 256,500. In the same paragraph, Josephus states that the lambs had to be slain between the ninth and the eleventh hour (3 to 5 p.m.). According to this explanation, Jesus and the Twelve may have partaken of the Passover meal on the first of the two evenings, and the Jews who next day feared defilement may have deferred their observance until the second………, ……… Some authorities assert that an error of one day had crept into the Jewish reckoning of time, and that Jesus ate the Passover on the true date, while the Jews were a day behind. If "the preparation of the Passover" (John 19: 14) on Friday, the day of Christ's crucifixion, means the slaughtering of the paschal lambs, our Lord, the real sacrifice of which all earlier altar victims had been but prototypes, died on the cross while the Passover lambs were being slain at the temple."

---

[158] JTC p 593

Talmage explains that the subject of the Passover has been controversial for centuries and that the interpretations are at best reached by what they think is inferred by the four gospels. He further states that his work is not at all an attempt to give an analysis of the divergent views of the biblical scholars.

Alfred Edersheim 1825-1889– a Jewish convert to Christianity and a Biblical scholar.

Farrar 1831-1903– Archdeacon of Westminster, Chaplin to the House of Commons, Dean of Canterbury.

Edward Gresswell – 1797-1869 English Churchman and Academic.

Samuel Andrews . 1817-1906 pastor of the catholic and Apostolic Church at Hartford, Conn.

Gresswell – 1797-1869 fellow at Corpus Christi College 1823-1869

These are just a few of the scholars and their works that has been held up as the unquestioned experts of so-called Biblical knowledge. While we admire, the information accumulated, and the <u>historical documentation</u> acquired, which, for some part seems to be accurate, we cannot help but notice their interpretation and manipulation of the scriptures, has a definite bias to prove their point of view, in regards to the seven-day chronology correct.

These scholarly masters of the 7-day chronology state; the 5th day afternoon, the preparation day, was when the lambs were sacrificed and the Passover meal was eaten on the night between the 5th and 6th day. Of course, this is correct, and this would make the 6th day the Passover feast day and the first day of unleavened bread. But the scholars turn right around in the next breath and state the 6th day is the preparation day for the Passover when the Lord was tried and crucified and the 7th day is the feast day of the Passover. The logic of this thinking escapes the mind.

For over fifteen hundred years on the eastern and western hemispheres, there appears to have been silence between the heavens and the earth. Of direct revelation from God to man during this long interval, we have no authentic record. As already shown, the period of apostolic ministry on the eastern continent probably terminated before the dawn of the second century of the Christian era. The passing of the apostles was followed by the rapid development of a universal apostasy as had been foreseen and predicted.[159]

In regards to the last days we find Nephi saw the colonization of America--the Revolutionary war and its outcome--the outcome of the war was under the divine guidance of God.[160] Nephi beheld the Gentiles had the Bible among them.

> *1 Nephi 13:20 And it came to pass that I, Nephi, beheld that they did prosper in the land; and I beheld a book, and it was carried forth among them.*
>
> *21 And the angel said unto me: Knowest thou the meaning of the book?*
>
> *22 And I said unto him: I know not.*
>
> *23 And he said: Behold it proceedeth out of the mouth of a Jew. And I, Nephi, beheld it; and he said unto me: The book that thou beholdest is a record of the Jews, which contains the covenants of the Lord, which he hath made unto the house of Israel; and it also containeth many of the prophecies of the holy prophets; and it is a record like unto the engravings which are upon the plates of brass, save there are not so many; nevertheless, <u>they contain the covenants of the Lord, which he hath made unto the house of Israel; wherefore, they are of great worth unto the Gentiles.</u>*
>
> *24 And the angel of the Lord said unto me: Thou hast beheld that the book proceeded forth from the mouth of a Jew; and when it proceeded forth from the mouth of a Jew it contained the fullness of the gospel of the Lord, of whom the twelve apostles bear record; and they bear record according to the truth which is in the Lamb of God.*
>
> *25 Wherefore, these things go forth from the Jews in purity unto the Gentiles, according to the truth which is in God.*

This confirms the record of the Old Testament came forth from the Jews in purity, and thereby could be trusted in its content. The Old Testament is virtually an undisputed historical record of Gods' revelations and dealings with His chosen people, and assures us we can have confidence in the Passover calendar and the

---

[159] JTC p745
[160] 1Nephi 13:12-19

performance and ordinances pertaining to the Law of Moses as laid out in Exodus, are reliable and accurate. This knowledge is of great value to us as it contains the undisputed Law of Moses along with the practices and ordinances. The exact time frame of the Lord's fulfillment of this Law should not be a confusion to us.

However, the New Testament is another story:

1 Nephi 13: 26 And after they go forth by the hand of the twelve apostles of the Lamb, from the Jews unto the Gentiles, thou seest the formation of that great and abominable church, which is most abominable above all other churches; for behold, they have taken away from the gospel of the Lamb many parts which are plain and most precious; and also many covenants of the Lord have they taken away.

27 And all this have they done that they might pervert the right ways of the Lord, that they might blind the eyes and harden the hearts of the children of men.

28 Wherefore, thou seest that after the book hath gone forth through the hands of the great and abominable church, that there are many plain and precious things taken away from the book, which is the book of the Lamb of God.

29 And after these plain and precious things were taken away it goeth forth unto all the nations of the Gentiles; and after it goeth forth unto all the nations of the Gentiles, yea, even across the many waters which thou hast seen with the Gentiles which have gone forth out of captivity, thou seest--because of the many plain and precious things which have been taken out of the book, which were plain unto the understanding of the children of men, according to the plainness which is in the Lamb of God--because of these things which are taken away out of the gospel of the Lamb, an exceedingly great many do stumble, yea, <u>insomuch that Satan hath great power over them.</u>

This graphic explanation tells us once the 12 Apostles were dead, a great an abominable church evolved, and proceeded to remove many precious parts and covenants of the Lord in order to blind the people to the truth and consequently gain power over them. Once this abominable church had perverted the right ways of the Lord and removed many of the plain and precious truths, what remained went out to all the nations of the Gentiles and a great many do stumble as they attempt to explain the scriptures to the people. Therefore, Satan takes advantage of this in order to gain power.

2 Nephi 28:3 For it shall come to pass in that day that the churches which are built up, and not unto the Lord, when the one shall say unto the other: Behold, I, I am the Lord's; and the others shall say: I, I am the Lord's; and thus shall every one say that hath built up churches, and not unto the Lord—

4 And they shall contend one with another; and their priests shall contend one with another, and they shall teach with their learning, and deny the Holy Ghost, which giveth utterance.

5 And they deny the power of God, the Holy One of Israel; and they say unto the people: Hearken unto us, and hear ye our precept; for behold there is no God today, for the Lord and the Redeemer hath done his work , and he hath given his power unto men;

6 Behold, hearken ye unto my precept; if they shall say there is a miracle wrought by the hand of the Lord, believe it not; for this day he is not a God of miracles; he hath done his work.

From a sermon given by the Prophet Joseph Smith in 1844:

If the whole tree is corrupt, are not its branches corrupt? If the Catholic religion is a false religion, how can any true religion come out of it? If the Catholic Church is bad, how can any good thing come out of it? The character of the old churches has always been slandered by all apostates since the world began. ….. It is in the order of heavenly things that God should always send a new dispensation into the world when men have apostatized from the truth and lost the priesthood; but when men come out and build upon other men's foundations, they do it on their own responsibility, without authority from God; and when the floods come and the winds blow, their foundations will be found to be sand, and their whole fabric will crumble to dust. (Sermon in a meeting in the grove, east of Nauvoo Temple, June 16, 1844)

When we place our confidence in the doctrines and apologists of the old third century universal church and its offshoots of today, we build our beliefs on a foundation of sand...

1 Nephi 13:32 Neither will the Lord God suffer that the Gentiles shall forever remain in that awful state of blindness, which thou beholdest they are in, because of the plain and most precious parts of the gospel of the Lamb which have been kept back by that abominable church, whose formation thou hast seen.

33 Wherefore saith the Lamb of God: I will be merciful unto the Gentiles, unto the visiting of the remnant of the house of Israel in great judgment.

34 And it came to pass that the angel of the Lord spake unto me, saying: Behold, saith the Lamb of God, after I have visited the remnant of the house of Israel--and this remnant of whom I speak is the seed of thy father--wherefore, after I have visited them in judgment, and smitten them by the hand of the Gentiles, and after the Gentiles do stumble exceedingly, because of the most plain and precious parts of the gospel of the Lamb which have been kept back by that abominable church, which is the mother of harlots, saith the Lamb--I will be merciful unto the Gentiles in that day, insomuch that I will bring forth unto them, in mine own power, much of my gospel, which shall be plain and precious, saith the Lamb.

35 For, behold, saith the Lamb: I will manifest myself unto thy seed, that they shall write many things which I shall minister unto them, which shall be plain and precious; and after thy seed shall be destroyed, and dwindle in unbelief, and also the seed of thy brethren, behold, these things shall be hid up, to come forth unto the Gentiles, by the gift and power of the Lamb.

36 And in them shall be written my gospel, saith the Lamb, and my rock and my salvation.

In these last days, the Lord, in spite of the fact that the abominable church has kept the people of the world ignorant and oppressed, has set his hand to be merciful unto the Gentiles and the House of Israel. After the Lord has visited the remnant of the tribes in the new world in judgment, He will bring forth to the stumbling Gentiles, the Book of Mormon that had been prepared for us by the hand of Nephi and all.

Once again, the plain and precious truths are being restored to us by the gift and power of the Lamb, so we might be blessed:

1 Nephi 13:37 And blessed are they who shall seek to bring forth my Zion at that day, for they shall have the gift and the power of the Holy Ghost; and if they endure unto the end they shall be lifted up at the last day, and shall be saved in the everlasting kingdom of the Lamb; and whoso shall publish peace, yea, tidings of great joy, how beautiful upon the mountains shall they be.

38 And it came to pass that I beheld the remnant of the seed of my brethren, and also the book of the Lamb of God, which had proceeded forth from the mouth of the Jew, that it came forth from the Gentiles unto the remnant of the seed of my brethren.

39 And after it had come forth unto them I beheld other books, which came forth by the power of the Lamb, from the Gentiles unto them, unto the convincing of the Gentiles and the remnant of the seed of my brethren, and also the Jews who were scattered upon all the face of the earth, that the records of the prophets and of the twelve apostles of the Lamb are true.

40 And the angel spake unto me, saying: These last records, which thou hast seen among the Gentiles, shall establish the truth of the first, which are of the twelve apostles of the Lamb, and shall make known the plain and precious things which have been taken away from them; and shall make known to all kindred, tongues, and people, that the Lamb of God is the Son of the Eternal Father, the Savior of the world; and that all men must come unto him, or they cannot be saved.

41 And they must come according to the words which shall be established by the mouth of the Lamb; and the words of the Lamb shall be made known in the records of thy seed, as well as in the records of the twelve apostles of the Lamb; wherefore they both shall be established in one; for there is one God and one Shepherd over all the earth.

42 And the time cometh that he shall manifest himself unto all nations, both unto the Jews and also unto the Gentiles; and after he has manifested himself unto the Jews and also unto the Gentiles, then he shall manifest himself unto the Gentiles and also unto the Jews, and the last shall be first, and the first shall be last.

The Book of Mormon, Doctrine & Covenants, The Pearl of Great Price and so much more have been continually coming to light, and by the Gift and Power of the Lamb our minds are constantly being opened to the plain and precious truths of the Gospel and Doctrine of Christ.

We feel that it is no mere coincidence that the representatives of the Catholic Church and others of her offspring, such as Edersheim and the likes, come forth with a sea of information and doctrine, just at the same time the gospel and authority of God is being restored to the world. Even though some of the historical information they provide may be correct, no longer need we rely on the doctrinal information that, as is said, "The Day of the Passover Feast. -- Controversy has been rife for many centuries as to the day of the Passover feast in the week of our Lord's death."

By properly combining the Old Testament Exodus revelation, which we know is true and gives a proper application of the New Testament, we are able to establish the crucifixion of the Savior on 20th of Nissan preparation day. According to the historian Josephus, the final sin sacrifice of the Passover is presented on the alter, at the 9th hour. It is no coincidence John tells us the Savior gave up his life at the same time. The next day was the High day Sabbath, and the final day of the Passover. Following along in the Passover calendar at the beginning of the chapter, we see this places the Savior in the tomb for 3 days and 3 night between the 11th and 14th days of the Passover. Allowing for the 3days and 3nights in the heart of the earth as prophesied in Matthew, we find that the resurrection would have been on the 15th day. We know this day to be the 1st day of the week, or Sunday. We now simply count backwards and, low and behold, we find that all scriptures dovetail and harmonize perfectly with the preceding 7day week for a grand total of 15 days instead of 7days.

This is not by accident nor by happen stance this harmony occurs, it is the perfect plan of salvation from God since the foundation of the world. With perfect understanding and foreknowledge, Jesus fulfilled the Law of Moses and brought to pass our immortality and possibility of Eternal Life.

While this seems complicated, but, if we follow the scripture table at the beginning of the chapter, we discover that the Old Testament gives us the exact and unquestionable Passover time frame of 12 days not 7. The New Testament is still intact enough to give us verification of the events and in the order as they occurred. It becomes quite clear as we study along, that the Prophets of old and new of this day, the book of Mormon, the Antiquities of Josephus and many other sources, whether knowingly or unknowingly, collaborate to arrive to the same conclusion.

Since Jesus has, through the mouths of the prophets established these facts and, since the Savior said He did not come to destroy the same, it will become abundantly clear that not one jot or tittle was to pass away and all would be fulfilled.

In the next chapter depicting the trials, we will begin to see how all the scriptures, which have long been in question, begin to fit properly into place.

Chapter 12
The Formal Trial

6th day, *15th Nissan*, (Friday)	Location	Matthew	Mark	Luke	John
Convocation, High day, Passover day, 1st day of unleavened bread	Jerusalem	Exodus 12			
7th day, *16th Nissan*, (Saturday) Feast day of First Fruits & regular 7th day sabbath	Jerusalem	Exodus 12			
8th day, *17th Nissan*, (Sunday)	Jerusalem				
The formal Trial				22:63-71	

    At the onset of this portion of our harmonizing of the four gospels, we feel it necessary to restate some of the premises for our discussion.

    First: We have established that the Old Testament given through the mouth of the Jew, as testified to by the twelve and Josephus, was pure and true. With the documentation from these sources, and others, we have established that the 15th of Nissan, the 6th day, was not the day of preparation but was indeed the "Feast day". We have further shown that the 16th day of Nissan, the 7th day, was the feast of the first fruits and also the 7th day Sabbath. Having established the correct day of the crucifixion, we can clearly see that the Jewish Priesthood would have been extensively occupied with the sacrifices and ordinances ordained by Jehovah for the above-mentioned days.

    Second: Controversy has been rife for centuries about the Passover days and how the events actually occurred. This confusion stems primarily from accepting the assumptive teachings codified in the 3rd century and conclusions postulated by an apostate clergy and apologist authors of these latter days. This confusion comes about, however, because religionists have incorrectly attempted to force all the scriptures into a 7-day chronology. Granted, some of their research has merit, but all must be perused with reasonable investigative doubt.

    Third: Many of the plain and precious truths of the New Testament have been lost in the Great Apostasy, but much has been restored, or brought to light, through the Book of Mormon and revelation now afforded us. By correlating old and modern scripture, and with prophetic guidance, we are able to obtain a more correct and understandable picture of what happened at the last Passover.[161]

    We can be grateful however for the research that has been brought forward for our study. The previously mentioned Chandlers Brief, gives a much greater understanding of the legal formalities that controlled the Jewish Justice System prevailing in the Saviors day.

Chandlers Brief lists the following illegalities:

    "Point 1: The arrest of Jesus was illegal, since it was effected by night, and through the treachery of Judas, an accomplice, both of which features were expressly forbidden in Jewish law of that day.

    "Point 2: The private examination of Jesus before Annas or Caiaphas was illegal; for (1) it was made by night; (2) the hearing of cause by a 'sole judge' was expressly forbidden; (3) as quoted by Salvador, 'A principle perpetually reproduced in the Hebrew scriptures relates to two conditions of publicity and liberty.'

    "Point 3: The indictment against Jesus was, in form, illegal. 'The entire criminal procedure of the Mosaic code rests upon four rules: certainty in the indictment; publicity in the discussion; full freedom granted to the

---
[161] Previous Chapters

accused; and assurance against all dangers or errors of testimony' – Salvador, p365. 'The Sanhedrin did not and could not originate the charges; it only investigated those brought before it.' – Edersheim, vol. 1, p. 309. The evidence of the leading witnesses constituted the charge. There was no other charge; no more formal indictment. Until they spoke and spoke in the public assembly, the prisoner was scarcely an accused man.' –Innes, p.41. 'The only prosecutors known to Talmudic criminal jurisprudence are the witnesses to the crime. Their duty is to bring the matter to the cognizance of the court, and to bear witness against the criminal. In capital cases they are the legal executioners also. Of an official accuser or prosecutor there is nowhere any trace in the laws of ancient Hebrews.' – Mendelshon, p. 110.

"Point 4: The proceedings of the Sanhedrin against Jesus were illegal because they were conducted at night. 'Let a capital offense be tried during the day, but suspended at night.' – Mishna, Sanhedrin 4:1. 'Criminal cases can be acted upon by the various courts during daytime only, by the Lesser Sanhedrin from the close of the morning service till noon, and by the Greater Sanhedrin till evening.' – Mendelsohn, p. 112.

"Point 5: The proceedings of the Sanhedrin against Jesus were illegal because the court convened before the offering of the morning sacrifice. 'The Sanhedrin sat from the close of the morning sacrifice to the time of the evening sacrifice.' – Talmud, Jer. San. 1:19. 'No session of the court could take place before the offering of the morning sacrifice.' – MM. Lemann, p.109. 'Since the morning sacrifice was offered at the dawn of day, it was hardly possible for the Sanhedrin to assemble until the hour after that time.'" – Mishnah, Tamid, ch.3.

"Point 6: The proceedings against Jesus were illegal because they were conducted on the day preceding a Jewish Sabbath; also, on the first day of unleavened bread and on the eve of the Passover. 'They shall not judge on the eve of the Sabbath nor on that of any festival. – Mishnah, San. 4:1. 'No court of justice in Israel was permitted to hold session on the Sabbath or any of the seven Biblical holidays. In cases of capital crime, no trial could be commenced on Friday or the day previous to any holiday, because it was not lawful either to adjourn such cases longer that overnight or to continues them on the Sabbath or holiday.' -- Rabbi Wise, Martyrdom of Jesus,' p. 67

"Point 7: The trial of Jesus was illegal because it was conducted in one day. 'A criminal resulting in the acquittal of the accused may terminate the same day on which the trial began. But if a sentence of death is to be pronounced, it cannot be concluded before the following day.' – Mishnah, San. 4:1.

"Point 8: The sentence of condemnation pronounced against Jesus by the Sanhedrin was illegal because it was founded upon His uncorroborated confession. 'We have it as a fundamental principle of our jurisprudence that no one can bring an accusation against himself. Should a man make a confession of guilt before a legally constituted tribunal, such confession is nor to be used against him unless properly attested by two other witnesses.' – Maimonides, 4:2. "Not only is self-condemnation never extorted from the defendant by means of torture, but no attempt is ever made to lead him on to self-incrimination. Moreover, a voluntary confession on his part is not admitted as evidence and therefore not competent to convict him, unless a legal number of witnesses minutely corroborate his self-accusation.' – Mendelsohn, p. 133.

"Point 9: The condemnation of Jesus was illegal because the verdict of the Sanhedrin was unanimous. A simultaneous and unanimous verdict of guilt rendered on the day of the trial has the effect of acquittal.' – Medelsohn, p. 141. 'If none of the judges defend the culprit, i.e., all pronounce him guilty, having no defender in the court, the verdict of guilty was invalid and the sentence of death could not be executed.' Rabbi Wise, 'Martyrdom of Jesus' p. 74.

"Point 10: The proceedings against Jesus were illegal in that: (1) The sentence of condemnation was pronounced in a place forbidden by law; (2) The high priest rent his clothes; (3) the balloting was irregular. "After leaving the hall Gazith, no sentence of death can be passed upon any one so ever.' – Talmud, Bab. 'Of Idolatry' 1;8. 'A sentence of death can be pronounced only so long as the Sanhedrin holds sessions in the appointed place.' –Maimonides, 14. See further Levit. 21:10; compare 10:6.'Let the judges each in his turn absolve or condemn.' – Mishnah, San. 15:5. 'The members of the Sanhedrin were seated in the form of a semicircle, at the extremity of which a secretary was placed, whose business it was to record votes. One of these secretaries recorded the votes in favor of the accused, the other those against him.' – Mishnah, San. 4; 3. 'In ordinary cases the judges voted according to seniority, the oldest commencing: in capital case the reverse order was followed.' – Benny, p. 73.

"Point 11: The members of the Great Sanhedrin were legally disqualified to try Jesus. 'Nor must there be on the judicial bench either a relation of a particular friend, or an enemy of either the accused or the accuser.' – Medlesohn, p. 108. 'Nor under any circumstances was a man known to be at enmity with the accused person permitted to occupy a position among the judges.' – Benny, p.37

"Point 12: the condemnation of Jesus was illegal because the merits of the defense were not considered. 'Then shalt thou enquire, and make search, and ask diligently. -- Deut. 13:14. 'The judges shall weigh the matter in the sincerity of their conscience.' – Mishnah, San. 4:5. 'The primary object of the Hebrew Judicial system was to render the conviction of an innocent person impossible. All the ingenuity of the Jewish legists was directed to the attainment of this end.' – Benny, p. 56." (Walter M. Chandler, *The Trial of Jesus from a Lawyer's Standpoint,* Vol. 1, *The Hebrew Trial,* quoted, *Talmage,* pp. 645-648).

We have entered Chandlers brief about the night trials, to show the confusion which exists regarding them. Supposed ecclesiastical authorities have gone into these points in great depth in order to prove their particular religious bias and views are correct.

Upon close examination of the scriptures, **WE FIND NOTHING IN THEM TO INDICATE ANY ILLEGAL NIGHT TRIAL.** The scriptures indicate only a gathering of the Sanhedrin, in groups of 10 to 20, observing the Passover according to custom. No doubt they were involved in the planning and the arrest of Jesus, but they were clever enough to let the Tribune and his band do it and bring Him in, this way they could claim they weren't responsible. It must be remembered, from this time forward the disciples or flock has been scattered, as Jesus said they would be. The information in the Gospels is rather limited at this point and, it must be remembered that many of the plain and precious truths have been taken out, in order to substantiate apostate views.

We have shown that the 6TH AND 7TH DAYS OF THE PASSOVER HAVE BEEN MISIDENTIFIED as the preparation day and the high day, thus creating a conundrum requiring a manipulation of the scriptures so as to fit them all into a 3-hour time frame.

The proponents of the seven-day chronology postulated this legal brief in order to show how illegally the Jewish hierarchy had acted, thus proving their interpretation of the scriptures are correct. Therefore, being correct, their religious convictions are true. These claims are the machinations of men, and we don't find them to be based in scriptural fact. When these apologists knowingly or unknowingly insist that the Passover is celebrated and observed in seven days, rather than for 1500 years it was 12 days, they are left with no other alternative but to adjust and lose scriptures, and advance fabricated legal theories to support their case.

We have previously pointed out the fallacy of this line of thinking. However, we applaud the effort and diligence that was required to accumulate and correlate all of this legal information. We appreciate these historical references to the laws of that time because it proves how meticulous the legal authorities were in the execution of their duties. We submit, that to a fault, the Jewish priesthood were fanatics in following the letter of the law, and in their own twisted way would not and did not violate their own laws.

The foregoing cited breaches of the Jewish laws are primarily hinged around two points: (1) The chronology of the seven days that denotes the Passover and the day of unleavened bread as the 6th day.
(2) Because of this, there are no other alternatives left than to assume that most of the trials and hearings took place at night. Any scriptures that differ or are contrary to this line of thinking are left out, misrepresented or not discussed.

We have already clearly established the Passover calendar that is the Lord's timetable for the expedient and final sacrifice of the chosen Lamb.[162] Jesus has left no doubt He is in control of the situation for, He told us clearly that He is the one who gave the Law of Moses, made the covenants, and He is the one who has fulfilled the Law.[163] We find it difficult to believe that the Savior would give the Law and the specific requirements as to

---

[162] Chapter 2
[163] 3 Nephi 15:5-10

the fulfillment, and then fulfill it in an entirely different manner. Even as deplorable as His captors were as a people, Jesus said, "forgive them Father, for they know not what they do."

Jesus further demonstrates His control of the situation surrounding the last supper, He dismisses Judas from the table to go do what he must do.[164] Then when they came to arrest Jesus in the Garden and Peter started to fight, Jesus told him to put up his sword, that if it were to be any different, the Father would send more than twelve legions of angles to protect them.[165] This is no happen-stance murder brought about by a group of renegade zealots; this is the final willing sacrifice in the Plan of Salvation set forth from the foundation of the world.

In regards to the Chandler brief:

***Point 1: The arrest of Jesus was illegal,** since it was effected by night, and through the treachery of Judas, an accomplice, both of which features were expressly forbidden in Jewish law of that day.*

There can be little doubt that Jesus was arrested at night. However, Jesus was a wanted criminal, the Pharisees had already put a warrant for his arrest.[166] The chief priests had personally covenanted with Judas Iscariot for the delivery of Jesus, for thirty pieces of silver.[167] The chief priests and the Pharisees had personally sent Judas and the band of soldiers to arrest a seditious malefactor.[168]

The Jewish leadership was gathered together at the palaces' of Annas and Caiaphas, sharing apparently, a common courtyard, celebrating the Passover meal and the first day of Unleavened Bread. Many of the chief priests and Pharisees would be gathered together in groups of 10-20 men, possibly having their loins girded, their shoes on and their staff in hand, eating in haste waiting the midnight hour, or in leisure depending on your point of view. When Jesus was delivered to them, early in the morning, the priests and scribes would most likely have been burning, or preparing to burn any remains of the Passover.[169] They were no doubt awaiting delivery of Jesus as per their orders. As far as it being against the law, they were the law!

Point 2: The private examination of Jesus before Annas or Caiaphas was illegal:

The hearing was not executed in private. There were soldiers, elders, scribes, multitudes of people and at least 2 of the disciples that witnessed the events that took place, not only by Annas but by Caiaphas as well, thus two judges.

The only thing that happened that night, before dawn, was a preliminary hearing to determine if Jesus could be bound over for trial. All four Gospels[170] agree that's what happened and then the cock crew and Peter wept, thus making it likely just at or before dawn.

Point 3: The indictment against Jesus was, in form, illegal

There was no formal indictment made that night. There is no scriptural record of night trial. The scriptures show only of two witnesses, false they may have been, which provided evidence of a personal information requirement to arrest and bind over for trial. Our trial system of today reflects approximately the same procedures.

Point 4: The proceedings of the Sanhedrin against Jesus were illegal because they were conducted at night.

There is no scriptural recordation of a trial at night, the only trial referred to, is the one in Luke 22:63-71 that records a formal daytime trial. Even though we would consider this supposed trial as a kangaroo court, it never the less had all the trappings of legality and was an all-day proceeding.

Point 5: The proceedings of the Sanhedrin against Jesus were illegal because the court convened before the offering of the morning sacrifice

This point totally presumes a nighttime trial, for which there is no evidence. We will present the trials later on in our analysis.

Point 6: The proceedings against Jesus were illegal because they were conducted on the day preceding a Jewish Sabbath; also, on the first day of unleavened bread and on the eve of the Passover.

This is a very interesting claim of breach of the law. Proponents of this brief, in order to support their belief in the 7-day chronology, claim this is the first day of unleavened bread and is at the same time the

---

[164] John 13:27-28
[165] Matt 26:51-54
[166] John 11:57
[167] Matt 26:15
[168] John 18:2-3
[169] Exodus 12:9-10
[170] Matt 26:57-69, Mark 14: 53-72, Luke 22:54-62, John 18:14-27

preparation day for the upcoming Passover, which they had just partaken of the night of the 5th day. On the other hand, they claim that Jesus was crucified on this same day, which we have shown was the feast day.

The scriptural references we have presented before, but needs repeating, unquestionably establishes the sixth day as the feast day:

John 12:1 ¶ **THEN Jesus six days before the Passover came to Bethany**, *where Lazarus was which had been dead, whom he raised from the dead.*

2 There they made him a supper; and Martha served: but Lazarus was one of them that sat at the table with him.

This record from John occurred the day before the first day of the Passover and thus establishes the 6th, 15 Nissan, as that day.

Matthew 26:2 **Ye know that after two days is [the feast of] the Passover, and the Son of man is betrayed to be crucified.**

3 Then assembled together the chief priests, and the scribes, and the elders of the people, unto the palace of the high priest, who was called Caiaphas,

4 And **consulted that they might take Jesus by subtlety, and kill [him]**.

5 But they said, **Not on the feast [day]**, *lest there be an uproar among the people.*

This record, as well as others, was given on the third day of the Passover and thus the 6th day is the feast day, all in harmony with the 12-day Passover calendar. So, we can see that the Jewish hierarchy was fully aware of the consequences of what might happen if they proceeded on a feast day, a holy convocation. Aside from the fact it would be against their law.

"Point 7: The trial of Jesus was illegal because it was conducted in one day.

There is no evidence that there was only one trial, even though we are glad they are admitting that there was a trial conducted in one day. We will show there were probably of at least three trials and two hearings.

Point 8: The sentence of condemnation pronounced against Jesus by the Sanhedrin was illegal because it was founded upon His uncorroborated confession.

There is no transcript or recordation of the trial in question, so any such claim is pure conjecture. We do know that Jesus confessed to claims that were true.

Point 9: The condemnation of Jesus was illegal because the verdict of the Sanhedrin was unanimous.

This is an unfounded claim. We know that many of the Jews believed in him,[171] and in particular, Joseph of Arimathea, a counselor and disciple of Jesus, as well as Nicodemus. These men and many other converts would have served in Jesus' defense at the formal trial.

Point 10: The proceedings against Jesus were illegal in that: (1) The sentence of condemnation was pronounced in a place forbidden by law; (2) The high priest rent his clothes; (3) the balloting was irregular.

There is no foundation for such a claim, as we will later show. This is strictly a presumption of a night trial.

Point 11: The members of the Great Sanhedrin were legally disqualified to try Jesus.

Tainted jury pool? Ideal principles, but in the real world it's an impossible dream. In the world at that time was, 'we make the rules' and it was obvious by the way they acted on all issues. Why do you think the Savior called them hypocrites, as well as other condemning appellations?

"Point 12: the condemnation of Jesus was illegal because the merits of the defense were not considered.

Who knows? We have reason to believe that at least a convoluted trial was adhered to on the 8th day for the sake of public appearances, as we will show later.

We have brought forth and dealt with, at least briefly, some of the issues regarding the Passover and sectarian claims of the group of 18th and 19th century authors and so called Biblical scholars. We are in awe of the lengths to which these authoritarians have gone to, to support and substantiate an 1800-year-old viewpoint.

We have every reason to believe that most if not all the forms of law and proceedings listed were observed, as well as the rest of the points of the brief that are so profusely mentioned. **There's nothing that we are aware of, in the scriptures to indicate otherwise.**

---

[171] John 12:11

Now begins the 6th day: (*15th Nissan*)

We have doubtlessly established, with incontrovertible scriptural evidence, that the 6th day was the Passover Feast day and the 1st day of Unleavened Bread.[172] There is very little written about the details of the Passover in the New Testament, other than what we have already discussed and are discussing now. To rename this day and the next by using John's text relating to the 7th day (20th Nissan) of Unleavened Bread and the last day of the Passover,[173] is further evidence of the misguided interpretation of the apologists of our day and the apostasy which has been created.

It should be remembered, that by this time of the morning (daylight), **all principal participants in this event have been up 24 hours or more.** The 6th day is a convocation day (solemn assembly) in which no servile work is to be performed.[174] It would only be reasonable to expect for all to be sleeping or otherwise resting, in preparation for the assembly and the sacrifices that would be made at 3: pm, as established by the Law of Moses. There is nothing written about this day, contrary or otherwise in the New Testament, or if there was it is something that has been lost. Thus, ends the 6th day.

7th day: (*16TH Nissan*):

The 7th day is the 2nd day of Unleavened Bread and the feast of the First Fruits. This day is a high holy day, as well as being the 7th day (Saturday) Sabbath. All of the Jewish Nation would have been making sacrifices and thanking God for their upcoming harvest, as well as resting and preparing for the daily sacrifices of the Passover.

We have already answered numerous points of Chandler's brief, and we have already and clearly shown by scriptural and historical evidence that the 6th and 7th days are a **convocational day** and a **regular Sabbath day**. Claims to the contrary, are nothing more than unfounded allegations put forth by misinterpretations of scholars in these last days to perpetuate a 3rd thru 5th century Nicene Philosophy.

Points 4 & 6 show:

4'Let a capital offense be tried during the day, but suspended at night.' – Mishnah, Sanhedrin 4:1. 'Criminal cases can be acted upon by the various courts during daytime only, by the Lesser Sanhedrin from the close of the morning service till noon, and by the Greater Sanhedrin till evening.' – Mendelsohn, p. 112.

And

6'They shall not judge on the eve of the Sabbath nor on that of any festival. – Mishnah, San. 4:1. 'No court of justice in Israel was permitted to hold session on the Sabbath or any of the seven Biblical holidays. In cases of capital crime, no trial could be commenced on Friday or the day previous to any holiday, because it was not lawful either to adjourn such cases longer that over-night or to continues them on the Sabbath or holiday.' -- Rabbi Wise, Martyrdom of Jesus,' p. 67

This is more evidence that the Jewish legal system would not have tried this case until after the 7th day. We must realize since the Savior had been arrested that the Apostles were scattered. However, they have given us in the days that followed, information if they were able to be at the right place and the right time to be able to obtain it. Often times, days and events are fragmented, run together, and are only separated by the words--then, when or now.

There is nothing written by the apostles specifically regarding activities on these two days as they too would have been observing the normal observance and performances of the Passover. The Lord expects us to be able to reason together to find the answers; otherwise we would lose our agency. There are, however, enough pertinent facts contained in what remains of the scriptures for us to be able to reason it out, if we take the prayerful time to do so. Other apologists disagree with Chandler and state the Jews would not have violated the law in this manner.

8th day: (*17th Nissan*)

---

[172] Capt. 2 & 4
[173] John 19:31
[174] Ibid Chap. 2-4

"Luke, who records no details of the night trial of Jesus, is the only Gospel-writer to give place to a circumstantial report of the morning session. He says: "And as soon as it was day, the elders of the people and the chief priests and the scribes came together, and led him into their council." Some Biblical scholars have construed the expression, "led him into their council," as signifying that Jesus was condemned by the Sanhedrin in the appointed meeting-place of the court, viz. Gazith or the Hall of Hewn Stones, as the law of the time required;"[175]

>Luke 22:63 ¶ And **the men that held Jesus mocked him, and smote [him]**.
>64 And when they had blindfolded him, they struck him on the face, and asked him, saying, Prophesy, who is it that smote thee?
>65 And many other things blasphemously spake they against him.
>
>66 <u>And as soon as it was day</u>, **the elders of the people and the chief priests and the scribes came together, and led him into their council, saying,**
>67 **Art thou the Christ**? tell us. And **he said unto them, If I tell you, ye will not believe**:
>68 And if I also ask [you], ye will not answer me, nor let [me] go.
>69 Hereafter shall the Son of man sit on the right hand of the power of God.
>70 Then said they all, Art thou then the Son of God? And he said unto them, Ye say that I am.
>71 And they said, What need we any further witness? for we ourselves have heard of his own mouth.

Scriptural authors all seem to agree that this was indeed the formal daytime trial. McConkie, (DNTC p 796,) states;

This is the formal Sanhedrin trial. "The following account or judicial procedure of the Sanhedrin in capital cases is abridged from Schurer, who follows the Mishnah. 'The members of the court sat in a semi-circle. A quorum of 223 was required. In front of them stood two clerks of the court, of whom the one on the right hand recorded the votes for acquittal, and the one on the left hand the votes for condemnation. The 'disciples of the wise' (pupils of the scribes) occupied three additional rows in the front. It was required to hear the reason for acquittal first (a regulation violated in the case of Jesus) and afterwards the reasons for condemnation. The 'disciples of the wise' could speak, but only in favor of the prisoner. Acquittal could be pronounced on the day of the trial, but condemnation not till the following day (this regulation was also violated, though some suppose that there were two meetings, one on Thursday night, and the other on Friday morning to render the proceedings technically legal). Each member stood to give his vote, and voting began with the youngest member. For acquittal, a simple majority would suffice; for condemnation, a majority of two was necessary." (Dummelow, p. 713)

Dummelow was another proponent of the 7-day chronology and you can see they still can't agree. However, this information shows how the court was held and it was an all-day trial.

We now refer to Chandler's brief:

Point 5. *'The Sanhedrin sat from the close of the morning sacrifice to the time of the evening sacrifice.' – Talmud, Jer. San. 1:19. 'No session of the court could take place before the offering of the morning sacrifice.' – MM. Lemann, p.109. 'Since the morning sacrifice was offered at the dawn of day, it was hardly possible for the Sanhedrin to assemble until the hour after that time.'' – Mishnah, Tamid, ch.3.*

AND:

Point 3. *'The entire criminal procedure of the Mosaic code rests upon four rules: certainty in the indictment; publicity in the discussion; full freedom granted to the accused; and assurance against all dangers or errors of testimony' – Salvador, p365. 'The Sanhedrin did not and could not originate the charges; it only investigated those brought before it.' – Edersheim, vol. 1, p. 309. The evidence of the leading witnesses constituted the charge. There was no other charge; no more formal indictment. Until they spoke and spoke in the public assembly, the prisoner was scarcely an accused man.' –Innes, p.41. 'The only prosecutors known to Talmudic criminal jurisprudence are the witnesses to the crime. Their duty is to bring the matter to the cognizance of the court, and to bear witness against the*

---
[175] JTC p 628

criminal. In capital cases they are the legal executioners also. Of an official accuser or prosecutor there is nowhere any trace in the laws of ancient Hebrews.' – Mendelshon, p. 110.

Chandler brought forth this brief in an effort to cast dispersion on the Jewish courts and to justify the theory of night trial to confirm the 7-day logic. Since Luke testifies of a day time trial, these points of law confirm how the trial was carried out.

It's obvious a strict law of performances and ordinances were required, and, we have shown how the Sanhedrin held their hypocritical court on the 8th day. In the following chapters, we will examine the trials and hearings before Pilate and Herod. It must be remembered, the Savior was before the formal trial after 6am and crucified at 9am, therefore, this trial and all we are about to discuss would have to occurred in 3 hours. Possible???

Chapter 13
Final Trials

9th day, 18th Nissan, (Monday)	Jerusalem	Matthew	Mark	Luke	John
Jesus before Pilate	Jerusalem	27:1-2	15:1-5	23:1-6	
Judas Hanged himself	Jerusalem	27:3-10			
Before Pilate Jesus taken to Herod	Jerusalem	27:11-14		23:7-8	
Herod-Many words	Jerusalem			23:9	
Jesus mocked & sent to Pilate the same day	Jerusalem			23:11-12	
10th day, 19th Nissan, (Tuesday)	Jerusalem				
Before Pilate 2nd time, (called people together and tried to release Jesus)	Jerusalem			23:13	18:28-32
Pilate and Herod found no guilt – wanted to release Jesus	Jerusalem	27:15-18	15:6-8	23:14-16	18:33-40
2nd time tried to release Jesus	Jerusalem	27:19-21	15:9-11	23:17-19	
Brought scourged Jesus before them	Jerusalem				19:1-7
3rd time tried to release Jesus	Jerusalem	27:22-23	15:12-14	23:20-25	19:8-12
Pilate washed hands- 6th hr.	Jerusalem	27:24-25			19:13-14
Released Barabbas and scourged Jesus	Jerusalem	27:26-28	15:15	23:26	19:15-16
Final scourging thru the night	Jerusalem		15:15-19		

NINTH DAY: 18th Nissan (Monday)

All four gospels begin to record the events on this day:

Mark 15:1 ¶ *AND* **straightway in the morning the chief priests held a consultation with the elders and scribes and the whole council, and bound Jesus, and carried [him] away, and delivered [him] to Pilate.**

2 And **Pilate asked him, Art thou the King of the Jews**? *And he answering said unto him, Thou sayest [it].*

3 And the **chief priests accused him of many things**: *but he answered nothing.*

4 And **Pilate asked** *him again, saying,* **Answerest thou nothing**? *behold how many things they witness against thee.*

5 But **Jesus yet answered nothing**; *so that Pilate marveled.*

John writes:

*

John 18:28 ¶ **Then led they Jesus** *from Caiaphas* **unto the hall of judgment: and it was early;** *and they themselves went not into the judgment hall, lest they should be defiled; but that they might eat the passover.*

*29 **Pilate** then went out unto them, and said, **What accusation bring ye against this man**?*

*30 They answered and said unto him**, If he were not a malefactor, we would not have delivered him up unto thee.***

*31 Then said Pilate unto them, **Take ye him, and judge him according to your law**. The Jews therefore said unto him, **It is not lawful for us to put any man to death**:*

*32 That the saying of Jesus might be fulfilled, which he spake, **signifying what death he should die**.*

*33 Then **Pilate** entered into the judgment hall again, and **called Jesus, and said unto him, Art thou the King of the Jews?***

*34 **Jesus answered** him, **Sayest thou this thing of thyself, or did others tell it thee of me?***

*35 Pilate answered, **Am I a Jew? Thine own nation and the chief priests have delivered thee unto me: what hast thou done?***

*36 **Jesus answered, My kingdom is not of this world:** if my kingdom were of this world, then would my servants fight, that I should not be delivered to the Jews: but now is my kingdom not from hence.*

*37 **Pilate therefore said unto him, Art thou a king then**? Jesus answered, Thou sayest that I am a king. To this end was I born, and for this cause came I into the world, that I should bear witness unto the truth. Every one that is of the truth heareth my voice.*

*38 **Pilate saith unto him, What is truth?** And when he had said this, he went out again unto the Jews, and saith unto them, **I find in him no fault [at all].***

AND

**Luke 23:1 ¶ AND the whole multitude of them arose, and led him unto Pilate.

*2 And they began to accuse him, saying, **We found this [fellow] perverting the nation, and forbidding to give tribute to Caesar, saying that he himself is Christ a King.***

3 And Pilate asked him, saying, Art thou the King of the Jews? And he answered him and said, Thou sayest [it].

*4 Then **said Pilate to the chief priests and [to] the people, I find no fault in this man.***

*5 And they were the more fierce, saying, **He stirreth up the people, teaching throughout all Jewry, beginning from Galilee to this place.***

6 When Pilate heard of Galilee, he asked whether the man were a Galilaean.

7 And as soon as he knew that he belonged unto Herod's jurisdiction, he sent him to Herod, who himself also was at Jerusalem at that time.

(compare also; Matt. 27:1-2, 11-14)

In our scripture chain, we see at the beginning of the **9th day**, the chief priests and the elders rose up early in the morning and agreed they wanted Jesus to be put to death. However, they didn't want to stone Him, as would be their form of execution, because they feared this would start a riot among the people.[176]

Christ's First Appearance Before Pilate

As we have supposedly learned, no Jewish tribunal had authority to inflict the death penalty; imperial Rome had reserved this prerogative as her own. The united acclaim of the Sanhedrists that Jesus was deserving of death, would be ineffective until sanctioned by the emperor's deputy, who at that time was Pontius Pilate, the governor, or more properly, procurator, of Judea, Samaria, and Idumea. Pilate maintained his official residence at Caesarea, on the Mediterranean shore; but it was his custom to be present in Jerusalem at the times of the great Hebrew feasts, probably in the interest of preserving order, or of promptly quelling any disturbance amongst the vast and heterogeneous multitudes by which the city was thronged on these festive occasions. The governor with his attendants was in Jerusalem at this momentous Passover season. Early on Friday (**note at end of this insert**)

---

[176] DNTC vol 1: p800

morning, the "whole council," that is to say, the Sanhedrin, led Jesus, bound, to the judgment hall of Pontius Pilate; but with strict scrupulosity they refrained from entering the hall lest they become defiled; for the judgment chamber was part of the house of a Gentile, and somewhere therein might be leavened bread, even to be near which would render them ceremonially unclean. Let everyone designate for himself the character of men afraid of the mere proximity of leaven, while thirsting for innocent blood!

In deference to their scruples Pilate came out from the palace; and, as they delivered up to him their Prisoner, asked: "What accusation bring ye against this man?" The question, though strictly proper and judicially necessary, surprised and disappointed the priestly rulers, who evidently had expected that the governor would simply approve their verdict as a matter of form and give sentence accordingly; but instead of doing so, Pilate was apparently about to exercise his authority of original jurisdiction. With poorly concealed chagrin, their spokesman, probably Caiaphas, answered: "If he were not a malefactor, we would not have delivered him up unto thee." It was now Pilate's turn to feel or at least to feign umbrage, and he replied in effect: Oh, very well; if you don't care to present the charge in proper order, take ye him, and judge him according to your law; don't trouble me with the matter. But the Jews rejoined: "It is not lawful for us to put any man to death."

John the apostle intimates in this last remark a determination on the part of the Jews to have Jesus put to death not only by Roman sanction but by Roman executioners for, as we readily may see, had Pilate approved the death sentence and handed the Prisoner over to the Jews for its infliction, Jesus would have been stoned, in accordance with the Hebrew penalty for blasphemy; whereas the Lord had plainly foretold that His death would be by crucifixion, which was a Roman method of execution, but one never practiced by the Jews. Furthermore, if Jesus had been put to death by the Jewish rulers, even with governmental sanction, an insurrection among the people might have resulted, for there were many who believed on Him. The crafty hierarchy were determined to bring about His death under Roman condemnation.

"And they began to accuse him, saying, we found this fellow perverting the nation, and forbidding to give tribute to Caesar, saying that he himself is Christ a King." It is important to note that no accusation of blasphemy was made to Pilate; had Such been presented, the governor, thoroughly pagan in heart and mind, would probably have dismissed the charge as utterly unworthy of a hearing; for Rome with her many gods, whose number was being steadily increased by current heathen deification of mortals, knew no such offense as blasphemy in the Jewish sense. The accusing Sanhedrists hesitated not to substitute for blasphemy, which was the greatest crime known to the Hebrew code, the charge of high treason, which was the gravest offense listed in the Roman category of crimes. To the vociferous accusations of the chief priests and elders, the calm and dignified Christ deigned no reply. To them He had spoken for the last time -- until the appointed season of another trial, in which He shall be the Judge, and they the prisoners at the bar.

Pilate was surprised at the submissive yet majestic demeanor of Jesus; there was certainly much that was kingly about the Man; never before had such a One stood before him. The charge, however, was a serious one; men who claimed title to kingship might prove dangerous to Rome; yet to the charge the Accused answered nothing. Entering the judgment hall, Pilate had Jesus called. That some of the disciples, and among them almost certainly John, also went in, is apparent from the detailed accounts of the proceedings preserved in the fourth Gospel. Anyone was at liberty to enter, for publicity was an actual and a widely-proclaimed feature of Roman trials.

Pilate, plainly without animosity or prejudice against Jesus, asked: "Art thou the King of the Jews? Jesus answered him, Sayest thou this thing of thyself, or did others tell it thee of me?" The Lord's counter-question, as Pilate's rejoinder shows, meant, and was understood to mean, as we might state it: Do you ask this in the Roman and literal sense -- as to whether I am a king of an earthly kingdom -- or with the Jewish and more spiritual meaning? A direct answer "Yes" would have been true in the Messianic sense, but untrue in the worldly signification; and "No" could have been inversely construed as true or untrue. "Pilate answered, Am I a Jew? Thine own nation and the chief priests have delivered thee unto me: what hast thou done? Jesus answered, my kingdom is not of this world: if my kingdom were of this world, then would my servants fight, that I should not be delivered to the Jews: but now is my kingdom not from hence. Pilate therefore said unto him, Art thou a king then? Jesus answered, thou sayest that I am a king. To this end was I born, and for this cause came I into the world, that I should bear witness unto the truth. Every one that is of the truth hearth my voice."

It was clear to the Roman governor that this wonderful Man, with His exalted views of a kingdom not of this world, and an empire of truth in which He was to reign, was no political insurrectionist; and that to consider Him a menace to Roman institutions would be absurd. Those last words -- about truth -- were of all the most puzzling; Pilate was restive, and perhaps a little frightened under their import. "What is truth?" He rather exclaimed in apprehension than inquired in expectation of an answer, as he started to leave the hall. To the Jews without he announced officially the acquittal of the Prisoner. "I find in him no fault at all" was the verdict.

But the chief priests and scribes and elders of the people were undeterred. Their thirst for the blood of the Holy One had developed into mania. Wildly and fiercely they shrieked: "He stireth up the people, teaching throughout all Jewry, beginning from Galilee to this place." The mention of Galilee suggested to Pilate a new course of procedure. Having confirmed by inquiry that Jesus was a Galilean, he determined to send the Prisoner to Herod, the Vassal ruler of that province, who was in Jerusalem at the time. By this action Pilate hoped to rid himself of further responsibility in the case, and moreover, Herod, with whom he had been at enmity, might be placated thereby.[177] **Note- the proper day would have been Monday, the 9th day**

Luke 23: *8 And **when Herod saw Jesus, he was exceeding glad:** for he was desirous to see him of a long [season], because he had heard many things of him; and **he hoped to have seen some miracle done by him.***

*9 Then **he questioned with him in many words;** but he answered him nothing.*

*10 And **the chief priests and scribes stood and vehemently accused him.***

*11 And **Herod with his men of war set him at nought, and mocked [him], and arrayed him in a gorgeous robe, and sent him again to Pilate.***

*12 **And the same day** Pilate and Herod were made friends together: for before they were at enmity between themselves.*

Christ before Herod

Herod Antipas, the degenerate son of his infamous sire, Herod the Great, was at this time tetrarch of Galilee and Perea, and by popular usage, though without imperial sanction, was flatteringly called king. He it was who, in fulfillment of an unholy vow inspired by a woman's voluptuous blandishments, had ordered the murder of John the Baptist. He ruled as a Roman vassal, and professed to be orthodox in the observances of Judaism. He had come up to Jerusalem, in state, to keep the feast of the Passover. Herod was pleased to have Jesus sent to him by Pilate; for, not only was the action a gracious one on the part of the procurator, constituting as after events proved a preliminary to reconciliation between the two rulers, but it was a means of gratifying Herod's curiosity to see Jesus, of whom he had heard so much, whose fame had terrified him, and by whom he now hoped to see some interesting miracle wrought.

Whatever fear Herod had once felt regarding Jesus, whom he had superstitiously thought to be the reincarnation of his murdered victim, John the Baptist, was replaced by amused interest when he saw the far-famed Prophet of Galilee in bonds before him, attended by a Roman guard, and accompanied by ecclesiastical officials. Herod began to question the Prisoner; but Jesus remained silent. The chief priests and scribes vehemently voiced their accusations; but not a word was uttered by the Lord. Herod is the only character in history to whom Jesus is known to have applied a personal epithet of contempt. "Go ye and tell that fox," He once said to certain Pharisees who had come to Him with the story that Herod intended to kill Him. As far as we know, Herod is further distinguished as the only being who saw Christ face to face and spoke to Him, yet never heard His voice. For penitent sinners, weeping women, prattling children, for the scribes, the Pharisees, the Sadducees, the rabbis, for the perjured high priest and his obsequious and insolent underling, and for Pilate the pagan, Christ had words -- of comfort or instruction, of warning or rebuke, of protest or denunciation -- yet for Herod the fox He had but disdainful and kingly silence. Thoroughly piqued, Herod turned from insulting questions to acts of malignant derision. He and his men-at-arms made sport of the suffering Christ, "set him at nought and mocked him"; then in travesty they "arrayed him in a gorgeous robe and sent him again to Pilate." Herod had found nothing in Jesus to warrant condemnation.[178]

---

[177] JTC pp 631-635
[178] JTC pp 635-636

We see in the foregoing that after Herod received Jesus, perhaps noon, he began a lengthy questioning of Him, as indicated by the phrase, "…questioned Him in many words; …" When Herod had finished with Jesus, the chief priests and scribes began, for the second day, to vehemently try Him and attack Him, all of which might have constituted a second trial. Herod then the same day returned Jesus to Pilate.

> *Matthew 27:3* **Then Judas, which had betrayed him, when he saw that he was condemned, repented himself, and brought again the thirty pieces of silver to the chief priests and elders,**
>
> *4 Saying,* **I have sinned** *in that I have betrayed the innocent blood. And* **they said, What [is that] to us? see thou [to that].**
>
> *5 And* **he cast down the pieces of silver in the temple, and departed, and went and hanged himself.**
>
> *6 And the* **chief priests took the silver pieces**, *and said, It is not lawful for to put them into the treasury, because it is the price of blood.*
>
> *7 And they took counsel, and* **bought with them the potter's field, to bury strangers in.**
>
> *8 Wherefore that field was called, The field of blood, unto this day.*
>
> *9* **Then was fulfilled that which was spoken by Jeremy the prophet, saying, And they took the thirty pieces of silver**, *the price of him that was valued, whom they of the children of Israel did value;*
>
> *10 And* **gave them for the potter's field, as the Lord appointed me**

When Judas Iscariot saw how terribly effective had been the outcome of his treachery, he became wildly remorseful. During Christ's trial before the Jewish authorities, with its associated humiliation and cruelty, the traitor had seen the seriousness of his action; and when the unresisting Sufferer had been delivered up to the Romans, and the fatal consummation had become a certainty, the enormity of his crime filled Judas with nameless horror.

Rushing into the presence of the chief priests and elders, while the final preparations for the crucifixion of the Lord were in progress, he implored the priestly rulers to take back the accursed wage they had paid him, crying in an agony of despair: "I have sinned, in that I have betrayed the innocent blood." He may have vaguely expected a word of sympathy from the conspirators in whose wickedly skillful hands he had been so ready and Serviceable a tool; possibly he hoped that his avowal might stem the current of their malignancy, and that they would ask for a reversal of the sentence. But the rulers in Israel repulsed him with disgust. "What is that to us?" they sneered, "see thou to that." He had served their purpose; they had paid him his price; they wished never to look upon his face again; and pitilessly they flung him back into the haunted blackness of his maddened conscience. Still clutching the bag of silver, the all too real remembrance of his frightful sin, he rushed into the temple, penetrating even to the precincts of priestly reservation, and dashed the silver pieces upon the floor of the sanctuary. Then, under the goading impulse of his master, the devil, to whom he had become a bond-slave, body and soul, he went out and hanged himself.

The chief priests gathered up the pieces of silver, and in sacrilegious scrupulosity, held a solemn council to determine what they should do with the "price of blood." As they deemed it unlawful to add the attainted coin to the sacred treasury, they bought with it a certain clay-yard, once the property of a potter, and the very place in which Judas had made of himself a suicide; this tract of ground they set apart as a burial place for aliens, strangers, and pagans. The body of Judas, the betrayer of the Christ, was probably the first to be there interred. And that field was called "Aceldama, that is to say, the field of blood".[179]

TENTH DAY: 19th Nissan, (Tuesday)

Pilate could no longer side step having to consider the case that was being thrust upon him:

Matthew 27:15 **Now at [that] feast the governor was wont to release unto the people a prisoner**, *whom they would.*

---

[179] Ibid p 634

*16 And they had then a **notable prisoner, called Barabbas.***

*17 **Therefore when they were gathered together,** Pilate said unto them, **Whom will ye that I release unto you?** Barabbas, or Jesus which is called Christ?*

*18 For **he knew that for envy they had delivered him.***

*19 When **he was set down on the judgment seat, his wife sent unto him, saying, Have thou nothing to do with that just man**: for I have suffered many things this day in a dream because of him.*

Mark *15:6 Now at [that] feast he released unto them one prisoner, whomsoever they desired.*

7 And there was [one] named Barabbas, [which lay] bound with them that had made insurrection with him, who had committed murder in the insurrection.

Luke *23:13 ¶ And Pilate, **when he had called together the chief priests and the rulers and the people,***

*Luke 23:14 Said unto them, Ye have brought this man unto me, as one that perverteth the people: and, behold, **I, having examined [him] before you, have found no fault in this man touching those things whereof ye accuse him:***

*15 **No, nor yet Herod**: for I sent you to him; and, lo, nothing worthy of death is done unto him.*

*16 **I will therefore chastise him, and release [him].***

17 (For of necessity he must release one unto them at the feast.)

The Roman procurator, finding that he could not evade further consideration of the case, **"called together the chief priests and the rulers and the people,"** and "said unto them, Ye have brought this man unto me, as one that perverteth the people: and, behold, I, having examined him before you, have found no fault in this man touching those things whereof ye accuse him: No, nor yet Herod: for I sent you to him; and, lo, nothing worthy of death is done unto him. I will therefore chastise him, and release him." **Pilate's desire to save Jesus from death was just and genuine;** his intention of scourging the Prisoner, whose innocence he had affirmed and reaffirmed, was an infamous concession to Jewish prejudice. He knew that the charge of sedition and treason was without foundation; and that even the framing of such an accusation by the Jewish hierarchy, whose simulated loyalty to Caesar was but a cloak for inherent and undying hatred, was ridiculous in the extreme; and he fully realized that the priestly rulers had delivered Jesus into his hands because of envy and malice.[180]

*Mark 15:8 And the multitude crying aloud began to **desire [him to do] as he had ever done unto them.***

*9 But Pilate answered them, saying, **Will ye that I release unto you the King of the Jews?***

*10 For he knew that the **chief priests had delivered him for envy**.*

It was the custom for the governor at the Passover season to pardon and release any one condemned prisoner whom the people might name. On that day there lay in durance, awaiting execution, "a notable prisoner, called Barabbas," who had been found guilty of sedition, in that he had incited the people to insurrection, and had committed murder. This man stood convicted of the very charge on which Pilate specifically and Herod by implication had pronounced Jesus innocent, and Barabbas was a murderer in addition. **Pilate thought to pacify the priests and people by releasing Jesus as the subject of Passover leniency**; this would be a tacit recognition of Christ's conviction before the ecclesiastical court, and practically an endorsement of the death sentence, superseded by official pardon. Therefore, he asked of them: "Whom will ye that I release unto you? Barabbas, or Jesus which is called Christ?"[181]

*I.V. Mark 10 **And the multitude, crying aloud, began to desire him to deliver Jesus unto them.***

---

[180] JTC p 637
[181] Ibid 637

There were those among the multitude who began to cry out for the release of Jesus. **Josephus recorded in history that there were tens of thousands, both Jew and Gentile, which were converted to Christianity.**

There appears to have been a brief interval between Pilate's question and the people's answer, during which the chief priests and elders busied themselves amongst the multitude, urging them to demand the release of the insurrectionist and murderer.[182]

Matthew 27:20 **But the chief priests and elders persuaded the multitude that they should ask Barabbas, and destroy Jesus.**

21 The **governor answered and said unto them, Whether of the twain** *will ye that I release unto you? They said, Barabbas.*

22 **Pilate saith unto them, What shall I do then with Jesus which is called Christ?** *[They] all say unto him,* **Let him be crucified**.

23 And the governor said, **Why, what evil hath he done?** *But they cried out the more, saying, Let him be crucified.*

Mark 15:11 But **the chief priests moved the people, that he should rather release Barabbas unto them.**

12 And Pilate answered and said again unto them, **What will ye then that I shall do [unto him] whom ye call the King of the Jews?**

13 And they cried out again, **Crucify him**.

14 Then Pilate said unto them, **Why, what evil hath he done?** *And they cried out the more exceedingly, Crucify him.*

So, when Pilate reiterated the question: "Whether of the twain will ye that I release unto you?" assembled Israel cried "Barabbas." Pilate, surprised, disappointed, and angered, then asked: "What shall I do then with Jesus which is called Christ? They all say unto him, let him be crucified. And the governor said, why, what evil hath he done? But they cried out the more, saying, Let him be crucified."[183]

*John 19:1 ¶ **THEN Pilate therefore took Jesus, and scourged [him].**

2 And the **soldiers platted a crown of thorns, and put [it] on his head, and they put on him a purple robe,**

3 And said, **Hail, King of the Jews! and they smote him with their hands**.

4 **Pilate therefore <u>went forth again</u>**, *and saith unto them,* **Behold, I bring him forth to you, that ye may know that I find no fault in him.**

5 Then came Jesus forth, wearing the crown of thorns, and the purple robe. And **[Pilate]** *saith unto them,* **Behold the man!**

Pilate had probably been a silent observer of this barbarous scene. He stopped it, and determined to make another attempt to touch the springs of Jewish pity, if such existed. He went outside, and to the multitude said: "Behold, I bring him forth to you, that ye may know that I find no fault in him." This was the governor's third definite proclamation of the Prisoner's innocence. "Then came Jesus forth, wearing the crown of thorns, and the purple robe. And Pilate saith unto them, Behold the man!" Pilate seems to have counted on the pitiful sight of the scourged and bleeding Christ to soften the hearts of the maddened Jews. But the effect failed. Think of the awful fact -- a heathen, a pagan, who knew not God, pleading with the priests and people of Israel for the life of their Lord and King! When, unmoved by the sight, the chief priests and officers cried with increasing vindictiveness, "crucify him, crucify him," Pilate pronounced the fatal sentence, "Take ye him and crucify him," but added with bitter emphasis: "I find no fault in him."[184]

*Luke 23:18 And they cried out all at once, saying, **Away with this [man], and release unto us Barabbas:**

---

[182] Ibid 637
[183] Ibid p 638
[184] Ibid p 639

19 (Who for a certain sedition made in the city, and for murder, was cast into prison.)
20 ***Pilate therefore, willing to release Jesus, spake again to them****.*

*John 19:6 When the ***chief priests therefore and officers saw him, they cried out, saying, crucify [him], crucify [him]****. Pilate saith unto them, Take ye him, and crucify [him]: for I find no fault in him.*

Jesus is innocent. Pilate knew it; Herod knew it; The Sanhedrin knew it; Caiaphas knew it; and the mob knew it – Satan knew it. Pilate still wanted to release Jesus so he told the mob "Take ye him and crucify him."

Luke 23:21 ***But they cried, saying, Crucify [him], crucify him****.*
Luke 23:22 ***And he said unto them*** <u>***the third time***</u>***, Why, what evil hath he done? I have found no cause of death in him: I will therefore chastise him, and let [him] go.***

23 And they were instant with loud voices, requiring ***that he might be crucified. And the voices of them and of the chief priest prevailed.***

It will be remembered that the only charge preferred against Christ before the Roman governor was that of sedition; the Jewish persecutors had carefully avoided even the mention of blasphemy, which was the offense for which they had adjudged Jesus worthy of death. Now that sentence of crucifixion had been extorted from Pilate, they brazenly attempted to make it appear that the governor's mandate was but a ratification of their own decree of death; therefore, they said:[185]

*John 19:7The Jews answered him, ***We have a law, and by our law he ought to die****, because he made himself the Son of God.*
8 When Pilate therefore heard that saying, he was the more afraid;
9 ***And went again into the judgment hall, and saith unto Jesus, Whence art thou?*** *But Jesus gave him no answer.*
10 Then saith Pilate unto him, ***Speakest thou not unto me? knowest thou not that I have power to crucify thee, and have power to release thee?***
11 Jesus answered, ***Thou couldest have no power [at all] against me, except it were given thee from above: therefore he that delivered me unto thee hath the greater sin****.*

"We have a law, and by our law he ought to die, because he made himself the Son of God." What did it mean? That awe-inspiring title, Son of God, struck yet deeper into Pilate's troubled conscience.
Once more he took Jesus into the judgment hall, and in trepidation asked, "Whence art thou?" The inquiry was as to whether Jesus was human or superhuman. A direct avowal of the Lord's divinity would have frightened but could not have enlightened the heathen ruler; therefore, Jesus gave no answer. Pilate was further surprised, and perhaps somewhat offended at this seeming disregard of his authority. He demanded an explanation, saying: "Speakest thou not unto me? knowest thou not that I have power to crucify thee, and have power to release thee?" Then Jesus replied: "Thou couldest have no power at all against me, except it were given thee from above: therefore, he that delivered me unto thee hath the greater sin." The positions were reversed; Christ was the Judge, and Pilate the subject of His decision. Though not found guiltless, the Roman was pronounced less culpable than he or those who had forced Jesus into his power, and who had demanded of him an unrighteous committal.[186]

Matthew 27:24 When Pilate saw that he could prevail nothing, but [that] rather a tumult was made, he took water, ***and washed [his] hands before the multitude****, saying, I am innocent of the blood of this just person: see ye [to it].*
25 Then <u>***answered all the people, and said, His blood [be] on us, and on our children.***</u>

The Roman governor was sorely troubled and inwardly afraid. To add to his perplexity, he received a warning message from his wife, even as he sat on the judgment seat: "Have thou nothing to do with that just man: for I have suffered many things this day in a dream because of him." Those who know not God are

---
[185] Ibid p 640
[186] Ibid p 640

characteristically superstitious. Pilate feared to think what dread portent his wife's dream might presage. But, finding that he could not prevail, and foreseeing a tumult among the people if he persisted in the defense of Christ, he called for water and washed his hands before the multitude -- a symbolic act of disclaiming responsibility, which they all understood -- proclaiming the while: "I am innocent of the blood of this just person: see ye to it." Then rose that awful self-condemnatory cry of the covenant people: "His blood be on us and on our children."[187]

> John 19:12 And from thenceforth Pilate sought to release him: but the Jews cried out, saying, If thou let this man go, thou art not Caesar's friend: whosoever maketh himself a king speaketh against Caesar.
>
> 13 When Pilate therefore heard that saying, he brought Jesus forth, and <u>sat down in the judgment seat</u> in a place that is called the Pavement, but in the Hebrew, Gabbatha.
>
> 14 **And it was the preparation of the passover, and <u>about the sixth hour:</u>** and he saith unto the Jews, Behold your King!
>
> 15 But they cried out, Away with [him], away with [him], crucify him. **Pilate saith unto them, Shall I crucify your King? The chief priests answered, We have no king but Caesar**.

The governor, though having pronounced sentence, yet sought means of releasing the submissive Sufferer. His first evidence of wavering was greeted by the Jews with the cry, "If thou let this man go, thou art not Caesar's friend: whosoever maketh himself a king speaketh against Caesar." Pilate took his place in the judgment seat, which was set up in the place of the Pavement, or Gabbatha, outside the hall. He was resentful against those Jews who had dared to intimate that he was no friend of Caesar, and whose intimation might lead to an embassy of complaint being sent to Rome to misrepresent him in exaggerated accusation. Pointing to Jesus, he exclaimed with unveiled sarcasm: "Behold your King!" But the Jews answered in threatening and ominous shouts: "Away with him, away with him, crucify him." In stinging reminder of their national subjugation, Pilate asked with yet more cutting irony, "Shall I crucify your King?" And the chief priests cried aloud: "We have no king but Caesar."

Even so was it and was to be. The people who had by covenant accepted Jehovah as their King, now rejected Him in Person, and acknowledged no sovereign but Caesar. Caesar's subjects and serfs, have they been through all the centuries since. Pitiable is the state of man or nation who in heart and spirit will have no king but Caesar!

Wherein lay the cause of Pilate's weakness? He was the emperor's representative, the imperial procurator with power to crucify or to save; officially he was an autocrat. His conviction of Christ's blamelessness and his desire to save Him from the cross are beyond question. Why did Pilate waver, hesitate, vacillate, and at length yield contrary to his Conscience and his will? Because, after all, he was more slave than freeman. He was in servitude to his past. He knew that should complaint be made of him at Rome, his corruption and cruelties, his extortions and the unjustifiable slaughter he had caused would all be brought against him. He was the Roman ruler, but the people over whom he exercised official dominion delighted in seeing him cringe, when they cracked, with vicious snap above his head, the whip of a threatened report about him to his imperial master, Tiberius.[188]

> Matthew 27:26 ¶ **Then released he Barabbas unto them: and when he had scourged Jesus, he delivered [him] to be crucified**.
>
> 27 **Then the soldiers of the governor took Jesus into the common hall, and gathered unto him the whole band [of soldiers]**.
>
> 28 And they stripped him, and put on him a scarlet robe.
>
> 29 And when they had platted a crown of thorns, they put [it] upon his head, and a reed in his right hand: and they bowed the knee before him, and mocked him, saying, Hail, King of the Jews!
>
> 30 And they spit upon him, and took the reed, and smote him on the head.
>
> ****Mark 15:16 And the soldiers led him away into the hall, called Praetorium**; and they call together the whole band.

---

[187] Ibid p 638
[188] Ibid p 640 - 641

17 And they clothed him with purple, and platted a crown of thorns, and put it about his [head],
*18 And **began to salute him, Hail, King of the Jews!***
19 And they smote him on the head with a reed, and did spit upon him, and bowing [their] knees worshipped him.

***Luke 23:24 And Pilate gave sentence that it should be as they required.**
*25 And **he released unto them him that for sedition and murder was cast into prison, whom they had desired; but he delivered Jesus to their will.***

Scourging was a frightful preliminary to death on the cross. The instrument of punishment was a whip of many thongs, loaded with metal and edged with jagged pieces of bone. Instances are of record in which the condemned died under the lash and so escaped the horrors of living crucifixion. In accordance with the brutal customs of the time, Jesus, weak and bleeding from the fearful scourging He had undergone, was given over to the half-savage soldiers for their amusement. He was no ordinary victim, So the whole band came together in the Praetorium, or great hall of the palace, to take part in the diabolical sport. They Stripped Jesus of His outer raiment, and placed upon Him a purple robe. Then with a sense of fiendish realism they platted a crown of thorns, and placed it about the Sufferer's brows; a reed was put into His right hand as a royal scepter; and, as they bowed in a mockery of homage, they saluted Him with: "Hail, King of the Jews!" Snatching away the reed or rod, they brutally smote Him with it upon the head, driving the cruel thorns into His quivering flesh; they Slapped Him with their hands, and spat upon Him in vile and vicious abandonment.[189]

Having little choice, Pilate returned Jesus to the Praetorium hall and to the band of 600 plus soldiers to await the final order of crucifixion. It's unimaginable what the Savior must have endured and suffered through that last long night, and the crucifixion is yet to begin.

Proponents of the 7day logic would have believe that all of these trials and activities, as well as the crucifixion to come, occurred in 3 hours or less. Really? Is it any wonder there is controversy when religious scholars attempt to place 4 days of incarceration, trials and crucifixion into the time frame of 3 hours!

REV

---

[189] Ibid p 638 - 639

Chapter 14
Crucifixion

11th day, 20th Nissan, (Wednesday)	Location	Matthew	Mark	Luke	John
Preparation Day- Crucifixion	Jerusalem		15:42		19:31
To Calvary- Simon bears cross	Jerusalem	27:31-32	15:20-21	23:26	19:16-17
Spoke to women following- weep for yourselves	Jerusalem			23:27-31	
CRUCIFIED --- 3rd Hr.	Golgotha	27:33-35	15:22-25	23:32-33	19:18,
His 1st Utterance – forgive them	Golgotha			23:34-	
Superscription by Pilate - Between two thieves – took His garments	Golgotha	27:36-38	15:26-28	23:38	19:19-22, 23-24
Mocking & scoffing	Golgotha	27:39-44	15:29-32	23:35-42	
2nd Utterance – today in paradise	Golgotha			23:43	
3rd utterance-behold thy son	Golgotha				19:25-27
Darkness over the earth – 6th to 9th Hr.	Golgotha	27:45	15:33	23:44-45	
4th Utterance-My God has thou forsaken Me?	Golgotha	27:46	15:34-35		
5th utterance- I thirst	Golgotha	27:47-49	15:36		19:28-29
6th utterance-it is finished	Golgotha				19:30
7th utterance-I commend my spirit		27:50	15:37	23:46	19:30
Great earthquake & graves opened	Golgotha	27:51-53	15:38	23:45	
Testimony of Centurion & women	Golgotha	27:54-56	15:39-41	23:47-49	

Days of the month (Nissan)														
10	11	12	13	14	15	16	17	18	19	20	21	22	23	24
Days of the Passover														
1	2	3	4	5	6	7	8	9	10	11**	12	13	14	15
Triumphal Entry	Cleanse Temple	Question Authority	Rest	Preparation Day & Last supper evening	Feast Day 1st day of unleavened bread	2nd day of unleavened bread & first fruits	Formal Trial	Pilate -- Herod	Pilate & Scourging	Preparation day & crucifixion	High Day & 7th Day of unleavened Jesus entombed	Jesus entombed	Jesus entombed	Resurrection
										½ nt	Day nt	Day & nt	Day & ½ nt	
Regular days of the week														
Sun	Mon	Tue	Wed	Thurs	Fri	Sat	Sun	Mon	Tue	Wed	Thurs	Fri	Sat	Sun

Now is the 11th day of the Passover, which is the last preparation day before the High Day Sabbath, the last Holy Convocation and the last day of unleavened bread.

> ***Mark 15:42** ¶ And now when the even was come, because it was the preparation, that is, the day before the sabbath,*
> ***John 19:31** ¶ The Jews therefore, because it was the preparation, that the bodies should not remain upon the cross on the sabbath day, (for that sabbath day was <u>an high day</u>,) besought Pilate that their legs might be broken, and [that] they might be taken away.*

Both Mark and John confirm this day of crucifixion as the preparation day, and in particular the day before the High Sabbath. Jesus was obviously not sacrificed on the 5th day, the preparation day before the Holy convocation on the 6$^{th\ day}$, then, this leaves the only remaining preparation day on the 11th, the preparation day before the Holy Convocation day on the 12th.

> ***Matthew 27:31** **and after that they had mocked him, they took the robe off from him, and put his own raiment on him, and led him away to crucify [him].***
>
> *32 And as they came out, they found a **man of Cyrene, Simon by name: him they compelled to bear his cross.***
>
> ****Mark 15:20 **And when they had mocked him, they took off the purple from him, and put his own clothes on him, and led him out to crucify him.***
> *21 And they **compel one Simon a Cyrenian, who passed by, coming out of the country, the father of Alexander and Rufus, to bear his cross.***
>
> *****Luke 23:26** ¶ And as they led him away, they laid hold upon one Simon, a Cyrenian, coming out of the country, and on him they laid the cross, that he might bear [it] after Jesus.*
>
> ******John 19:16** ¶ Then delivered he him therefore unto them to be crucified. And they took Jesus, and led [him] away.*

Pontius Pilate, having reluctantly surrendered to the clamorous demands of the Jews, issued the fatal order; and Jesus, divested of the purple robe and arrayed in His own apparel, was led away to be crucified. After a night of excruciating agony and abuse, the soldiers emerged from the Praetorium hall with Jesus attired in his own clothes and bearing His own cross.

The sentence of death by crucifixion required that the Condemned person carry the cross upon which he was to suffer. Jesus started on the way bearing His cross. The terrible strain of the preceding hours, the agony in Gethsemane, the barbarous treatment He had suffered in the palace of the high priest, the humiliation and cruel usage to which He had been subjected before Herod, the frightful Scourging under Pilate's order, the brutal treatment by the inhuman soldiery, together with the extreme humiliation and the mental agony of it all, had so weakened His physical organism that He moved but slowly under the burden of the cross. The soldiers, impatient at the delay, peremptorily impressed into service a man whom they met coming into Jerusalem from the country, and him they compelled to carry the cross of Jesus.

> *Luke 23:27 And **there followed him a great company of people, and of women, which also bewailed and lamented him.***

There were as many as 2 to 3 million people in Jerusalem at this time, attending the Passover, and a great company of people followed Him, and of women, which also bewailed and lamented Him. Jesus had remained mostly silent under the inquisition of the trials he had gone through, and completely silent while enduring the mockery and buffetings of Herod and his underlings, now responded to the lamentations of the women. Jesus uttered this prophetic warning:

> *Luke 23:28 But **Jesus turning unto them said, Daughters of Jerusalem, weep not for me, but weep for yourselves, and for your children.***
> *29 For, behold, the days are coming, in the which **they shall say, Blessed [are] the barren, and the wombs that never bare, and the paps which never gave suck.***
> *30 Then shall they begin **to say to the mountains, Fall on us; and to the hills, Cover us.***

31 For if they do these things in a green tree, what shall be done in the dry?

It was the Lord's last testimony of the impending holocaust of destruction that was to follow the nation's rejection of her King. Although motherhood was the glory of every Jewish woman's life, yet in the terrible scenes, which many of those there weeping would live to witness, barrenness would be accounted a blessing; for the childless would have fewer to weep over, and at least would be spared the horror of seeing their offspring die of starvation or by violence; for so dreadful would be that day, that people would fain welcome the falling of the mountains upon them to end their sufferings. If Israel's oppressors could do what was then in process of doing to the "Green Tree," who bore the leafage of freedom and truth and offered the priceless fruit of life eternal, what would the powers of evil not do to the withered branches and dried trunk of apostate Judaism?[190]

Mark 15:22 ¶ And **they bring him unto the place Golgotha**, which is, being interpreted, The place of a skull.
23 And **they gave him to drink wine mingled with myrrh: but he received [it] not.**
24 And when **they had crucified him, they parted his garments, casting lots upon them,** what every man should take.
25 And it was the <u>third hour</u>, **and they crucified him**.

Luke 23:32* ¶ And there **were also two other, malefactors, led with him to be put to death.
33 And when they were come to the place, which is called Calvary, there they **crucified him, and the malefactors, one on the right hand, and the other on the left.**

***John 19: 17* And **he bearing his cross went forth into a place called [the place] of a skull,** which is called in the Hebrew Golgotha:
18 Where they crucified him, and two other with him, on either side one, and Jesus in the midst.

At Calvary, the official crucifiers proceeded without delay to carry into effect the dread sentence pronounced upon Jesus and upon the two criminals. Preparatory to affixing the condemned to the cross, it was the custom to offer each a narcotic draught of sour wine or vinegar mingled with myrrh and possibly containing other anodyne ingredients, for the merciful purpose of deadening the Sensibility of the victim. … When the drugged cup was presented to Jesus, He put it to His lips, but having ascertained the nature of its contents refused to drink, and so demonstrated His determination to meet death with faculties alert and mind unclouded.

Then they crucified Him, on the central cross of three, and placed one of the condemned malefactors on His right hand, the other on His left. Thus, was realized Isaiah's vision of the Messiah numbered among the transgressors. But few details of the actual crucifixion are given us. We know however that our Lord was nailed to the cross by spikes driven through the hands and feet, as was the Roman method, and not bound only by cords as was the custom in inflicting this form of punishment among some other nations.[191]

Crucifixion was unanimously considered the most horrible form of death. "A death by crucifixion seems to include all that pain and death can have of the horrible and ghastly – dizziness, cramp, thirst, starvation, sleeplessness, traumatic fever, tetanus, publicity of shame, long continuance of torment, horror of anticipation, mortification of unattended wounds, all intensified just up to the point at which they can be endured at all, but stopping just short of the point which would give the sufferer the relief of unconsciousness."[192]

"They part my garments among them, and cast lots upon my vesture"[193] – contains two parts: (1) His garments are to be divided among them; and (2) For His vesture they are to cast lots. A Messianic prophecy given to David over a thousand years before, giving the minute detail of what the soldiers would do on this dread occasion. We can plainly see this action of crucifixion took place at the **3rd hr.** in the morning. **(9am)**

A party of four soldiers watches the crucified,[194] with their centurion.[195]

---

[190] JTC p 654
[191] JTC p 655
[192] Farrar's 'Life of Christ'
[193] Psalm 22:18
[194] John 19:23
[195] Matt. 27:54

As the crucifiers proceeded with their awful task, not unlikely with roughness and taunts, for killing was their trade and to scenes of anguish they had grown callous through long familiarity, the agonized Sufferer, void of resentment but full of pity for their heartlessness and capacity for cruelty, voiced the first of the seven utterances delivered from the cross. In the spirit of God-like mercy He prayed:

The First utterance

> *I.V. Luke 23:35 Then said Jesus,* **Father, forgive them; for they know not what they do,** *(*Meaning the soldiers who crucified Him.*)*

These words are as important for what they don't say as well as for what they do say. Jesus is the Son of God and as such has the power to forgive sins, a power that he had freely used in proper cases.[196]

A superscription of the offense of the criminal would be written a tablet that would have been carried by a herald or placed around the neck of the condemned, and then placed on the cross at the crucifixion.

> *John 19:19 ¶ And* **Pilate wrote a title, and put [it] on the cross. And the writing was, JESUS OF NAZARETH THE KING OF THE JEWS.**
> *20 This title then read many of the Jews: for the place where Jesus was crucified was nigh to the city:* **and it was written in Hebrew, [and] Greek, [and] Latin.**
> *21 Then said the chief priests of the Jews to Pilate,* **Write not, The King of the Jews; but that he said, I am King of the Jews.**
> *22 Pilate answered,* **What I have written I have written.**

As we can see the chief priests did not want it to be known that He was the king but only that He said He was. The pleadings of the Jews fell on deaf ears. Knowingly or unknowingly Pilate had it correct.

The mocking and reviling began:
> *Matthew 27:39 And* **they that passed by reviled him**, *wagging their heads,*
> *40 And saying, Thou that destroyest the temple, and buildest [it] in three days,* **save thyself. If thou be the Son of God, come down from the cross.**
> *41 Likewise* **also the chief priests mocking [him], with the scribes and elders, said,**
> *42* **He saved others; himself he cannot save.** *If he be the King of Israel, let him now come down from the cross, and we will believe him.*
> *43* **He trusted in God;** *let him deliver him now, if he will have him: for he said,* **I am the Son of God.**[197]

The soldiers whose duty it was to guard the crosses, until loitering death would relieve the crucified of their increasing anguish, jested among themselves, and derided the Christ, pledging Him in their cups of sour wine in tragic mockery. Looking at the title affixed above the Sufferer's head, they bellowed forth the devil-inspired challenge: "If thou be the king of the Jews, save thyself."[198]

But worst of all, the chief priests and the scribes, the elders of the people, the unvenerable Sanhedrists, became ringleaders of the inhuman mob as they gloatingly exulted and cried aloud: "He saved others; himself he cannot save. If he be the King of Israel, let him now come down from the cross, and we will believe him. He trusted in God; let him deliver him now, if he will have him: for he said, I am the Son of God." Though uttered in ribald mockery, the declaration of the rulers in Israel stands as an attestation that Christ had saved others, and as an intended ironical but a literally true proclamation that He was the King of Israel.[199]

Thus, again fulfilling the Messianic prophecy: "All they that see me, laugh me to scorn: . . . They gaped upon me with their mouths, as a ravening and a roaring lion."[200] And another: "He trusted on the Lord that he would deliver him: let

---

[196] Matt. 9:2-8
[197] Mark 15:29-32, Luke 23:35-42
[198] Luke 23:36-37
[199] JTC p 658
[200] Psalm 22:7 13.

him deliver him, seeing he delighted in him."[201] It also becomes more and more apparent that every facet of the Passover and the crucifixion is well planned, known and executed to the last jot and tittle.

The two malefactors, each hanging from his cross, joined in the general derision, and "cast the same in his teeth." One of them, in the desperation incident to approaching death, echoed the taunts of the priests and people:

*Luke 23:39 And **one of the malefactors** which were hanged **railed on him, saying, If thou be Christ, save thyself and us.***

*40 But the **other answering rebuked him, saying, Dost not thou fear God, seeing thou art in the same condemnation?***

*41 And we indeed justly; **for we receive the due reward of our deeds: but this man hath done nothing amiss.***

42 And he said unto Jesus, Lord, remember me when thou comest into thy kingdom.

Then one of the crucified thieves, softened into penitence by the Savior's uncomplaining fortitude, and perceiving in the divine Sufferer's demeanor something more than human, rebuked his railing fellow. His confession of guilt and his acknowledgment of the justice of his own condemnation led to incipient repentance, and to faith in the Lord Jesus, his companion in agony.

To the appeal of penitence, the Lord replied with such a promise as He alone could make, His <u>second utterance</u> from the cross:

*Luke 23:43 **And Jesus said unto him, Verily I say unto thee, To day shalt thou be with me in paradise.***

This malefactor had within his heart the seeds of faith and repentance, sufficient enough to seek salvation. Pleased that here was one, even in death, who would seek him and desire his blessings, Jesus uttered the marvelous, though hidden and enigmatic statement, "This day thou shalt be with me in paradise." The abode of righteous spirits, as they await the day of resurrection; paradise—a place of peace and rest where sorrows and trials of his life have been shuffled off, and where the saints continue to prepare for a celestial heaven. There Jesus was going this day and there the so-called penitent will also find himself.

Jesus cast his eyes about and saw his weeping mother, as she stood with John at the foot of the cross and spoke the <u>3rd utterance</u> from the cross:

*John 19:26 When **Jesus therefore saw his mother, and the disciple standing by**, whom he loved, he saith unto his mother, **Woman, behold thy son!***

*27 **Then saith he to the disciple, Behold thy mother! And from that hour that disciple took her unto his own [home].***

Jesus' attention is now turned to a scene of sorrow and despair. By the cross stands his mother, the Virgin of Galilee, the one chosen of God to bear his Son, the one who bad suckled and cradled and reared Israel's Messiah. With her are three other faithful women -- her sister, Salome, the wife of Zebedee and the mother of James and John (who thus were cousins of Jesus); Mary the wife of Cleophas; and Mary Magdalene. On the resurrection morn Jesus, will pay to Mary Magdalene one of the greatest compliments ever given a mortal being: he will appear to her first, even ahead of Peter and the Twelve. But now his concern is his mother. A sword is piercing her soul as the saintly Simeon had prophesied that day in the temple. How the mother must have suffered to see her Son bear the infinite burden placed upon him!

With these four sisters was the Beloved John, the one who leaned on Jesus' breast and for whom the Master had greater love than for any other. It is clear that Joseph, the husband of Mary, had passed on; it appears also that Mary's other sons had not yet joined the household of faith and accepted Jesus, their brother, as the Son of God; and we are led to believe that the apostle John had a home in Jerusalem. Clearly, Mary's future lot must be cast with the Twelve and the Church and the apostolic witnesses whom Jesus will soon command to carry his message to all the world. Thus, to his mother he says:

---

[201] Psalm 22:8

"Woman, behold thy son!" And to John the word is given: "Behold thy mother!" These words comprise the third utterance from the cross. "And from that hour that disciple took her unto his own home."[202]

> *Luke 23:44 ¶ And it was about the <u>sixth hour</u>, and there was a darkness over all the earth <u>until the ninth hour</u>.*
> *45 And the sun was darkened, and the veil of the temple was rent in the midst.*

All three gospel writers, Matthew, Mark and Luke, record the same event.

At noontide, the light of the sun was obscured, and black darkness spread over the whole land. The terrifying gloom continued for a period of three hours. This remarkable phenomenon has received no satisfactory explanation from science. It could not have been due to a solar eclipse, as has been suggested in ignorance, for the time was that of full moon; indeed, the Passover season was determined by the first occurrence of full moon after the spring equinox. The darkness was brought about by miraculous operation of natural laws directed by divine power. It was a fitting sign of the earth's deep mourning over the impending death of her Creator. Of the mortal agony through which the Lord passed while upon the cross the Gospel-scribes are reverently reticent.[203]

During that time, there were great earthquakes around the entire earth. The Book of Mormon describes the event in great detail:

> *3 Nephi 8:6 And there was also a great and terrible tempest; and there was terrible thunder, insomuch that it did shake the whole earth as if it was about to divide asunder.*
> *7 And there were exceedingly sharp lightnings, such as never had been known in all the land.*
> *8 And the city of Zarahemla did take fire.*
> *9 And the city of Moroni did sink into the depths of the sea, and the inhabitants thereof were drowned.*
> *10 And the earth was carried up upon the city of Moronihah, that in the place of the city there became a great mountain.*
> *11 And there was a great and terrible destruction in the land southward.*
> *12 But behold, there was a more great and terrible destruction in the land northward; for behold, the whole face of the land was changed, because of the tempest and the whirlwinds, and the thunderings and the lightnings, and the exceedingly great quaking of the whole earth;*
> *13 And the highways were broken up, and the level roads were spoiled, and many smooth places became rough.*
> *14 And many great and notable cities were sunk, and many were burned, and many were shaken till the buildings thereof had fallen to the earth, and the inhabitants thereof were slain, and the places were left desolate.*
> *15 And there were some cities which remained; but the damage thereof was exceedingly great, and there were many in them who were slain.*
> *16 And there were some who were carried away in the whirlwind; and whither they went no man knoweth, save they know that they were carried away.*
> *17 And thus the face of the whole earth became deformed, because of the tempests, and the thunderings, and the lightnings, and the quaking of the earth.*
> *18 And behold, the rocks were rent in twain; they were broken up upon the face of the whole earth, insomuch that they were found in broken fragments, and in seams and in cracks, upon all the face of the land.*
> *19 And it came to pass that when the thunderings, and the lightnings, and the storm, and the tempest, and the quakings of the earth did cease--for behold, they did last for about the space of three hours; and it was said by some that the time was greater; nevertheless, all*

---

[202] Mortal Messiah Vol. 4-141
[203] JTC p 660

these great and terrible things were done in about the space of three hours--and then behold, there was darkness upon the face of the land.

While there was darkness and an earthquake in the old world, it appears that the devastation was far more severe in the Americas.

About the 9th hour the 4th <u>utterance</u> of the Lord was heard:

> *Matthew 27:46 And about the ninth hour Jesus cried with a loud voice, saying, Eli, Eli, lama sabachthani? that is to say, My God, my God, why hast thou forsaken me?*
> *47 Some of them that stood there, when they heard [that], said, This [man] calleth for Elias.*

These are the exact words of the Messianic prophecy found in Psalm 22:1.

"What mind of man can fathom the significance of that awful cry? It seems, that in addition to the fearful suffering incident to crucifixion, the agony of Gethsemane had recurred, intensified beyond human power to endure. In that bitterest hour, the dying Christ was alone, alone in most terrible reality. That the supreme sacrifice of the Son might be consummated in all its fullness, the Father seems to have withdrawn the support of His immediate presence, leaving to the Savior of men the glory of complete victory over the forces of sin and death."[204]

His 5th <u>utterance</u>:

> **John 19:28 After this, Jesus knowing that all things were now accomplished, that the scripture might be fulfilled, saith, I thirst.*
> *29 Now there was set a vessel full of vinegar: and they filled a spunge with vinegar, and put [it] upon hyssop, and put [it] to his mouth.*

> ***Matthew 27:48 And straightway one of them ran, and took a spunge, and filled [it] with vinegar, and put [it] on a reed, and gave him to drink.*
> *49 The rest said, Let be, let us see whether Elias will come to save him.*

Another detailed Messianic prophecy is fulfilled: *"They gave me also gall for my meat; and in my thirst they gave me vinegar to drink."*[205]

The period of faintness, the conception of utter forsakenness soon passed, and the natural cravings of the body reasserted themselves. The maddening thirst, which constituted one of the worst of the crucifixion agonies, wrung from the Savior's lips His one recorded utterance expressive of physical suffering. *"I thirst"*

His 6th <u>utterance</u>:

"Father, it is finished, thy will be done."[206] Jesus' mortal work was done; he paid the price for the sins of the world; Man was ransomed from the spiritual and temporal death brought upon him by the fall; the infinite and eternal atoning sacrifice had been made – all according to the will of the Father.[207]

His 7th <u>utterance</u>:

With His final breath; "Father, into thy hands I commend my spirit": and having said thus, he gave up the ghost.[208] Thus fulfilling the Messianic prophecies: "Into thy hand I commit my spirit: thou has redeemed me, O lord God of truth"[209] and, I lay down my life. …No man taketh it from me, but I lay down of myself."[210]

> *John 19:28 After this, Jesus knowing that all things were now accomplished, that the scripture might be fulfilled, saith, I thirst.*

---

[204] JTC p 661
[205] Psalm 69:21
[206] I.V. Matt. 54
[207] DNTC 829
[208] Luke 23:46
[209] Psalm 31:5
[210] John 10:17-18

29 Now there was set a vessel full of vinegar: and they filled a spunge with vinegar, and put [it] upon hyssop, and put [it] to his mouth.

30 When Jesus therefore had received the vinegar, he said, <u>It is finished</u>: and he bowed his head, and gave up the ghost.

Jesus addressed the Father saying: *"Father, into thy hands I commend my spirit."*
Matthew 27:50 ¶ Jesus, when he had cried again with a loud voice, yielded up the ghost.
*51 And, **behold, the veil of the temple was rent in twain from the top to the bottom; and the earth did quake, and the rocks rent***
*52 **And the graves were opened; and many bodies of the saints which slept arose**,*

Jesus Christ had given up his life and was dead. The earth responded to the death of her creator with violent quakes and threw down the mighty hills. The graves of the saints were opened and, worst of all to the Jews, the veil of the temple was rent from top to bottom, thus revealing the Holy of Holies for the world to see. The Mosaic dispensation had come to an end, and was now replaced by apostolic administration of Christianity.

Thereupon Jesus made his final earthly report to the one who had sent him. 'Father, it is finished, thy will is done,' he said; and this is the sixth utterance from the cross. How, does a God die? It is a voluntary act; no man taketh his life from him; he lays it down of himself; he has power to lay it down and power to take it again. Jesus makes his seventh utterance from the cross. He says simply: "Father, into thy hands I commend my spirit," quoting thus, as was his wont, the Messianic word concerning himself. (Ps. 31:5 :) "And having said thus, he gave up the ghost." He did not taste of death, for it was sweet unto him. As he, with the Eleven, had sung in the Hallel the night before: "Precious in the sight of the Lord is the death of his saints." (Ps. 116:15.)

As Jesus passed through the door from mortality to the spirit world; as his eternal spirit divested itself of its tenement of clay; as he left his mortal remains to be cared for by the loving persons whose friend he was -- two portentous events marked his glorious victory. For one, "the earth did quake, and the rocks rent"; and, for another, "the veil of the temple was rent in twain from the top to the bottom."

As to the earthquake, it came in fulfillment of Enoch's word. He, among others of the ancients, had seen "the Son of Man lifted up on the cross, after the manner of men; and he heard a loud voice; and the heavens were veiled; and all the creations of God mourned; and the earth groaned; and rocks were rent." (Moses 7:55-56.) Had the earthquake among the Jews been as it was among the Nephites, Jerusalem itself would have scarcely survived.

As to the rending of the veil of the temple, it was the thing that would symbolize, in power, the end of the old Jewish dispensation and the beginning of the new Christian day. The veil itself -- shielding the Holy of Holies from the gaze of any but the high priest, and from him except once a year, on the day of atonement, when he entered the sacred portal to atone for the sins of the people -- the veil is said to have been sixty feet long, thirty feet wide, "of the thickness of the palm of the hand, and wrought in 72 squares, which were joined together." It was so heavy that it took hundreds of priests to manipulate it. "If the Veil was at all such as is described in the Talmud, it could not have been in twain by a mere earthquake or the fall of the lintel, although its composition in squares fastened together might explain, how the rent might be as described in the Gospel.[211]

Bruce R. McConkie, The Mortal Messiah, Vol.4, p.229 - p.230
"Indeed, everything seems to indicate that, although the earthquake might furnish the physical basis, the rent of the Temple-Veil was -- with reverence be it said -- really made by the Hand of God. As we compute, it may just have been the time when, at the Evening Sacrifice, the officiating Priesthood entered the Holy Place, either to burn the incense or to do other sacred service there. To see before them, not as the aged Zacharias at the beginning of this story the Angel Gabriel, but the Veil of the Holy Place rent from top to bottom -- that beyond it they could scarcely have seen -- and hanging in two parts from its fastenings above and at the side, was, indeed, a terrible portent, which would soon become generally known, and must, in some form or other, have been preserved in tradition. And they all must have understood, that it meant that Gods own Hand had rent the Veil, and forever deserted and thrown open that Most Holy Place where He had so long dwelt in the

---
[211] Mortal Messiah Vol. 4-143-144

mysterious gloom, only lit up once a year by the glow of the censer of him, who made atonement for the sins of the people."[212]

And the earth did quake, and the rocks rent, and the graves of the saints were opened and they went into Jerusalem and appeared too many.[213] Enoch foresaw these scenes: he "beheld the Son of Man lifted up on the cross, after the manner of men; and heard a loud voice; and the heavens were veiled; and all the creations of God mourned; and the earth groaned; and the rocks were rent."[214] Also Samuel the Lamanite (Hela. 14:24; 19:12). Also, Nephi and Zenos (1 Ne. 1 2:4, 19:12) and (3 Ne. 8:18-19; 10:9)

Matt. 27:54 Now when **the centurion, and they that were with him, watching Jesus, saw the earthquake, and those things that were done, **they feared greatly, saying, Truly this was the Son of God.***

*55 And **many women were there beholding afar off**, which followed Jesus from Galilee, **ministering unto him**:*

56 Among which was Mary Magdalene, and Mary the mother of James and Joses, and the mother of Zebedee's children.

Luke 23:47 Now when the **centurion saw what was done, he glorified God, saying, **Certainly this was a righteous man**.*

*48 And all **the people that came together to that sight, beholding the things which were done, smote their breasts, and returned.***

49 And all his acquaintance, and the women that followed him from Galilee, stood afar off, beholding these things.

After seeing all the outward circumstances, that caused even the heaven and the earth to speak forth, the centurion and others were basically forced to glorify God and confess that Jesus was the Son of God. What value is a forced testimony?

*Alma 32:13 **And now, because ye are compelled to be humble blessed are ye;** for a man sometimes, if he is compelled to be humble, seecatch repentance; **and now surely, whosoever repenteth shall find mercy; and he that findeth mercy and endureth to the end the same shall be saved.***

*14 And now, as I said unto you, that because ye were compelled to be humble ye were blessed, **do ye not suppose that they are more blessed who truly humble themselves because of the word?***

*15 Yea, **he that truly humbleth himself, and repenteth of his sins, and endureth to the end, the same shall be blessed--yea, much more blessed than they who are compelled to be humble because of their exceeding poverty**.*

*16 Therefore, blessed are they who humble themselves without being compelled to be humble; or rather, in other words, **blessed is he that believeth in the word of God, and is baptized without stubbornness of heart, yea, without being brought to know the word, or even compelled to know, before they will believe.***

This 11th day of the Passover, however, is not only the day of the crucifixion but it is also **preparation day or the day before the 7th day, which day is the last day of unleavened bread and the final Passover convocation**. The final Paschal Lamb is sacrificed in perfect accordance with the Passover law. It is no coincidence the Savior gave up the ghost that at the 9th hour, at the exact same time the final Sin Sacrifice, the Lamb of the goat, is offered up in accordance with the Passover Law.

But Christ is now sacrificed; the law is fulfilled; the Mosaic dispensation is dead; the fullness of the gospel has come with all its light and power; and so – to dramatize, in a way which all Jewry would recognize, that the kingdom had been taken from them and given to others – Deity rent the veil of the temple "from top to bottom."

---

[212] Eldership 2:611-612
[213] Matt. 27:51-53
[214] Moses 7:55-57

The Holy of Holies is now open to all, and all, through the atoning blood of the Lamb, can enter into the highest and holiest of places, that kingdom where eternal life is found.[215]

To all this the centurion and his soldiers were witnesses, and when they saw it all, they agreed they feared and said: "truly, this was the Son of God." And the centurion himself glorified God -Perhaps in praising and prayer -And said: "certainly this was a righteous man."

Nor were the centurion and his soldiers alone in their fearful and awe-filled feelings. A congregation of the friends and acquaintances and disciples of Jesus had now gathered at the cross, many of them being and Galileans. They "smote their breasts," and were sorrowful. Particular mention is made of "the women that followed him from Galilee." They had come to minister unto him "for his burial," And among them were Mary Magdalene, Mary the mother of James the younger and Joses, and Salome and the mother of James and John. The Blessed Virgin is not mentioned, leaving us to suppose that John has by now taken her to his home so she will no longer be a personal witness of the agonies of her Son. Since Jesus' friends were there, we take the liberty of assuming this included the Ten; surely all of them, scattered at Gethsemane, would have long since rallied again around his side.

But now, "the sun was westering as the darkness away from the completed sacrifice. They who had not thought it a pollution to inaugurate their feast by the murder of their Messiah, were seriously alarmed lest the sanctity of the following day—which began at sunset—should be compromised by the hanging of the corpses on the cross. And, horrible to relate, the crucified often live for many hours—nay, even for two or three days---in their torture." (Farrar. 711-12)

17 ¶ Now the LORD had prepared a great fish to swallow up Jonah. And Jonah was in the belly of the fish three days and three nights.
(Jonah 1:17)
40 For as Jonas was three days and three nights in the whale's belly; so shall the Son of man be three days and three nights in the heart of the earth.
(Matthew 12:40)
21 ¶ From that time forth began Jesus to shew unto his disciples, how that he must go unto Jerusalem, and suffer many things of the elders and chief priests and scribes, and be killed, and be raised again the third day.
(Matthew 16:21)
3 And they shall kill him, and the third day he shall be raised again. And they were exceeding sorry.
(Matthew 17:23)
1 And he began to teach them, that the Son of man must suffer many things, and be rejected of the elders, and *of* the chief priests, and scribes, and be killed, and after three days rise again.
(Mark 8:31)
1 For he taught his disciples, and said unto them, The Son of man is delivered into the hands of men, and they shall kill him; and after that he is killed, he shall rise the third day.
(Mark 9:31)
4 And they shall mock him, and shall scourge him, and shall spit upon him, and shall kill him: and the third day he shall rise again.
(Mark 10:34)
3 And they shall scourge *him,* and put him to death: and the third day he shall rise again.
(Luke 18:33)

What is a Day? 1. One period of the earth's revolution on its axis (24 hours) is called a day. (Gen.7:24) Hebrew days were calculated "from even unto even" (Lev. 23:32)., Meaning from sunset to sunset. The Lord's Day is the first day of the week. (D'&C 59:9-14). **2.** That period between dawn and dark is the day as distinguished from the night. (Gen.8:22; Ps. 19:2).

---

[215] DNTC p. 830

"Are there not twelve hours in the day?" (John ll:9). **3.** A day is a specified age, time or period…. (Job 19:25)…. This must be correct in calculating the days of the Atonement.

These are just a few quotes of the thousands of scriptures written, that are either a similitude or an actual precursor of the Saviors circumstances surrounding His fulfillment of the Atonement. Jesus Christ himself, established the details of this sacrifice down to the last jot and tittle, which, He would fulfill with impeccable exactness. Why?
So, we might know with certainty that He is the only one that can reveal the true path to immortality and Eternal life.

REV

Chapter 15
Burial

12th day, 21st *Nissan*, (Thursday Night)	Location	Matthew	Mark	Luke	John
Day of preparation-bodies must be removed-next day was high day	Jerusalem	27:62	15:42	23:54	19:31-37,42
Joseph of Arimathea begged the body of Jesus	Golgotha	27:57-58	15:43-45	23:50-52	19:38
Prepared Jesus for burial-Nicodemus 100 weight of Aloes & rolled stone closed	New tomb	27:59-60	15:46	23:53-54	19:38-41
Women observed where	New tomb	27:61	15:47	23:55	
12th day, 21st *Nissan*, (Thursday) High Day Convocation	Jerusalem High Day observance	Exodus	0	0	0
Priests & Pharisees wanted a guard set	Jerusalem	27:62-66			
13th day, 22nd *Nissan*, (Friday)	Jerusalem				
Women prepared spices & ointments	Jerusalem			23:56	

12th day: 21th Nissan (Thursday)
After 6pm Evening time.

In spite of the turmoil surrounding these disruptive events, the Jewish hierarchy was portentously and dogmatically pleading with Pilate to remove Jesus from the cross:

John 19:31 ¶ The Jews therefore, **because it was the preparation,** *that the bodies should not remain upon the cross on the Sabbath day,* **(for that Sabbath day was an high day,)** *besought Pilate that their legs might be broken, and [that] they might be taken away.*[216]

Pilate marveled that Jesus was already dead and so he sent a centurion to find out:[217]

32 Then came the soldiers, and brake the legs of the first, and of the other which was crucified with him.

33 **But when they came to Jesus, and saw that he was dead already, they brake not his legs:**

34 But **one of the soldiers with a spear pierced his side, and forthwith came there out blood and water.**

35 And **he that saw [it] bare record, and his record is true: and he knoweth that he saith true, that ye might believe.**

36 For these things were done, that the **scripture should be fulfilled, A bone of him shall not be broken.**

37 And again **another scripture saith, They shall look on him whom they pierced.**

Christ, the great Passover sacrifice, of whom all altar victims had been but suggestive prototypes, died through violence yet without a bone of His body being broken, as was a prescribed condition of the slain paschal lambs. One of the soldiers, to make sure that Jesus was actually dead, or to surely kill Him if He was yet alive, drove a spear into His Side, making a wound large enough to permit a man's hand to be thrust there into. The withdrawal of the spear was followed by an outflow of blood and water an occurrence so surprising that John, who was an eye-witness, bears specific personal testimony to the fact, and cites the scriptures thereby fulfilled.[218]

---

[216] Luke 23:54
[217] Mark 15:44
[218] JTC p 663

Mark 15:42 ¶ *And **now when the even was come,** because it **was <u>the preparation, that is, the day before the sabbath,</u>***

This day was the 11th day of the Passover and the 20th day of Nissan. This day was the final preparation day before the Holy Convocation required on the 21st day of Nissan.

*43 **Joseph of Arimathaea, an honourable counsellor, which also waited for the kingdom of God, came, and went in boldly unto Pilate, and craved the body of Jesus.***

*44 And Pilate marveled if he were already dead: **and calling [unto him] the centurion, he asked him whether he had been any while dead.***

Luke 23:50* ¶ *And, **behold, [there was] a man named Joseph, a counsellor; [and he was] a good man, and a just:*

*51 (The same had not consented to the counsel and deed of them;) [he was] of **Arimathaea, a city of the Jews: who also himself waited for the kingdom of God**.*

*52 This [man] went unto Pilate, **and begged the body of Jesus.***

Joseph of Arimathaea, a member of the Sanhedrin, a counselor and a just man, was one who defended Jesus and did not consent to the deed of them concerning the trials. This man being a disciple of Christ, awaiting the kingdom of God, but hesitated to openly confess it for fear of the Jews. Never-the-less Joseph went boldly to Pilate and begged the body of Jesus so that he might give the Savior a decent burial. Pilate was still surprised that Jesus was dead, but when the centurion confirmed this fact, Pilate commanded the body of Christ to be delivered to Joseph.

*Mark15: 45 And when he knew [it] of the centurion, **he gave the body to Joseph**.*

*46 And **he bought fine linen, and took him down, and wrapped him in the linen, and laid him in a sepulchre** which was hewn out of a rock, **and rolled a stone unto the door of the sepulchre.***

*47 And **Mary Magdalene and Mary [the mother] of Joses beheld where he was laid.***

*Luke 23:53 And **he took it down, and wrapped it in linen, and laid it in a sepulchre that was hewn in stone,** wherein never man before was laid.*

*54 **And that day was the preparation, and the sabbath drew on.***

*55 And **the women also, which came with him from Galilee, followed after, and beheld the sepulchre, and how his body was laid.***

****John 19:38* ¶ *And after this **Joseph of Arimathaea, being a disciple of Jesus,** but secretly for fear of the Jews, besought Pilate that he might take away the body of Jesus: and Pilate gave [him] leave. **He came therefore, and took the body of Jesus.***

*39 And **there came also Nicodemus**, which at the first came to Jesus by night, and **brought a mixture of myrrh and aloes, <u>about an hundred pound [weight]</u>.***

*40 Then **took they the body of Jesus, and wound it in linen clothes with the spices, as the manner of the Jews is to bury.***

41 Now in the place where he was crucified there was a garden; and in the garden a new sepulchre, wherein was never man yet laid.

*42 **There laid they Jesus therefore because of the Jews' preparation [day];** for the sepulchre was nigh at hand.*

*****Matthew 27:57- 60 And **laid it in his own new tomb**, which he had hewn out in the rock: and **he rolled a great stone to the door of the sepulchre, and departed.***

*61 And there was **Mary Magdalene, and the other Mary, sitting over against the sepulchre.***

Joseph removed Jesus from the cross and was assisted by Nicodemus, another ruling member of the Sanhedrin, the same who had come to Jesus by night three years before, and who at the conspiracy meetings of the council had protested against the unlawful condemnation of Jesus without a hearing.[219]

These two disciples, knowing full well they would not be purified to partake of the Passover proceedings the next day, moved with tenderness and care to prepare the Son of God for burial. Nicodemus brought a large quantity of myrrh and aloes, about a hundred-pound weight. This expensive mixture of spices and fine linen was highly esteemed for anointing and embalming, but its high cost restricted its use to the wealthy.

There was a garden nearby where Joseph had his own newly hewn tomb, wherein a man had never been laid, there he and Nicodemus began the task of preparing the body of Jesus 'as the manner of the Jews is to bury.' This burial process is not done hastily and, considering the great respect these two men had for their Christ and they had started after dark, they could not have been finished till after midnight some time.

After they finished preparing the body they rolled 'a great stone to the door of the sepulcher and departed.' Mary Magdalene and the other Mary, being totally grief stricken, were sitting over against the sepulcher until Josephus had the great stone rolled to the door.[220] As we have pointed out, this would have been around 2am or 3am in the morning.

The **12th day** (Thursday) of the Passover, which would be the High Sabbath day, would also be a day of mourning for the bereaved and exhausted followers of Jesus. Even though this was the **7th** day of the Passover, and last day of **unleavened bread and the last convocation day**, there were Jewish leaders concerned about the promise of resurrection:

> *Matthew 27:62 Now **the next day, that followed the day of the preparation, the chief priests and Pharisees came together unto Pilate,***
>
> *63 Saying, Sir, **we remember that that deceiver said, while he was yet alive, <u>After three days</u> I will rise again.***
>
> *64 Command therefore that the **sepulchre be made sure until the third day, lest his disciples come by night, and steal him away,** and say unto the people, He is risen from the dead: **so, the last error shall be worse than the first**.*
>
> *65 Pilate said unto them, **Ye have a watch: go your way, make [it] as sure** as ye can.*
>
> *66 So **they went, and made the sepulchre sure, sealing the stone, and setting a watch.***

The chief priests and Pharisees were gravely concerned if Jesus, in their minds the deceiver had said, he would rise again after **3 days**, (not the next day but in three days), and they were afraid his followers would come and steal him at night and claim He had risen from the dead. Pilate, not sympathetic to their concerns, told them to assign their own guards and security to watch over the sepulcher. So, they went and set their own watch to try and make sure this could not happen.

Jewish leadership was painfully aware that Jesus had said that **<u>after 3 days</u>** He would rise from the grave. On one occasion when confronting Jesus, they asked for a sign of His claims to divinity and He answered them:

> *Matthew 12:39 But **he answered** and said unto them, **An evil and adulterous generation seeketh after a sign; and there shall no sign be given to it, but the sign of the prophet Jonas:***
>
> *40 **For as Jonas was three days and three nights in the whale's belly; so, shall the Son of man <u>be three days and three nights</u> in the heart of the earth.***
>
> *41 The men of Nineveh shall rise in judgment with this generation, and shall condemn it: because **they repented at the preaching of Jonas; and, behold, a greater than Jonas [is] here.***

Also Matt. 16:21; 17:22-23; 20:18-19 & John 2:19. The Book of Mormon in 3 Nephi completely verifies happenings of this day and the length of the burial in detail:

> *3 Nephi 8:19 And it came to pass that when the **thunderings, and the lightnings, and the storm, and the tempest, and the quakings of the earth did cease--for behold, they did last for about the space of three hours;** and it was said by some that the time was greater; nevertheless,*

---

[219] John 3:1-2
[220] Matt. 27:60-61

*all these great and terrible things were done in about the space of three hours--and **then behold, there was darkness upon the face of the land.***

*20 And it came to pass that there was **thick darkness upon all the face of the land,** insomuch that the inhabitants thereof who had not fallen could feel the vapor of darkness;*

21 And there could be no light, because of the darkness, neither candles, neither torches; neither could there be fire kindled with their fine and exceedingly dry wood, so that there could not be any light at all;

22 And there was not any light seen, neither fire, nor glimmer, <u>neither the sun, nor the moon, nor the stars</u>, for so great were the mists of darkness which were upon the face of the land.

23 And it came to pass that it <u>did last for the space of three days</u> that there was no light seen; and there was great mourning and howling and weeping among all the people continually; yea, great were the groanings of the people, because of the darkness and the great destruction which had come upon them.

Truly the Light of the world was absent for 3 days and 3 nights, or a time span of 72 hours or more. This is significant in the fact, that in order to satisfy the Jewish superstitions and beliefs, a body had to be dead for at least 3 days and 3 nights or the spirit could re-enter on its own accord.

Then out of the darkness a voice is heard:

*3 Nephi 9:15 **Behold, I am Jesus Christ the Son of God**. I created the heavens and the earth, and all things that in them are. I was with the Father from the beginning. I am in the Father, and the Father in me; **and in me hath the Father glorified his name**.*

*16 I came unto my own, and my own received me not. **And the scriptures concerning my coming are fulfilled.***

*17 And as many as have received me, to them have I given to become the sons of God; and even so will I to as many as shall believe on my name, for behold, by me redemption cometh, **and in me is the law of Moses fulfilled.***

This verifies what the comparison calendar has clearly shown us, Jesus was in the tomb early in the morning while it was yet dark of the **12th day**, until early in the morning while it was yet dark of the **15th day**, thus making up the 72-hour time frame.[221]

On the **12th day**, the final day of the Passover and as we have shown would have been a Thursday, there would have been no servile work performed. The disciples, both men and women, had already been up for 24 hours or more and would have been mourning and fitfully trying to rest or sleep this day and night.

The next day was Friday:

*Luke 23:55 And the **women also, which came with him from Galilee, followed after, and beheld the sepulchre, and how his body was laid.***

*56 And **they returned, and prepared spices and ointments; and rested the sabbath day according to the commandment.***

These are the women of Galilee who had accepted the responsibility for the final preparation of the body, and would not have been able to purchase and prepare the necessary ingredients on the previous day as it was the Convocation High Day. However, on this **22nd** day of Nissan (Friday), after the Passover was finished, they were able to procure and prepare the spices and ointments necessary to complete the task of interment. The next day which was the **23rd** day of Nissan, was the regular Saturday Sabbath, and they rested according to commandment.

As Jesus hung on the cross between two malefactors:

*Luke 23:39 And **one of the malefactors** which were hanged railed on him, saying, **If thou be Christ, save thyself and us.***

*40 But **the other answering rebuked him, saying, Dost not thou fear God**, seeing thou art in the same condemnation?*

---

[221] John 20:1

41 And we indeed justly; for we receive the due reward of our deeds: but this man hath done nothing amiss.

42 And he said unto Jesus, Lord, remember me when thou comest into thy kingdom.

43 And Jesus said unto him, Verily I say unto thee, To day shalt thou be with me in paradise.

Jesus stated clearly that he and this malefactor would be **in paradise together**. Both would then be dead, and there would be physical dissolution in which the immortal spirit and the body of flesh and bones would be separated.

Where is paradise?

*Alma 40:11 Now, **concerning the state of the soul between death and the resurrection--Behold, it has been made known unto me by an angel, that the spirits of all men, as soon as they are departed from this mortal body,** yea, the spirits of all men, whether they be good or evil, are taken home to that God who gave them life.*

*12 And then shall it come to pass, **that the spirits of those who are righteous are received into a state of happiness, which is called paradise,** a state of rest, a state of peace, where they shall rest from all their troubles and from all care, and sorrow.*

*13 And then shall it come to pass, that the **spirits of the wicked, yea, who are evil--for behold, they have no part nor portion of the Spirit of the Lord;** for behold, they chose evil works rather than good; therefore the spirit of the devil did enter into them, and take possession of their house--**and these shall be cast out into outer darkness; there shall be weeping, and wailing, and gnashing of teeth, and this because of their own iniquity, being led captive by the will of the devil.***

*14 Now this is the state of the souls of the wicked, yea, in darkness, and a state of awful, fearful looking for the fiery indignation of the wrath of God upon them; **thus, they remain in this state, as well as the righteous in paradise, until the time of their resurrection.***

Peter confirms this conclusion:

1 Peter 3:18 ¶ For **Christ also hath once suffered for sins, the just for the unjust, that he might bring us to God, **being put to death in the flesh, but quickened by the Spirit**:*

*19 By **which also he went and preached unto the spirits in prison**:*

*20 Which **sometime were disobedient, when once the long suffering of God waited in the days of Noah,** while the ark was a preparing, wherein few, that is, eight souls were saved by water.*

**1 Peter 4:5 Who shall give account to him that is ready to judge the quick and the dead.

*6 **For, for this cause was the gospel preached also to them that are dead, that they might be judged according to men in the flesh,** but live according to God in the spirit.*

On the third day following, Jesus, then a resurrected Being, positively stated to the weeping Magdalene: "I am not yet ascended to my Father." **He had gone to paradise but not to the place where God dwells. Paradise, therefore, is not Heaven**, if by the latter term we understand it to be the abode of the Eternal Father and His celestial children.

Three days earlier: "And he bowed his head, and gave up the ghost."[222] In that brief moment between life and death, His eternal body that was housed in this tenement of clay, He stepped over to live in another realm, that we call death. Because Jesus had the power over immortality, and no man could take his life from him, chose to live in an unembodied state in the realm of the departed. He entered into the paradise of God, and as other men,

---

[222] (John 19: 30.)

to await the day of his resurrection, when the eternal spirit would be reunited with its body, and having a body of flesh and bones, thereafter to live eternally in immortal Glory. The testimonies of the prophets establish that the Savior spent three days and three nights, of our time, teaching the spirits in prison, and informing His apostles and the people, that He had fulfilled the Law of Moses and the work for them now can go forward.

The ministry of Christ among the disembodied was foreseen, predicted, and accomplished; and then it was that He began to "proclaim liberty to the captives, and the opening of the prison to them that are bound"; [223] then the work commenced "to bring out the prisoners from the prison, and them that sit in darkness out of the prison house";[224] He had now suffered for our sins, the Just for the unjust, having been put to death in the flesh but continuing to live in the spirit, "went and preached to the spirits in prison".[225]

The fact that the gospel was preached to the dead necessarily implies the possibility of the dead accepting the same, and availing themselves of the saving opportunities thereof. In the merciful providence of the Almighty, provision has been made for vicarious service by the living for the dead, in the ordinances essential to salvation; so that all who in the spirit-world accept the word of God as preached to them, develop true faith in Jesus Christ as the one and only Savior, and contritely repent of their transgressions, shall be brought under the saving effect of baptism by water for the remission of sins, and be recipients of the baptism of the Spirit or the bestowal of the Holy Ghost. Paul cites the principle and practice of baptism by the living for the dead, as proof of the actuality of the resurrection: "Else what shall they do which are baptized for the dead, if the dead rise not at all? Why are they then baptized for the dead?" Free agency, the divine birthright of every human soul, will not be annulled by death. Only as the spirits of the dead become penitent and faithful will they be benefited by the vicarious service rendered in their behalf on earth.[226]

> *And there were gathered together in one place an innumerable company of the spirits of the just, who had been faithful in the testimony of Jesus while they lived in mortality; And who had offered sacrifice in the similitude of the great sacrifice of the Son of God, and had suffered tribulation in their Redeemer's name. All these had departed the mortal life, firm in the hope of a glorious resurrection….*
>
> *I beheld that they were filled with joy and gladness, and were rejoicing together because the day of their deliverance was at hand. They were assembled awaiting the advent of the Son of God into the spirit world, to declare their redemption from the bands of death.*
>
> *While this vast multitude waited and conversed, rejoicing in the hour of their deliverance from the chains of death, the Son of God appeared, declaring liberty to the captives who had been faithful; And there he preached to them the everlasting gospel, the doctrine of the resurrection and the redemption of mankind from the fall, and from individual sins on conditions of repentance. But unto the wicked he did not go….*
>
> *And the saints rejoiced in their redemption, and bowed the knee and acknowledged the Son of God as their Redeemer and Deliverer from death and the chains of hell. Their countenances shone, and the radiance from the presence of the Lord rested upon them, and they sang praises unto his holy name.*[227]

> *John 10;16 tells us "And other sheep I have, which are not of this fold: them also I must bring, and they shall hear my voice……". 3 Nephi 15, in speaking of his church in Israel tells us "And they understood me not, for they suppose it had been the Gentiles; they understood not that the Gentiles should be converted through their preaching." ….. "And verily, verily, I say unto you that I have other sheep, which are not of this land, neither of the land of Jerusalem, neither in any parts of the land round about whither I have been to minister."*

This and much more, reveals that Jesus is the savior and redeemer of our entire world. However, that's another story!

---

[223] Isa. 61:1
[224] Isa. 42:7
[225] 1 Pet. 3:18-20
[226] JTC 675
[227] D&C 138:12-34

Chapter 16

The Resurrection

	Location	Matthew	Mark	Luke	John
14th day, *23rd Nissan*, (Saturday)	Jerusalem				
Regular Sabbath	Jerusalem				
15th day, *24th Nissan*, (Sunday) Resurrection	Jerusalem & Tomb				
Mary Magdalene & Mary–while it was still dark	Tomb				20:1
Ran & told Peter & John, who ran to the tomb	Jerusalem				20:2-10
Mary & other Mary were ahead of other women	Jerusalem & Tomb	28:1			
Women went to sepulcher & was told of resurrection	Tomb	28:2-8	16:1-8	24:1-8	
Mary outside sepulcher & Jesus appeared to her	Tomb		16:9		20:11-17
Jesus appeared to women	Tomb	28:9-10			
Mary & Women told them of the resurrection	Jerusalem		16:10-11	24:9-11	20:18
Peter returned to tomb	Tomb			24:12	
Guards went to priests	Jerusalem	28:11-15			
Appeared to other two			16:12-13	24:13-35	
Same day appeared to apostles	Jerusalem		16:14-18--	24:36-48	20:19-23

Saturday, the Jewish Sabbath has now passed, and the most memorable Sunday in the history of mankind is about to be recorded. In an early morning hour before dawn, while a Guard kept watch, the earth began to quake and an angle of the Lord rolled back the massive stone from the entrance of the tomb. The soldiers paralyzed with fear fell to the ground as dead men.

Because Jesus came from the grave on the first day of the week, to commemorate that day and to keep in remembrance the glorious reality of the resurrection, the ancient apostles, as guided by the spirit, changed the Sabbath to Sunday.

72 hours after His interment, three days and three nights the son of man will be in the heart of the earth as prophesied, from early morning hour of the 21st of Nissan to the early morning hour of the 24th of Nissan.

*Mark 16:1 ¶ AND **when the sabbath was past**, Mary Magdalene, and Mary the [mother] of James, and Salome, **had bought sweet spices, that they might come and anoint him.** **The Sabbath spoken of here was the Saturday (7th day).**

John 20:1 ¶ <u>**THE first [day] of the week cometh Mary Magdalene early, when it was yet dark,**</u> unto the sepulchre, and seeth the stone taken away from the sepulchre.

2 Then **she runneth, and cometh to Simon Peter, and to the other disciple**, whom Jesus loved, and **saith unto them, They have taken away the Lord out of the sepulchre**, and **we know not where they have laid him.**

While the morning was yet dark, Mary Magdalene and Mary, the mother of James and Salome, proceeded to the sepulcher where they had seen Jesus laid, with preparations they had bought for his anointing. When they arrived at the sepulcher they found the stone rolled away and the Savior gone. Mary Magdalene immediately turned and ran to tell Peter and James that they had taken our Lord out of the tomb and we, she and the other Mary, don't know where He has been laid.

John 20:3 **Peter therefore went forth, and that other disciple, and came to the sepulchre.**

4 So **they ran both together: and the other disciple did outrun Peter**, and came first to the sepulchre.

5 And **he stooping down**, [and looking in], saw the linen clothes lying; **yet went he not in.**

6 Then cometh **Simon Peter following him, and went into the sepulchre,** and seeth the linen clothes lie,

7 **And the napkin**, that was about his head, not lying with the linen clothes, but **wrapped together in a place by itself**.

8 **Then went in also that other disciple**, which came first to the sepulchre, and he saw, and believed.

9 For as yet they knew not the scripture, that he must rise again from the dead.

10 Then **the disciples went away again unto their own home.**

Upon receiving the startling news of the resurrection both apostles ran forth to see for themselves. John out ran Peter, but he waited for Peter to go in first. They found Jesus not there and his head clothes neatly wrapped separately by them-selves. They now believed Mary that the tomb was empty, but they apparently did not understand clearly that He was to rise again from the dead on the third day. Because it was still early in the morning they returned to their homes, most perplexed and confused.

Now as dawn broke forth, Mary Magdalene had returned and rejoined with the other Mary, in order to see if they could locate where the Saviors body had been taken.

* *Matthew 28:1* ¶ IN the end of the sabbath, **as it began to dawn toward the first [day] of the week, came Mary Magdalene and the other Mary to see the sepulchre**.

2 And, behold, there was a great earthquake: for **the angel of the Lord descended from heaven, and came and rolled back the stone from the door**, and sat upon it.

3 **His countenance was like lightning, and his raiment white as snow:**

4 And **for fear of him the keepers did shake, and became as dead [men].**

The two Mary's were unaware that an earthquake caused by the angel of the Lord had rolled back the stone door and they still believed it to be the work of men who had removed the body. As the two Mary's returned to the tomb a little ahead of the rest of the other faithful women of Galilee, who were totally unaware of what had just transpired and were also on the way to the sepulcher to fulfill their duties of bodily preparation. The Guard had already revived and ran back to town.

Mark 16:2 And very **early in the morning the first [day] of the week, they came unto the sepulchre at the rising of the sun.**

3 And they said among themselves, **Who shall roll us away the stone** from the door of the sepulchre?

4 And when they looked, **they saw that the stone was rolled away**: for it was very great.

5 And **entering into the sepulchre, they saw a young man sitting on the right side, clothed in a long white garment; and they were affrighted.**

6 And he saith unto them, **Be not affrighted: Ye seek Jesus of Nazareth, which was crucified: he is risen;** he is not here: behold the place where they laid him.

7 **But go your way, tell his disciples and Peter that he goeth before you into Galilee**: there shall ye see him, as he said unto you.

8 And **they went out quickly, and fled from the sepulchre**; for they trembled and were amazed: neither said they any thing to any [man]; for they were afraid.

***Luke 24:1* ¶ NOW upon the first [day] of the week, very early in the morning, they came unto the sepulchre, bringing the spices which they had prepared, and certain [others] with them.

2 And they found the stone rolled away from the sepulchre.

3 And they entered in, and found not the body of the Lord Jesus.

*4 **And it came to pass, as they were much perplexed thereabout, behold, two men stood by them in shining garments:***

*5 And as they were afraid, and bowed down [their] faces to the earth, they said unto them, **Why seek ye the living among the dead?***

*6 **He is not here, but is risen:** remember how he spake unto you when he was yet in Galilee,*

*7 Saying, **The Son of man must be delivered into the hands of sinful men, and be crucified, and the third day rise again.***

8 And they remembered his words,

****Matthew 28:5 And the angel answered and said unto the women, Fear not ye: for **I know that ye seek Jesus, which was crucified.***

*6 He is not here: for he is risen, as he said. **Come, see the place where the Lord lay.***

*7 And **go quickly, and tell his disciples that he is risen from the dead; and, behold, he goeth before you into Galilee**; there shall ye see him: lo, I have told you.*

*8 And **they departed quickly from the sepulchre** with fear and great joy; and did run to bring his disciples word.*

At the rising of the sun, the devoted and faithful women of Galilee set out for the tomb, bearing spices and ointments which they had prepared for the further anointing of the body of Jesus. Some of them had been witnesses of the burial, and where He had been laid away by Joseph and Nicodemus, just before the beginning of the Holy Convocation Sabbath; and now these adoring women came early to render loving service, in a more thorough anointing and external embalmment of the body. On the way as they sorrowfully conversed, they seemingly for the first time thought of the difficulty of entering the tomb. "Who shall roll us away the stone from the door of the sepulcher?" they asked one of another. Evidently, they knew nothing of the seal and the guard of soldiery. At the tomb they saw the angel, and were afraid; but he said unto them: "Fear not ye: for I know that ye seek Jesus, which was crucified. He is not here: for he is risen, as he said. "Come, see the place where the Lord lay. And go quickly, and tell his disciples that he is risen from the dead; and, behold, he goeth before you into Galilee; there shall ye see him: lo, I have told you." The women, though favored by angelic visitation and assurance, left the place amazed and frightened.

But Mary Magdalene, who had been ahead of the others in returning to the sepulcher, remained:

*John20:11 ¶ But **Mary stood without at the sepulchre weeping**: and **as she wept, she stooped down, [and looked] into the sepulchre**,*

*12 And **seeth two angels in white sitting**, the one at the head, and the other at the feet, **where the body of Jesus had lain.***

*13 And they say unto her, **Woman, why weepest thou?** She saith unto them, **Because they have taken away my Lord, and I know not where they have laid him.***

*14 And when she had thus said**, she turned herself back, and saw Jesus standing, and knew not that it was Jesus.***

*15 Jesus saith unto her, **Woman, why weepest thou? whom seekest thou?** She, **supposing him to be the gardener, saith** unto him, **Sir, if thou have borne him hence, tell me where thou hast laid him,** and I will take him away.*

*16 Jesus saith unto her, **Mary. She turned herself, and saith unto him, Rabboni; which is to say, Master.***

*17 Jesus saith unto her, **Touch me not; for I am not yet ascended to my Father: but go to my brethren, and say unto them, I ascend unto my Father, and your Father; and [to] my God, and your God.***

As Mary looked into the sepulcher she saw two personages, angels in white; one sat "at the head, and the other at the feet, where the body of Jesus had lain." In accents of tenderness they asked of her: "Woman, why weepest thou?" In reply she could but voice anew her overwhelming sorrow: "Because they have taken away my Lord, and I know not where they have laid him." The absence of the body, which she thought to be all that was left on earth of Him whom she loved so deeply, was a personal bereavement. There is a volume of pathos and affection in her words, "They have taken away my Lord."

Turning from the vault, which, though at that moment illumined by angelic presence, was to her void and desolate, she became aware of another Personage, standing near. She heard His sympathizing inquiry: "Woman, why weepest thou? Whom seekest thou?" Scarcely lifting her tearful countenance to look at the Questioner, but vaguely supposing that He was the caretaker of the garden, and that He might have knowledge of what had been done with the body of her Lord, she exclaimed: "Sir, if thou have borne him hence, tell me where thou hast laid him, and I will take him away." She knew that Jesus had been interred in a borrowed tomb; and if the body had been dispossessed of that resting place, she was prepared to provide another. "Tell me where thou hast laid him," she pleaded.

It was Jesus to whom she spake, her beloved Lord, though she knew it not. One word from His living lips changed her agonized grief into ecstatic joy. "Jesus saith unto her, Mary." The voice, the tone, the tender accent she had heard and loved in the earlier days lifted her from the despairing depths into which she had sunk. She turned, and saw the Lord. In a transport of joy, she reached out her arms to embrace Him, uttering only the endearing and worshipful word, "Rabboni," meaning my beloved Master.

Jesus restrained her impulsive manifestation of reverent love, saying, "Touch me not; for I am not yet ascended to my Father," and adding, "but go to my brethren, and say unto them, I ascend unto my Father, and your Father; and to my God, and your God." To a woman, to Mary of Magdala, was given the honor of being the first among mortals to behold a resurrected Soul, and that Soul, the Lord Jesus.[228]

The other women had been affrighted by the presence of the angel at the tomb, and had departed with mingled fear and joy.

> *Matthew 28:8 And **as they went to tell his disciples, behold, Jesus met them, saying, All hail. And they came and held him by the feet, and worshipped him.***
>
> ***9** Then said Jesus unto them,* **Be not afraid: go tell my brethren that they go into Galilee, and there shall they see me.**

And they remembered His words. As they were returning to the city to deliver the message to the disciples, "Jesus met them, saying, All hail. And they came and held him by the feet, and worshipped him. It appears that between Mary's impulsive attempt to touch Jesus and the action of the other women to hold His feet, Christ had ascended to the Father and was now immortal. Now continuing His ministry Jesus said unto them, "Be not afraid: go tell my brethren that they go into Galilee, and there shall they see me."[229]

> **Luke 24:8 And **they remembered his words,***
>
> *9 And returned from the sepulchre, and **told all these things unto the eleven, and to all the rest.***
>
> *10 It was **Mary Magdalene, and Joanna, and Mary [the mother] of James, and other [women that were] with them, which told these things unto the apostles.***
>
> *11 And **their words seemed to them as idle tales, and they believed them not.***

> ***Mark16:9 ¶ Now when [Jesus] was risen early the first [day] of the week, he **appeared first to Mary Magdalene**, out of whom he had cast seven devils.*
>
> *10 [And] **she went and told them that had been with him, as they mourned and wept.***
>
> *11 And they, **when they had heard that he was alive, and had been seen of her, believed not.***

---

[228] JTC pp. 681-682
[229] JTC 682

***John 20:18** **Mary Magdalene came and told the disciples that she had seen the Lord, and [that] he had spoken these things unto her.**

Mary Magdalene and the other women told the wonderful story of their several experiences to the disciples, but the brethren could not credit their words, which "seemed to them as idle tales, and they believed them not." After all that Christ had taught concerning His rising from the dead on that third day the apostles were unable to accept the actuality of the occurrence; to their minds the resurrection was some mysterious and remote event, not a present possibility. The grief and the sense of irreparable loss which had characterized the yesterday Sabbath, were replaced by profound perplexity and contending doubts on this first day of the week. But while the apostles hesitated to believe that Christ had actually risen, the women, less skeptical, more trustful, knew, for they had both seen Him and heard His voice, and some of them had touched His feet.

Matt 28:11 ¶ *Now when they were going, behold,* **some of the watch came into the city, and shewed unto the chief priests all the things that were done.**
12 And when **they were assembled with the elders,** *and had taken counsel,* **they gave large money unto the soldiers,**
13 Saying, **Say ye, His disciples came by night, and stole him away while we slept.**
14 And if this come to the governor's ears, we will persuade him, and secure you.
15 So they took the money, and did as they were taught: and **this saying is commonly reported among the Jews until this day.**

While the resurrection had actually taken place, the hierarchy of the Jewish establishment paid off the soldiers to protect them and started the saying that the people had stolen the body and hid it away. To this day this story is still believed.

Luke 24:12 **Then arose Peter, and ran unto the sepulchre; and stooping down, he beheld the linen clothes laid by themselves, and departed, wondering in himself at that which was come to pass.**

Peter, however, giving some credence to the words of the women, arose from his rest and, returned to the tomb, perhaps hoping to see the Savior. Never-the-less, he departed from the tomb still in wonderment as to what has happened. However, at some time during the day the Lord had appeared to Simon and eased his mind.

Luke 24:13 ¶ *And,* **behold, two of them went that same day to a village called Emmaus,** *which was from Jerusalem [about] threescore furlongs.*
14 And **they talked together of all these things which had happened**.
15 And it came to pass, that, **while they communed [together] and reasoned, Jesus himself drew near, and went with them.**
16 But **their eyes were holden** *that they should not know him.*
17 And he said unto them, **What manner of communications [are] these** *that ye have one to another, as* **ye walk, and are sad?**
18 And the one of them, whose name was Cleopas, answering said unto him, **Art thou only a stranger in Jerusalem, and hast not known the things which are come to pass there in these days?**
19 And he said unto them, **What things?** *And they said unto him,* **Concerning Jesus of Nazareth, which was a prophet mighty in deed and word** *before God and all the people:*
20 And how **the chief priests and our rulers delivered him to be condemned to death, and have crucified him.**
21 **But we trusted** *that it had* **been he which should have redeemed Israel:** *and beside all this,* **today is the third day since these things were done.**
22 Yea, and **certain women also of our company made us astonished,** *which were early at the sepulchre;*

*23 And when **they found not his body**, they came, saying, that **they had also seen a vision of angels, which said that he was alive**.*

*24 And **certain of them which were with us went to the sepulchre, and found [it] even so as the women had said: but him they saw not**.*

*25 Then **he said unto them, O fools, and slow of heart to believe all that the prophets have spoken**:*

*26 **Ought not Christ to have suffered these things**, and to enter into his glory?*

*27 And beginning at Moses and all the prophets, **he expounded unto them in all the scriptures the things concerning himself**.*

*28 And **they drew nigh unto the village**, whither they went: and **he made as though he would have gone further**.*

*29 But they constrained him, saying, **Abide with us: for it is toward evening, and the day is far spent. And he went in to tarry with them**.*

*30 And it came to pass, as **he sat at meat with them, he took bread, and blessed [it], and brake, and gave to them**.*

*31 And **their eyes were opened, and they knew him; and he vanished out of their sight**.*

32 And they said one to another, Did not our heart burn within us, while he talked with us by the way, and while he opened to us the scriptures?

*33 And **they rose up the same hour, and returned to Jerusalem, and found the eleven gathered together, and them that were with them**,*

*34 Saying, **The Lord is risen indeed, and hath appeared to Simon**.*

*35 And **they told what things [were done] in the way, and how he was known of them in breaking of bread**.*

During the afternoon of that same Sunday, two disciples, not of the apostles, left the little band of believers in Jerusalem and set out for Emmaus, a village between seven and eight miles from the city. There was but one topic of conversation; as they walked and talked about the Lord's life, they dwelt particularly upon the facts of His death and marveled deeply over the incomprehensible testimony of the women concerning His reappearance as a living Soul. As they went, engrossed in sorrowful and profound discourse, another Wayfarer joined them and it was the Lord Jesus, *16 But their eyes were holden that they should not know him.* In courteous interest, He asked: *What manner of communications [are] these that ye have one to another, as ye walk, and are sad?*

Cleopas replied with surprise for the Stranger's seeming ignorance: *Art thou only a stranger in Jerusalem, and hast not known the things which are come to pass there in these days?* Christ asked them, *what things?* They could not be reticent. *And they said unto him, Concerning Jesus of Nazareth, which was a prophet mighty in deed and word before God and all the people:* In sorrowful mood they went on to tell how they had trusted that the now crucified Jesus would have proved to be the Messiah sent to redeem Israel; but alas! this was the third day since He had been slain. Yet still perplexed, they told of certain women of their company who had astonished them that morning by saying that they had visited the sepulcher early and had discovered that the Lord's body was not there. But, *that they had also seen a vision of angels, which said that he was alive.* Moreover, others besides the women had gone to the tomb, and had verified the absence of the body but had not seen the Lord.

Then Jesus, gently chiding His fellow travelers as foolish men and slow of heart in their hesitating acceptance of what the prophets had spoken, asked impressively, *26 Ought not Christ to have suffered these things, and to enter into his glory?* Beginning with the inspired predictions of Moses, He expounded to them the scriptures, touching upon all the prophetic utterances concerning the Savior's mission.

When they reached the little town of Emmaus, they entreated Him to join them for supper. When their simple meal was prepared, Jesus seated himself with them at the table. As the Guest of Honor, He took the loaf *blessed [it], and brake, and gave to them.* There may have been something in the fervency of the blessing, or in the manner of the breaking and distributing the bread, that revived memories of former days; or, possibly, they caught sight of the pierced hands; but, whatever the immediate cause, they looked intently upon their Guest, *and their eyes were opened, and they knew him; and he vanished out of their sight.* In a fullness of joyful wonderment, they rose from the table, surprised at themselves for not having recognized Him sooner. Straightway they started to retrace their steps and hastened back to Jerusalem to confirm by their witness what, before, the brethren had been slow to believe.

Why did the risen Lord take this means to appear to Cleopas and his companion? Why did he keep his identity hidden? Why walk and talk with them for some time?

Obviously to show what a resurrected being is like. So much did he seem like any other wayfaring teacher, in demeanor, in dress, in speech, in physical appearance, in conversation, that they did not recognize him as Jesus whom they assumed was dead?

When Cleopas and his companion were returned that night to Jerusalem, they found the apostles and other believers gathered in service behind closed doors.

John 20:19 ¶ Then **the same day at evening, being the first [day] of the week,** *when the doors were shut where the disciples were assembled for fear of the Jews, came* **Jesus and stood in the midst, and saith unto them, Peace [be] unto you.**

Luke 24:36 ¶ *And* **as they thus spake, Jesus himself stood in the midst of them, and saith unto them, Peace [be] unto you.**

37 **But they were terrified and affrighted, and supposed that they had seen a spirit.**

38 And he said unto them, **Why are ye troubled? and why do thoughts arise in your hearts?**

39 **Behold my hands and my feet, that it is I myself: handle me, and see; for a spirit hath not flesh and bones, as ye see me have.**

40 And when he had thus spoken, **he shewed them [his] hands and [his] feet.**

41 And **while they yet believed not for joy, and wondered, he said unto them, Have ye here any meat?**

42 And they **gave him a piece of a broiled fish, and of an honeycomb**.

43 **And he took [it], and did eat before them**.

44 And he said unto them, **These [are] the words which I spake unto you**, *while I was yet with you, that all things must be fulfilled,* which were written in the law of Moses, and [in] the prophets, and [in] the psalms, concerning me.

45 **Then opened he their understanding**, *that they might understand the scriptures,*

46 And said unto them, Thus **it is written, and thus it behoved Christ to suffer, and to rise from the dead the third day:**

47 And **that repentance and remission of sins should be preached in his name among all nations, beginning at Jerusalem.**

48 And **ye are witnesses of these things**.

As the little company communed together, "Jesus himself stood in the midst of them, and saith unto them, Peace be unto you." They were affrighted, supposing with superstitious dread that a ghost had intruded amongst them. But the Lord comforted them, saying "Why are ye troubled? And why do thoughts rise in your hearts? Behold my hands and my feet, that it is I myself: handle me, and see; for a spirit hath not flesh and bones, as ye see me have." Then He showed them the wounds in His hands and feet and side. "They yet believed not for joy," which is to say, they thought the reality, to which they all were witnesses, too good, too glorious, to be true. To further assure them that He was no shadowy form, no immaterial being of tenuous substance,

but a living Personage with bodily organs internal as well as outward, He asked, "Have ye here any meat?" They gave Him a piece of broiled fish and other food which He took "and did eat before them."

These unquestionable evidences of their Visitant's corporeity calmed and made rational the minds of the disciples; and now that they were composed and receptive the Lord reminded them that all things that had happened to Him were in accordance with what He had told them while He had lived amongst them. In His divine presence their understanding was quickened and enlarged so that they comprehended as never before the scriptures -- the Law of Moses, the books of the prophets and the psalms -- concerning Him. That His now accomplished death was a necessity, He attested as fully as He had predicted and affirmed the same aforetime. Then He said unto them: "Thus it is written, and thus it behooved Christ to suffer, and to rise from the dead the third day: and that repentance and remission of sins should be preached in his name among all nations, beginning at Jerusalem. And ye are witnesses of these things."

Then were the disciples glad. As He was about to depart the Lord gave them His blessing, saying, "Peace be unto you: as my Father hath sent me, even so send I you." This specification of men sent by authority points directly to the apostles; "And when he had said this, he breathed on them, and saith unto them, Receive ye the Holy Ghost: who so ever sins ye remit, they are remitted unto them; and who so ever sins ye retain, they are retained."[230]

We now begin to see the apostolic ministry start to blossom forth on the eastern world. But wait! There are others!

*John 10:15 As the Father knoweth me, even so know I the Father: and **I lay down my life for the sheep.***

16 And <u>other sheep I have, which are not of this fold</u>: them also I must bring, and they shall hear my voice; and there shall be one-fold, [and] one shepherd.

*17 Therefore doth my Father love me, because **I lay down my life, that I might take it again.***

*"Genesis 49:22 Joseph is a fruitful bough, **even a fruitful bough by a well; whose branches run over the wall:**"*

The people of the western hemisphere were one of those branches which ran over the wall and was transplanted in the Americas in 600 BC and flourished. The time has now come for this fold to be brought to the knowledge of the Good Shepherd so they can become as one.

This is a small part of their testimony from the Book of Mormon, a second witness:

*3 Nephi 11:1 AND now it came to pass that **there were a great multitude gathered together, of the people of Nephi, round about the temple which was in the land Bountiful**; and **they were marveling and wondering** one with another, **and were showing one to another the great and marvelous change which had taken place.***

*2 **And they were also conversing about this Jesus Christ, of whom the sign had been given concerning his death.***

*3 And it came to pass **that while they were thus conversing one with another, they heard a voice as if it came out of heaven**; and they cast their eyes round about, for **they understood not the voice which they heard; and it was not a harsh voice, neither was it a loud voice; nevertheless, and notwithstanding it being a small voice it did pierce them that did hear to the center**, insomuch that there was no part of their frame that it did not cause to quake; yea, it did pierce them to the very soul, and did cause their hearts to burn.*

*4 And it came to pass that **again they heard the voice, and they understood it not.***

*5 And **again the third time they did hear the voice**, and did open their ears to hear it; and their eyes were towards the sound thereof; and they did look steadfastly towards heaven, from whence the sound came.*

*6 And behold, **the third time they did understand the voice which they heard; and it said unto them:***

*7 **Behold my Beloved Son, in whom I am well pleased, in whom I have glorified my name--hear ye him.***

*8 And it came to pass**, as they understood they cast their eyes up again towards heaven; and behold, they saw a Man descending out of heaven; and he was clothed in a white robe**; and he came down and stood in the midst of them; and **the eyes of the whole multitude***

---

[230] JTC p 689

*were turned upon him, and they durst not open their mouths, even one to another, and wist not what it meant, **for they thought it was an angel that had appeared unto them.***

9 And it came to pass that he stretched forth his hand and spake unto the people, saying:

*10 **Behold, I am Jesus Christ, whom the prophets testified shall come into the world.***

*11 **And behold, I am the light and the life of the world; and I have drunk out of that bitter cup which the Father hath given me, and have glorified the Father in taking upon me the sins of the world, in the which I have suffered the will of the Father in all things from the beginning.***

*12 And it came to pass that when Jesus had spoken these words **the whole multitude fell to the earth; for they remembered that it had been prophesied among them that Christ should show himself unto them after his ascension into heaven.***

*13 And it came to pass that the **Lord spake unto them saying**:*

*14 **Arise and come forth unto me, that ye may thrust your hands into my side, and also that ye may feel the prints of the nails in my hands and in my feet, that ye may know that I am the God of Israel, and the God of the whole earth, and have been slain for the sins of the world.***

*15 And it came to pass that the multitude went forth, and thrust their hands into his side, and did feel the prints of the nails in his hands and in his feet; and this they did do, going forth one by one until they had all gone forth, and did see with their eyes and did feel with their hands, and **did know of a surety and did bear record, that it was he, of whom it was written by the prophets, that should come**.*

*16 And when they had all gone forth and had witnessed for themselves, **they did cry out with one accord, saying:***

*17 **Hosanna! Blessed be the name of the Most High God! And they did fall down at the feet of Jesus, and did worship him.***

The people of Nephi, another sheep of the Savior, had just suffered through devastating earth quakes, destruction of unimaginable proportions and three days and three nights of suffocating darkness. The sun rose on the fourth day and revealed great and marvelous changes that made the people gaze about in wonderment.

They were conversing about the fact that this was the sign portending the death of Jesus Christ, when a small voice came from out of heaven. It was not a loud voice nor a harsh voice but it did strike to the very center of their soul and cause their hearts to burn. The people did not understand this voice the first time nor the second time, however the third time they understood it clearly as the Father said; **Behold my Beloved Son, in whom I am well pleased, in whom I have glorified my name--hear ye him.**

As their eyes gazed to the heavens they saw a man descending and came and stood in their midst. At first everyone thought He was an angle until Jesus identified Himself as the one who their Prophets testified to as the Light and Life of the world, and would come into the world and fulfill the will of the Father and accomplish the Law of Moses. In order that they might know with surety He was the fulfillment of their Prophets prophesies, Jesus invited all to come forward to thrust their hands into his side and feel the nail prints in His hands and as they did they knew '*it was he, of whom it was written by the prophets, that should come.*' His ministry could now begin in earnest in the Western world!

But wait! Is this all?
3 Nephi 16:1 ***AND** verily, verily, I say unto you that I have other sheep, which are not of this land, neither of the land of Jerusalem, neither in any parts of that land round about whither I have been to minister.*

*2 For they of whom I speak are they who have not as yet heard my voice; **neither have I at any time manifested myself unto them.***

*3 But **I have received a commandment of the Father that I shall go unto them**, and that they shall hear my voice, and shall be numbered among my sheep**, that there may be one fold and one shepherd; therefore, I go to show myself unto them**.*

*4 **And I command you that ye shall write these sayings after I am gone**, that **if it so be that my people at Jerusalem**, they who have seen me and been with me in my ministry, do not ask the Father in my name, that they **may receive a knowledge of you by the Holy Ghost**, and also of the other tribes whom they know not of, **that these sayings** which ye shall write **shall be kept and shall be manifested unto the Gentiles**, that through the fullness of the Gentiles, **the remnant of their seed**, who shall be scattered forth upon the face of the earth because of their unbelief, **may be brought in, or may be brought to a knowledge of me, their Redeemer.***

*5 And **then will I gather them in from the four quarters of the earth; and then will I fulfil the covenant which the Father hath made unto all the people of the house of Israel**.*

*6 And **blessed are the Gentiles, because of their belief in me, in and of the Holy Ghost**, which witnesses unto them of me and of the Father.*

*7 Behold**, because of their belief in me, saith the Father, and because of the unbelief of you, O house of Israel, in the latter day shall the truth come unto the Gentiles, that the fullness of these things shall be made known unto them.***

The Savior informed them that there were other sheep which weren't of this land or of Jerusalem to which the Father has commanded Him to go. Jesus commanded this people to write and keep a record so Jerusalem and the Gentiles and the four quarters of the earth may be brought to a knowledge of the truth. It can honestly be said Jesus Christ is the Savior of all nations and all mankind whom the Father has given Him that Jesus may glorify the Father and be glorified in Him. Untold false religions and false Saviors have been manifested unto the world since Satan has been allowed to tempt mankind, however there is but one tomb left unfilled and there has been but one resurrected Savior. There is but one who has fulfilled the Law of Moses and paved the path for immortality and eternal life.

Moses 1:39 **For behold, this is my work and my glory--to bring to pass the immortality and eternal life of man.**

"God himself" The Prophet says, "finding he was in the midst of spirits and glory, because he was more intelligent, saw proper to institute laws whereby the rest could have a privilege to advance themselves. The relationship we have with God places us in a situation to advance in knowledge. He has powers to institute laws to instruct the weaker intelligences, that they may be exalted with himself, so that they might have one glory upon another, and all that knowledge, power, glory, and intelligence, which is requisite in order to save them in the world of spirits."[231] Thus the plan of salvation (of redemption, and exaltation) comprises all the laws, ordinances, principles, and doctrines by conformity to which the spirit offspring of God have power to progress to the high state of exaltation enjoyed by the Father.

Nothing in the entire plan of salvation compares in any way in importance with the most transcendent of all events, the atoning sacrifice of our Lord. It is the most important single thing that has ever occurred in the entire history of created things; it is the rock foundation upon which the gospel and other all things rest. Indeed all "things *which* pertain to our religion are only appendages to it.*"*[232]

"Adam fell that men might be; and men are, that they might have joy: Lehi says. "And the Messiah cometh in the fullness of time, that he may redeem the children of men from the fall."[233] "The atonement, King Benjamin explains, "was prepared from the foundation of the world for all mankind, which ever were since the fall of Adam, or who are, or whoever shall be, even to the end of the world."[234]

---

[231] Teachings p. 534
[232] Ibid p.121
[233] 2 Ne. 2:25-26
[234] Mosiah 4:7

Alama 34:8-12 ***"For it is expedient that there should be a great and a last sacrifice; yea, not a sacrifice of man, neither of beast, neither any manner of foul; for it shall not be a human sacrifice; but it must be an infinite and eternal sacrifice. Now there is not any man that can sacrifice his blood which will atone for the sins of another.... Therefore, there can be nothing short of an infinite atonement which shall will suffice for the sins of the world."***

The world has always been awash in sacrifices, both human and animal, all with the effort to placate the demands of a God and entice the blessing of a God upon the people involved.

So, there could be no question as to the identity of the Savior of mankind, Jesus Christ (Jehovah) spoke directly to Moses face to face and instituted the Passover, which was to commemorate the deliverance of Israelites from Egyptian bondage as well as the deliverance of their firstborn from physical death. The deeper intent of the Passover was to point to the exactness of the sacrifice to be made by Jesus Christ for the salvation and exaltation of mankind.

This Jesus accomplished as He fulfilled to the last Jot and Tittle of the Law of Moses as referred to in both ancient and modern prophecies.

REV

Chapter 17
Ministry & Ascension

24th Nissan & after	Location	Matthew	Mark	Luke	John	Acts
Doubting Thomas	Jerusalem				20:24-25	
After 8 days Christ appeared to Thomas & gathered apostles	Galilee				20:26-29	
Many other signs – not written	Galilee				20:30-31	
Peter, I go a fishing	Tiberias				21:1-3	
Jesus stood on shore- said cast your net 3rd appearance	Tiberias				21:4	
Have ye any meat? Cast your net on the right	Tiberias				21:5-13	
Third appearance to apostles	Tiberias				21:14	
Appointment at mountain	Mountain	28:16-18				
Peter, feed my sheep	Mountain				21:15-17	
Signifies Peters death	Mountain				21:18-19	
John to tarry till Jesus comes	Mountain				21:20-23	
Johns Testimony	Mountain				21:23-24	
Ministered to them for 40 days	Galilee					1:1-3
Told to Remain in Jerusalem	Bethany			24:49		1:4-8
Led them as far as Bethany	Bethany			24:50		
Preach to the world	Bethany	28:19-20				
Christ sits on right hand of God	Bethany		16:19-20	24:51		1:9
They returned to Jerusalem	Jerusalem			24:52-53		

    The angel at the sepulcher instructed the faithful women of Galilee to tell the apostles that Jesus had risen and they were to go to Galilee.[235] No doubt these faithful women were members of the disciple's family and would have to prepare for the journey. The Savior that same day in the evening appeared to brethren as they gathered and upbraided them for not believing the testimony they had received.[236] The Sea of Galilee would be their destination and was approximately 80 miles distance.

---

[235] Mathew 28:7,

[236] Mark 16:14-18

The disciples had, along with their families, reached their destination, around Tiberias, between Lower Galilee and Upper Galilee, and were once again together in their native province.

For the second time the savior revealed Himself to them:
*John 20:26 ¶ And **after eight days again his disciples were within, and Thomas with them:** then came Jesus, the doors being shut, and stood in the midst, and said, Peace be unto you.*
*27 Then **saith he to Thomas, Reach hither thy finger, and behold my hands; and reach hither thy hand, and thrust it into my side: and be not faithless, but believing.***

After eight days the apostles were gathered together again and Jesus came to them again for the second time. This time Thomas, who had not believed or understood that Jesus came forth in a tangible body of flesh and bone, was with them. Thomas had heard the testimony of the others as to the resurrection, which he most likely believed, but he did not understand the corporeal nature of it. When Thomas felt the body of the Savior and the marks of the crucifixion, Thomas exclaimed 'my Lord and my God'! The Savior said to Thomas 'because you have seen me you believe, but more blessed are those who have not seen and yet they believe.[237] It is sad commentary indeed that many who call themselves Christians today, believe that Jesus exists only as some kind of spiritual form or essence and not corporeal in nature. Then Jesus proceeded to show the disciples many other signs, signs so they might believe He was the Christ, the son of the living God. However, they are not written in this book.[238]

*John 21:1 After these things **Jesus shewed himself again to the disciples at the sea of Tiberias; and on this wise shewed he himself.***
*2 There were **together Simon Peter, and Thomas called Didymus, and Nathanael of Cana in Galilee, and the sons of Zebedee, and two other of his disciples.***
*3 Simon **Peter saith unto them, I go a fishing**. They say unto him, **We also go with thee. They went forth, and entered into a ship immediately; and that night they caught nothing.***

After the Savior had shown Himself to the disciples this Second time and explained many marvelous things, He encouraged them to get engaged in their ministry. However, it appears Peter and some of the others were concerned and perhaps how to proceed, but also about the physical welfare of their families. These good disciples just naturally returned to their trade as fishermen for sustenance and finances.

They had cast their nets all night and yet had caught nothing.
*John 21:4 But when **the morning was now come, Jesus stood on the shore: but the disciples knew not that it was Jesus.***
*5 Then Jesus saith unto them, **Children, have ye any meat? They answered him, No.***
*6 And he said unto them, **Cast the net on the right side of the ship, and ye shall find. They cast therefore, and now they were not able to draw it for the multitude of fishes**.*

In the Sea of Galilee, the best fishing results are accomplished at night. Seven of the disciples were coming in about mid-morning and Jesus was standing on the shore of Galilee near Tiberias watching them. They did not recognize Him when He queried as to whether they had caught any fish? When they replied that had caught nothing, Jesus instructed them cast on the right side and when they did they filled the nets so full they could not draw them into the boats. Jesus was fully aware of their situation and by this action He showed the disciples, if they followed His instructions their needs would be taken care of.

*John 21:7 Therefore **that disciple whom Jesus loved saith unto Peter, it is the Lord**. Now when **Simon Peter heard that it was the Lord**, he girt his fisher's coat unto him, (for he was naked,) and **did cast himself into the sea.***
*8 And **the other disciples came in a little ship**; (for they were not far from land, but as it were two hundred cubits,) **dragging the net with fishes**.*
*9 As soon then **as they were come to land, they saw a fire of coals there, and fish laid thereon, and bread**.*

---
[237] John 20:28-29
[238] John 20:30-31

However, John the beloved quickly recognized the Savior by this action and told Peter, 'it is the Lord!' Impulsive Peter threw on his fisherman's coat and jumped into the sea and swam to shore so he could be quickly with Jesus. When the rest of the men jumped into a smaller boat and finally dragged the net close into the shore they could see that Jesus, knowing they would be tired and hungry, had prepared warm meal for them.

John 21:10 **Jesus saith unto them, Bring of the fish which ye have now caught.**

11 Simon Peter went up, **and drew the net to land full of great fishes**, *an hundred and fifty and three: and for all there were so many,* **yet was not the net broken**.

Jesus instructed them to bring their catch on shore and secure it. When Peter had made a count there were 153 great fish, which was a huge catch indeed, and yet in spite of the size the net was not damaged.

12 Jesus saith unto them, **Come and dine**. *And none of* **the disciples durst ask him, Who art thou? knowing that it was the Lord.**

13 Jesus then cometh, and taketh bread, and giveth them, and fish likewise.

14 **This is now the third time that Jesus shewed himself to his disciples, after that he was risen from the dead.**

Even though this was the third time Jesus had appeared to them, His resurrected form was enough different to them that they did not recognize Him, but they dared not ask Him who he was, and yet they knew it was the Savior. When their boats and catch was secure He bid them to partake of the prepared meal of bread and fish. This assistance rendered in catching a huge haul of great fish shows the Savior was well aware of the physical needs and well-being of their families and, when properly prepared and salted, this good fortune would take care of their family for an extended period of time. The work involved would take a few days and Jesus made or reaffirmed the appointment for His appearance on the Mount in Galilee.

Matthew 28:16 ¶ **Then the eleven disciples went away into Galilee, into a mountain where Jesus had appointed them.**

17 And when **they saw him, they worshipped him: but some doubted.**

18 And **Jesus came and spake unto them, saying, All power is given unto me in heaven and in earth**.

1 Corinthians 15:6 After that, **he was seen of above five hundred brethren at once;** *of whom the greater part remain unto this present, but some are fallen asleep.*

7 **After that, he was seen of James; then of all the apostles**.

While preparing their catch of fish over the next few days, the disciples had time to acquaint others of the appearance of Jesus and inform them of the appointment at the mountain. The day came when everyone went into the interior of Galilee and met with the savior. When they saw the Savior, they worshiped Him, even though some of the 500[239] among whom some doubted, and were not yet convinced of the actual corporeity of His resurrection. Jesus reassured them all power in Heaven and Earth had been given to Him, affirming His absolute God ship, and they became living witnesses.[240]

John 21:15 ¶ So **when they had dined, Jesus saith to Simon Peter,** *Simon, son of Jonas,* **lovest thou me more than these?** *He saith unto him,* **Yea, Lord**; *thou knowest that I love thee.* **He saith unto him, Feed my lambs**.

16 He saith to him again **the second time, Simon, son of Jonas, lovest thou me?** *He saith unto him,* **Yea, Lord; thou knowest that I love thee**. *He saith unto him,* **Feed my sheep.**

17 He saith unto him **the third time,** *Simon, son of Jonas,* **lovest thou me?** *Peter was grieved because he said unto him the third time, Lovest thou me? And he said unto him,* **Lord, thou knowest all things; thou knowest that I love thee**. *Jesus saith unto him,* **Feed my sheep.**

After completion of convincing instruction, Jesus assured all in attendance of His supreme authority and those commissioned by Him were to minister in His name, and by a power that no man could give or take away.

---

[239] 1 Cor. 15:6
[240] JTC p.694

When they had dinned, and were gazing out over His tender flock of disciples, Jesus, knowing Peter was not fully converted yet, called upon him three times to assert his love for Him. Peter reassured Jesus that he did love Him, and each time the Savior adjured him to "feed my sheep", and in so doing Peter was given his commission as chief Apostle and the opportunity to erase the fact he averred thrice, "he knew not the Man".

> *John 21:18 Verily, verily, I say unto thee,* **When thou wast young, thou girdedst thyself, and walkedst whither thou wouldest: but when thou shalt be old, thou shalt stretch forth thy hands, and another shall gird thee, and carry thee whither thou wouldest not.*
>
> *19 This spake he,* **signifying by what death he should glorify God**. *And when he had spoken this, he saith unto him, Follow me.*

Peter had pledged, "I will lay down my life for thy sake."[241] Jesus reminded Peter when he was young he went whenever and wherever he desired to go. Since Peter had vowed to lay down his life for the Savior, then when he is old this disciple will truly do so. This analogy points to crucifixion and thus signifies the death by which Peter should find a place among the martyrs. Peter would truly follow the Savior and be crucified with hands stretched forth on the cross, girded with the loin cloth of the criminal and carried to his execution.

> *John 21:20 Then* **Peter, turning about, seeth the disciple whom Jesus loved** *following; which also leaned on his breast at supper, and said, Lord, which is he that betrayeth thee?*
>
> *21 Peter seeing him saith to Jesus,* **Lord, and what shall this man do?**
>
> *22* **Jesus saith unto him, If I will that he tarry till I come, what is that to thee?** *follow thou me.*
>
> *23* **Then went this saying** *abroad among the brethren,* **that that disciple should not die:** *yet Jesus* <u>said not</u> *unto him, He shall not die; but,* **If I will that he tarry till I come,** *what is that to thee?*

Peter accepting his fate turned and, looking back over his shoulder, inquired what was to become of John? Jesus said, what difference does this make to you, but he shall not die and I will that he should tarry here till I come? This was an admonition to Peter to follow his own course and the road charted for him by the Master.

> *D&C 7:1 And the Lord said unto me:* **John, my beloved, what desirest thou?** *For if you shall ask what you will, it shall be granted unto you.*
>
> *2 And I said unto him:* **Lord, give unto me power over death, that I may live and bring souls unto thee.**
>
> *3 And the Lord said unto me:* **Verily, verily, I say unto thee, because thou desirest this thou shalt tarry until I come in my glory**, *and shalt prophesy before nations, kindreds, tongues and people.*
>
> *4 And* **for this cause the Lord said unto Peter: If I will that he tarry till I come, what is that to thee?** *For he desired of me that he might bring souls unto me, but thou desiredst that thou mightest speedily come unto me in my kingdom.*

Thus, we know John lives in his embodied state and shall remain in the flesh until the Lord's yet future advent. John continues to bring souls to the Lord.

To this, John adds his testimony;

> *John 21:24* **This is the disciple which testifieth of these things, and wrote these things: and we know that his testimony is true.**
>
> *25 And* **there are also many other things which Jesus did**, *the which, if they should be written every one, I suppose that* **even the world itself could not contain the books that should be written**. *Amen.*

John states clearly, that which he has written is true but however, it is only a small portion of what Jesus did. There are many things written which won't be dealt with here.

> *Acts 1:2* **Until the day in which he was taken up, after that he through the Holy Ghost had given commandments unto the apostles whom he had chosen:**
>
> *3 To whom* **also he shewed himself alive after his passion** *by many infallible proofs,* **being seen of them** <u>**forty days**</u>, *and speaking of the things pertaining to the kingdom of God:*

---

[241] John 13:36-38

After His resurrection, and before He was taken up, the Savior showed individuals and groups of people infallible proofs that He had a body and was indeed immortal. Jesus instructed them of the many things in this regard and much else that pertained to their relationship, and how they should conduct themselves, concerning the needed requirements to enter the kingdom of heaven. Jesus thus administered to them forty days before He was taken up to take His rightful place with our Father.

*Luke 24:49 ¶ And, behold, **I send the promise of my Father upon you: but tarry ye in the city of Jerusalem, until ye be endued with power from on high.***

*Acts 1:4 And, being assembled together with them, **commanded them that they should not depart from Jerusalem, but wait for the promise of the Father, which, saith he, ye have heard of me.***
*5 For John truly baptized with water; but **ye shall be baptized with the Holy Ghost not many days hence***

As the apostles and those that were with them had been organizing the church structure, doing some missionary work and receiving instruction, they all had eventually traveled from Galilee back to Jerusalem. The Savior instructed them to remain there and the promise of the Father would be realized, at which time they would be endued with power from high and be baptized with the coming of the Holy Ghost.

*Luke 24:50 ¶ And **he led them out as far as to Bethany, and he lifted up his hands, and blessed them.***

*Acts 1:6 When they therefore were come together, they asked of him, saying, Lord, **wilt thou at this time restore again the kingdom to Israel?***
*7 And he said unto them, It is not for you to know the times or the seasons, which the **Father hath put in his own power.***
*8 But **ye shall receive power, after that the Holy Ghost is come upon you: and ye shall be witnesses unto me both in Jerusalem, and in all Judæa, and in Samaria, and unto the uttermost part of the earth.***

The Lord had led them as far as Bethany, there was question still in the minds many "wilt thou at this time restore again the kingdom of Israel?" Jesus answered them by telling them, this is reserved to Gods' power and it will be at His time and it is not for you to know. However, Jesus assured them they would receive power from the Holy Ghost to be witnesses of Him and what He has done, and they should go forth unto the uttermost part of the earth.

*Matt 28:19 ¶ **Go ye therefore, and teach all nations, baptizing them in the name of the Father, and of the Son, and of the Holy Ghost:***
*20 **Teaching them to observe all things whatsoever I have commanded you: and, lo, I am with you alway, even unto the end of the world. Amen.***

As the time of His ascension drew nigh, the Lord said unto the eleven apostles: "Go ye into all the world, and preach the gospel to every creature. He that believeth and is baptized shall be saved; but he that believeth not shall be damned. And these signs shall follow them that believe; in my name, shall they cast out devils; they shall speak with new tongues; they shall take up serpents; and if they drink any deadly thing, it shall not hurt them; they shall lay hands on the sick, and they shall recover." In contrast with their earlier commission, under which they were sent only "to the lost sheep of the house of Israel," they were now to go to Jew and Gentile, bond and free, to mankind at large, of whatever nation, country, or tongue. Salvation, through faith in Jesus the Christ, followed by repentance and baptism, was to be freely offered to all; the rejection of the offer thenceforth would bring condemnation. Signs and miracles were promised to "follow them that believe," thus confirming their faith in the power divine; but no intimation was given that such manifestations were to precede belief, as baits to catch the credulous wonder-seeker.[242]

---
[242] JTC p.605

And with this power they were to go forth not only to Jerusalem, Judea and Samaria, but to the uttermost parts of the world, teaching about Jesus the Christ and the commandments of God and baptizing them in the name of the Father, and of the son, and of the Holy Ghost. Jesus reminded them He would be with always, even to the end of the world.

*Mark 16:19 ¶ **So then after the Lord had spoken unto them, he was received up into heaven, and sat on the right hand of God.***

*Luke 24:51 **And it came to pass**, while he blessed them, **he was parted from them, and carried up into heaven.***
*Luke 24:52 And **they worshipped him, and returned to Jerusalem with great joy:***

*Acts 1:9 And when he had spoken these things, **while they beheld, he was taken up; and a cloud received him out of their sight.***
*10 And **while they looked steadfastly toward heaven as he went up**, behold, **two men stood by them in white apparel;***
*11 Which also said, **Ye men of Galilee, why stand ye gazing up into heaven?** this same Jesus, which is taken up from you into heaven, **shall so come in like manner as ye have seen him go into heaven.***
*12 Then **returned they unto Jerusalem** from the mount called Olivet, which is from Jerusalem a sabbath day's journey.*

While the apostles stood gazing upward, two men in white apparel assured them that this same Jesus will return in a like manner as ye have seen him go into heaven.

Worshipfully and with great joy the apostles returned to Jerusalem, there to await the coming of the Comforter. The Lord's ascension was accomplished; it was truly a literal departure of a material Being as His resurrection had been an actual return of His spirit to His own corporeal body, theretofore dead. With the world abode and yet abides the promise, that Jesus the Christ, the same Being who ascended from Olivet in His immortalized of flesh and bones, shall return, descending from the heavens, in similarly material form and substance.[243]

*Acts1:13 And **when they were come in, they went up into an upper room**, where abode both Peter, and James, and John, and Andrew, Philip, and Thomas, Bartholomew, and Matthew, James the son of Alphæus, and Simon Zelotes, and Judas the brother of James.*
*Acts 1:14 **These all continued with one accord in prayer and supplication, with the women, and Mary the mother of Jesus, and with his brethren.***

*Luke 24:53 **And were continually in the temple**, praising and blessing God. Amen.*

*Mark 16:20 **And they went forth, and preached everywhere, the Lord working with them, and confirming the word with signs following. Amen.***

As Jesus was sent by the Father into the world, He now sends those He has been given, past and present, into the world to declare the truth. The Savior prays they will be able to consecrate their lives by the example and teaching as He has. The Son prays for all the disciples and those who believe in their words to become one in obtaining their salvation.

And thus begins the Apostolic Ministry!

REV

---

[243] JTC p.697

Final Harmony of the 4 Gospels

Supper @ Bethany

Event	Location	Matt.	Mark	Luke	John
Caiaphas prophesy that Jesus should die for the nation					11:47-52
To Jerusalem for Passover					11:55-57

7th day Sabbath (Saturday)	Location	Matthew	Mark	Luke	John
The Sixth day before Passover	Bethany				12:1
A supper at Martha & Mary's	Bethany				12:2
Jesus anointed by Mary	Bethany	(26:6-13}	(14:3-9)		12:3
Judas Protest-Jesus, let her alone	Bethany				12:4-8
Conspiracy against Lazarus	Bethany & Jerusalem				12:9-11

Triumphal Entry

1st day, - 10 Nissan,- (Sunday)	Location	Matthew	Mark	Luke	John
Prophecy fulfilled-ride in on an ass & a colt	Mount of Olives	21:1-7	11:1-7	19:28-35	
Triumphal Entry	Jerusalem	21:8-11	11:8-10	19:36-38	12:12-18
Pharisees Disapprove	Jerusalem			19:39-40	12:19
Visits Temple	Jerusalem		11:11		
Greeks desired to see Jesus	Out-side Temple				12:20-22
Jesus declare His mission & Then hid himself	Out-side Temple				12:23-36
Returned to Bethany	Bethany		11:11		

Return to Jerusalem-Cleanses Temple

2nd day, -11 Nissan, (Monday)	Location	Matthew	Mark	Luke	John
Returns to Jerusalem &wept				19:41-44	
Curses fig tree	Mount		11:12-14		
Moneychangers cast out	Temple	21:12-14	11:15-17	19:45-46	
Priests & scribes displeased	Temple	21:15-16	11:18	19:47-48	
Returns to Bethany	Bethany	21:17	11:19		

Return to Jerusalem-Day of Authority

3rd day, 12 Nissan, (Tuesday)	Location	Matthew	Mark	Luke	John
Withered fig tree and discourse on faith	Road to Jerusalem	21:18-22	11:20-26		
Priests challenge Jesus' authority	Temple	21:23-27	11:27-33	20:1-8	
Parable of two sons	Temple	21:28-32			
Wicked husbandmen	Temple	21:33-41	12:1-9	20:9-16	
Rejected corner stone	Temple	21:42-46	12:10-12	20:17-18	
Royal Marriage	Temple	22:1-14			
Question on tribute to Caesar	Temple	22:-15-22	12:13-17	20:19-26	
Marriage after resurrection	Temple	22:23-33	12:18-27	20:27-38	

Sadducees					
Great commandment Pharisees	Temple	22:34-40	12:28-34		
Who is the Father of Christ	Temple	22:41-46	12:35-37	20:39-44	
Scribes & Pharisees condemned	Temple	23:1-36	12:38-40	20:45-47	
Jesus Lament over Jerusalem	Temple	23:37-39			12:37-41
Some believed	Temple				12:42-43

Afternoon 3rd day

The widows mite	Against the treasury		12:41-44	21:1-4	
Destruction of Temple	Depart Temple	24:1-2	13:1-2	21:5-6	
Olivet Discourse		JST 24			
False Christs & False Prophets & Great calamities	Mount of Olives	24: 3-31	13:3-31	21:7-28	
Parable of fig tree -watch	Mount of Olives	24: 32-41	13:32-37	21:29-33	
Watch therefore	Mount of Olives	24:42-51	13:38	21:34-38	
Parable of Ten Virgins	Mount of Olives	25:1-13			
Parable of entrusted Talents	Mount of Olives	25:14-30			
Final and inevitable Judgment	Mount of Olives	25:31-46			

Day of Rest, Preparation & Betrayal

4th day, 13th Nisssan, (Wednesday)	Location	Matthew	Mark	Luke	John
Preparing the Lamb	Bethany	Exodus			
Feast day in Two days	Bethany	26:1-2			
Jesus betrayal foretold	Bethany	26:2			
Chief priests plot to kill Jesus- not on feast day	Jerusalem	26:3-5	14:1-2	22:1-2	
Woman anoints Jesus	Bethany (reminder)	26:5-13	14:3-9		
Judas-final arrangements to betray Jesus	Jerusalem	26:14-16	14:10-11	22:3-6	

Paschal Lamb Sacrifice and Last Supper

5th day, 14th Nissan, (Thursday)	Location	Matthew	Mark	Luke	John
Preparing the Passover	Jerusalem	26:17-19	14:12-16	22:7-13	
One will betray me (as they ate)	Jerusalem	26:20-25	14:17-21	22:14-18	13:1-3
Instituted the sacrament	Jerusalem	26:26-29	14:22-25	22:19-20	
Jesus washes their feet	Jerusalem				13:4-11
Jesus explains service	Jerusalem				13:12-17
Jesus dismisses Judas from table	Jerusalem			22:21-23	13:18-30
Strife at table	Jerusalem			22:24-30	
Ye can't go where I go, so Love one another	Jerusalem				13:31-35
Peter to deny Jesus	Jerusalem			22;31-34	13:36-38
Buy a sword	Jerusalem			22:35-38	

Night on the Mount of Olives & Intercessory Prayer

AM 6th day, *15th Nissan*, (Thursday)	Location	Matthew	Mark	Luke	John
Went to Mount of Olives	Mount	26:30	14:26	22:39	
Let not your heart be troubled (many mansions)	Mount				14:1-5
I am the way (show us the father)					14:6-14
Keep my commandments (Father to give another comforter)	Mount				14:15-31
Jesus the vine (ye are the branches)	Mount				15:1-9
Keep the commandments & Love one another	Mount				15:10-17
World will hate you	Mount				15:18-25
Send the comforter	Mount				15:26-27
All ye shall be offended	Mount	26:31-32	14:27-28		16:1-6
Peter, I will not be offended	Mount	26:33-35	14:29-31		
Jesus to Leave & send the Holy Ghost	Mount				16:7
Mission of the Holy Ghost	Mount				16:8-15
Sorrow of His death & Joy in His Resurrection	Mount				16:16-22
Relationship between the Father & Son & Apostles	Mount				16:23-30
Apostles to be scattered	Mount				16:31-33
Intercessory Prayer (Eternal Life, prays for Apostles & Saints, Son & Father & all are one)	Gethsemane				17:1-5, 6-19, 20-26

Prayer @ Gethsemane & Arrest

AM 6th day, *15th Nissan*, (Thursday)	Location	Matthew	Mark	Luke	John
Enter Gethsemane	Gethsemane	26:36	14:32	22:40	18:1
Sit ye here, while I pray	Gethsemane	26:37-44	14:32-41	22:41-46	
Judas Betrayal	Gethsemane	26:45-50	14:42-46	22:47-48	18:2-3
Whom seek ye? They fell backwards	Gethsemane				18:4-7
Let these go	Gethsemane				18:8-9
Peter defend Jesus w/sword	Gethsemane	26:51-54	14:47	22:49-51	18:10-11
Jesus arrested & disciples flee	Gethsemane	26:55-56	14:48-52	22:51-53	18:12
Jesus before Annas &Caiaphas	Jerusalem	26:57-68	14:53-65	22:54-55	18:13-14 18:19-24
Denial by Peter (1st, 2nd & 3rd time)	Jerusalem	26:69-75	14:66-72	22:56-62	18:15-18 18:25-27

Convocation Day & First Day of Unleavened Bread

6th day, *15th Nissan*, (Friday)	Location	Matthew	Mark	Luke	John

| Convocation, High day, Passover day, 1st day of unleavened bread | Jerusalem (kill not on feast day) | Exodus 12 (as per law) (26:3-5) | (14: 1-2) | (22:1-2) | |

First Fruits & Regular 7th day Sabbath

7th day, *16th Nissan*, (Saturday)	**Location**	**Matthew**	**Mark**	**Luke**	**John**
Feast day of First Fruits & regular 7th day Sabbath	Jerusalem	Exodus 12 (as per law)			

Formal Trial

8th day, *17th Nissan*, (Sunday)	**Jerusalem**	**Matthew**	**Mark**	**Luke**	**John**
The formal Trial	Jerusalem			22:63-71	

Before Pilate & Herod

9th day, *18th Nissan*, (Monday)	**Location**	**Matthew**	**Mark**	**Luke**	**John**
Jesus before Pilate	Jerusalem	27:1-2	15:1-5	23:1-6	
Judas Hanged himself	Jerusalem	27:3-10			
Jesus sent to Herod (Many words)	Jerusalem	27:11-14		23:7-9	
Accused by Priests & Scribes	Jerusalem			23:10	
Jesus mocked by soldiers & sent to Pilate the same day	Jerusalem			23:11-12	

Trial before Pilate

10th day, *19th Nissan*, (Tuesday)	**Location**	**Matthew**	**Mark**	**Luke**	**John**
Pilate 2nd time, (called people together and tried to release Jesus)	Jerusalem			23:13	18:28-32
Pilate and Herod found no guilt – wanted to release Jesus	Jerusalem	27:15-18	15:6-8	23:14-16	18:33-40
2nd time to release Jesus	Jerusalem	27:19-21	15:9-11	23:17-19	
Brought scourged Jesus before them	Jerusalem				19:1-7
3rd time tried to release Jesus	Jerusalem	27:22-23	15:12-14	23:20-25	19:8-12
Pilate washed hands- 6th hr.	Jerusalem	27:24-25			19:13-15
Released Barabbas and scourged Jesus	Jerusalem	27:26-28	15:15	23:26	19:16
Final scourging thru the night	Jerusalem		15:15-19		

Crucifixion on Preparation Day

11th day, 20th Nissan, (Wednesday)	*Location*	*Matthew*	*Mark*	*Luke*	*John*
Preparation Day			15:42		19:31
To Calvary- Simon bears cross	Jerusalem	27:31-32	15:20-21	23:26	19:16-17
Spoke to women following- weep for yourselves	Jerusalem			23:27-31	
CRUCIFIED --- 3rd Hr.	Golgotha	27:33-35	15:23-25	23:32-33	19:18,

	Location	Matthew	Mark	Luke	John
His 1st Utterance – forgive them	Golgotha			23:34	
Superscription – Between to thieves – took garments	Golgotha	27:36-38	15:26-28	23:38	19:19-22, 23-24
Mocking & scoffing	Golgotha	27:39-44	15:29-32	23:35-42	
2nd Utterance – today in paradise	Golgotha			23:43	
3rd utterance-behold thy son	Golgotha				19:25-27
Darkness over the earth – 6th to 9th Hr.	Golgotha	27:45	15:33	23:44-45	
4th Utterance-My God has thou forsaken Me?	Golgotha	27:46	15:34-35		
5th utterance- I thirst	Golgotha	27:47-49	15:36		19:28-29
6th utterance-it is finished	Golgotha				19:30
7th utterance-I commend my spirit		27:50	15:37	23:46	19:30
Great earthquake & graves opened & veil rent	Golgotha	27:51-53	15:38		
Testimony of Centurion & women	Golgotha	27:54-56	15:39-41	23:46-49	

Burial

11th day, 20th Nissan, (Wednesday Night)	Location	Matthew	Mark	Luke	John
Preparation Day	Jerusalem	27:62	15:42	23:54	19:31-37,42
Joseph of Arimathaea begged the body of Jesus	Golgotha	27:57-58	15:43-45	23:50-52	19:38
Prepared Jesus for burial-Nicodemus 100 weight of Aloes & rolled stone closed	New tomb	27:59-60	15:46	23:53-53	19:39-42
Women observed where	New tomb	27:61	15:47	23:55	

Convocation Day

12th day, 21st Nissan, (Thursday)	Location	Matthew	Mark	Luke	John
High Day Convocation	Jerusalem High Day observance		0	0	0
Priests & Pharisees wanted a guard set	Jerusalem	27:62-66			

Regular Week Day

13th day, 22nd Nissan, (Friday)	Jerusalem				
Women prepared spices & ointments	Jerusalem			23:55-56	

7th Day Sabbath Jerusalem

14th day, 23rd Nissan, (Saturday)	Location	Matthew	Mark	Luke	John
Women rested on Sabbath	Jerusalem			23-56	

Resurrection

15th day, 24th Nissan, (Sunday)	*Location*	*Matthew*	*Mark*	*Luke*	*John*
Mary Magdalene & Mary—while it was still dark	Tomb				20:1
Ran & told Peter & John, who ran to the tomb	Jerusalem				20:2-10
Mary & other Mary were ahead of other women	Jerusalem & Tomb	28:1			
Women went to sepulcher & was told of resurrection	Tomb	28:2-8	16:1-8	24:1-8	
Mary outside sepulcher & Jesus appeared to her	Tomb		16:9		20:11-17
Jesus appeared to women	Tomb	28:9-10			
Mary & Women told them of the resurrection	Jerusalem		16:10-11	24:9-11	20:18
Peter returned to tomb	Tomb			24:12	
Guards went to priests	Jerusalem	28:11-15			
Appeared to other two			16:12-13	24:13-35	
Same day appeared to apostles	Jerusalem		16:14-18	24:36-48	20:19-23

Ministry & Ascension						
14th *Nissan* & after	Location	Mathew	Mark	Luke	John	Acts
Doubting Thomas	Jerusalem				20:24-25	
After 8 days Christ appeared to Thomas & gathered apostles	Galilee				20:26-29	
Many other signs – not written in this book	Galilee				20:30-31	
Peter, I go a fishing – caught nothing	Galilee				21:1-3	
Jesus stood on shore – they knew him not	Galilee				21:4	
Have ye any meat? Cast your net on the right	Galilee				21:5-7	
Recognized Him, great catch of fish, dined Him in	Galilee				21:8-13	
Third appearance to apostles	Galilee				21:14	
Peter, feed my sheep	Galilee				21:15-17	
Signifies Peters death	Galilee				21:18-19	
John to tarry till Jesus comes	Galilee				21:20-23	
Johns Testimony	Galilee				21:23-24	
Appointment at mountain	Galilee	28:16-18				

Ministered to them for 40 days	Eventually to Jerusalem					1:1-3
Told to Remain in Jerusalem When Israel to be restored	Jerusalem			24:49		1:4-8
Led them as far as Bethany	Bethany			24:50		
Preach to the world	Bethany	28:19-20				
Christ sits on right hand of God			16:19-20	24:51		1:9
They returned to Jerusalem	Jerusalem			24:52-53		

Compiled by:
Gordon L Ormesher
Cocolalla, Idaho
208 946-0998

The Law of Moses

"All Things Denote There Is a God" An all-wise Creator has structured all the creations of his hands in such a way, not only to call attention to himself as the Maker, Preserver, and Upholder of all things, but to bear record of the nature and kind of Being he is.

Then comes the question: " Unto what shall I liken these kingdoms, that ye may understand? " There follows a parable which teaches that he will visit " every kingdom " — and the inhabitants thereof — " in its hour, and in its time, and in its season. " But our immediate concern is the divine announcement: " All these are kingdoms, and any man who hath seen any or the least of these hath seen God moving in his majesty and power. I say unto you, he hath seen him; nevertheless, he who came unto his own was not comprehended. " It is then said that in a future day the faithful shall " comprehend even God, " as pertaining to which time it is written: " Then shall ye know that ye have seen me. " (D & C 88: 40 - 62.)

Gospel Taught with Similitudes.

To crystallize in our minds the eternal verities which we must accept and believe to be saved, to dramatize their true meaning and import with an impact never to be forgotten, to center our attention on these saving truths, again and again and again, the Lord uses similitudes. Abstract principles may easily be forgotten or their deep meaning overlooked, but visual performances and actual experiences are registered on the mind in such a way as never to be lost. It is one thing to talk of faith as an abstract principle, another to see the Red Sea parted by its power. It is one thing to talk of the word of God coming down from heaven, another to actually gather and taste the angelic manna. It is one thing to teach that God is our Father in an abstract and impersonal way, thus expecting all Christendom to envision that he is a personal being in whose image man is created. It is another thing to say: Here is his Son; he is in the express image of his Father's person; he is in the similitude of the Father; observe what he does and see how he acts and you will know what the Father is like, for God is in Christ manifesting himself to men.

" I . . . am the Lord thy God, " is the introduction of Jehovah to his people. Such is the voice of him who knows all things, reveals what he will, and chooses what his children shall be taught. How, then, does he present his message? " I have also spoken by the prophets, " he says, " and I have multiplied visions, and used similitudes, by the ministry of the prophets. " (Hosea 12: 9 - 10.) He uses ordinances, rites, acts, and performances; he uses similarities, resemblances, and similitudes so that whatever is done will remind all who are aware of it of a greater and more important reality. He uses similes; he uses parables; he uses allegories. If two things have the same semblance or form, if they are like each other in appearance, if they correspond in qualities, it may suit his purposes to compare them. To liken one thing to another is one of the best teaching procedures.

" My soul delighteth in proving unto my people the truth of the coming of Christ, " says Jacob, the Nephite, " for, for this end hath the law of Moses been given; and all things which have been given of God from the beginning of the world, unto man, are the typifying of him. " (2 Ne. 11: 4.) It follows that if we had sufficient insight, we would see in every gospel ordinance, in every rite that is part of revealed religion, in every performance commanded of God, in all things Deity gives his people, something that typifies the eternal ministry of the Eternal Christ. The performance of all such ordinances or acts, from Adam to Christ, falls thereby into the category of Messianic acts and performances. We shall now consider samples of these matters and note some of their Messianic implications.

" Why Dost Thou Offer Sacrifices? " In point of time one of the first great symbolic ordinances was that of sacrifice, animal sacrifice, the shedding of the blood of chosen beasts in similitude of that which was to be in time's meridian. After Adam and Eve were cast out of Eden to till the dust whence they came and to gain the experiences available only in a mortal probation, the Lord " gave unto them commandments, that they should worship the Lord their God, and should offer the firstlings of their flocks, for an offering unto the Lord. And Adam was obedient unto the commandments of the Lord. " He complied with the heavenly commandments and worshiped the Lord, in manner and form, as that holy being had directed, including the offering of sacrifices. We do not know the details and specifics of his worship, except that the gospel plan was given to him, line upon line and precept upon precept, until he was the possessor of its everlasting fullness.

….." an angel of the Lord appeared unto Adam, saying: Why dost thou offer sacrifices unto the Lord? And Adam said unto him: I know not, save the Lord commanded me. "

In any event, " the angel spake, saying: This thing is a similitude of the sacrifice of the Only Begotten of the Father, which is full of grace and truth. Wherefore, thou shalt do all that thou doest in the name of the Son, and thou shalt repent and call upon God in the name of the Son forevermore. " (Moses 5: 4 - 8.)

There we have it. Sacrifice is a similitude. It is performed to typify the coming sacrifice of the Son of God. For four thousand long years, from Adam to that bleak day when our Lord was lifted up by sinful men, all of his righteous followers sought remission of their sins through sacrifice. It was an ordinance of the Melchizedek Priesthood; it antedated the law of Moses by two and a half millenniums,

For our purposes now it suffices to say that such Messianic utterances as that of Isaiah, that the Messiah should " make his soul an offering for sin " (Isa. 53: 10), or that of Lehi, that " he offereth himself a sacrifice for sin " (2 Ne. 2 : 7) , were well and perfectly understood by all Israel and all others in whose hearts the light of truth dwelt, and that the righteous of all ages looked forward with hope to the day when the Lamb of God should be slain for the sins of the world. After the final great sacrifice on the cross, the use for the similitude that looked forward to our Lord's death ceased. Blood sacrifices became a thing of the past.

" Behold the Lamb of God " As the prophets sought for similitudes to use in teaching the great and eternal truths of salvation to the people, how natural it was for them to designate him who should sacrifice himself for the sins of the world as the Lamb of God. He was to be God's Son. He would bear " the sin of many. " (Isa. 53: 12.) He would lay down his life for his people. Through his atoning sacrifice the way would be open to gain a remission of sins. Sacrifices were performed in similitude of his infinite and eternal sacrifice. In large measure the firstlings of the flocks slain on the altars of sacrifice were lambs, lambs without spot or blemish. What could be more appropriate than to name Him who would make the supreme sacrifice, whose own shed blood would give efficacy and force to four thousand years of sacrificial ordinances, to designate him who came from God to sacrifice his soul as the Lamb of God.

And so, it was. In point of time, the first Messianic designation of Christ as the Lamb of which we have record came from the lips of Enoch, who " saw the day of the coming of the Son of Man, even in the flesh; and his soul rejoiced, saying: The Righteous is lifted up, and the Lamb is slain from the foundation of the world. " (Moses 7: 47.)

Thus, when Nephi saw in vision the Virgin of Nazareth who was to be " the mother of the Son of God, after the manner of the flesh, " and when he saw her " bearing a child in her arms, " he was also privileged to hear the angelic proclamation: " Behold the Lamb of God, yea, even the Son of the Eternal Father! " (1 Ne. 11: 13 - 21.)

Our New Testament accounts pick up the same manner of identifying Him who laid down his life in sacrifice for the sins of the world. As Lehi had foreseen, John the Baptist testified: " Behold the Lamb of God, which taketh away the sin of the world. " (John 1: 29.)

" This Do in Remembrance of Me "

Lest they forget, the Lord gave them the ordinance of sacrifice, an ordinance perfectly designed to keep them in remembrance of that which was to be. " This thing, " the angelic voice proclaimed, " is a similitude of the sacrifice of the Only Begotten of the Father. " (Moses 5: 7.)

As four thousand years of sacrifices kept the Lord's people in remembrance of what their Messiah would do for them in a garden and on a cross, so two thousand years of sacramental administrations have kept them in remembrance of what he did for them in time's meridian.

This sacred ordinance in which bread is eaten, in similitude and remembrance of our Lord's broken flesh, and in which water or wine is drunk, in similitude and remembrance of his spilt blood, will be found among the Lord's people so long as the earth shall stand.

As it is written: " He that will harden his heart, the same receiveth the lesser portion of the word; and he that will not harden his heart, to him is given the greater portion of the word, until it is given unto him to know the mysteries of God until he knows them in full. " (Alma 12: 9 – 10,)

The Law of Christ and the Law of Moses.

There are two laws — the law of Christ and the law of Moses. The one is the gospel, the other is the preparatory gospel. There are two sets of commandments — the commandments which assure a celestial inheritance, and the law of carnal commandments, which, standing alone, carry no such assurance of eternal reward. The one is for those who are " anxiously engaged in a good cause, " who " do many things of their own free will, " who use their agency to " bring to pass much righteousness "; the other is for those who are slothful and rebellious by nature, who need to be commanded in all things, who neglect good works unless they are compelled to perform them. (D & C 58: 26 - 27.) Of these two laws, John wrote " The law was given through Moses, but life and truth came through Jesus Christ. For the law was after a carnal commandment, to the administration of death; but the gospel was after the power of an endless life, through Jesus Christ, the Only Begotten Son, who is in the bosom of the Father. " (JST John 1: 17 - 18.)

And by conformity to its ordinances, all mankind may gain a celestial inheritance. It is, in fact, the law of a celestial kingdom and has been given to us mortals to qualify us to go where God and Christ and holy beings are " And they who are not sanctified through the law which I have given unto you, the Lord says, " even the law of Christ, must inherit another kingdom, even that of a terrestrial kingdom, or that of a telestial kingdom. For he who is not able to abide the law of a celestial kingdom cannot abide a celestial glory. " (D & C 88: 21 - 22.) Moses' law is the law of carnal commandments, or in other words the law which is concerned, in detail and specifically, with carnal and evil acts — warning, exhorting, encouraging, commanding, all to the end that men will be left without excuse and, hopefully, will avoid the snares of the evil one. Paul uses the name " the law of a carnal commandment " (Heb. 7: 16) to describe it, and also calls it " the law of commandments contained in ordinances " (Eph. 2: 15). Abinadi speaks of it as " a law of performances and of ordinances, a law which they were to observe strictly from day to day, to keep them in remembrance of God and their duty towards him. " (Mosiah 13: 30.) Our revelation, speaking of the preparatory gospel, says: " Which gospel is the gospel of repentance and of baptism, and the remission of sins, and the law of carnal commandments, which the Lord in his wrath caused to continue with the house of Aaron among the children of Israel until John. " (D & C 84: 27.) Historically, this law first came into being when Israel rejected the gospel and failed to live as Jehovah, their Lord, commanded them to do. Moses, having destroyed the tablets of stone on which the law as first revealed was written , received this commandment from the Lord: " Hew thee two other tables of stone , like unto the first , and I will write upon them also , the words of the law , according as they were written at the first on the tables which thou brakest; but it shall not be according to the first, for I will take away the priesthood out of their midst ; therefore my holy order , and the ordinances thereof , shall not go before them ; for my presence shall not go up in their midst , lest I destroy them . But I will give unto them the law as at the first, but it shall be after the law of a carnal commandment; for I have sworn in my wrath, that they shall not enter into my presence, into my rest, in the days of their pilgrimage. " (JST Ex. 34: 1 - 2)

Why There Was a Law of Moses

Why was there a law of Moses? Two reasons are apparent:

1. It was a divine and uplifting system of goodness and right. Those who obeyed its precepts and kept its ordinances bettered themselves temporally and spiritually. They were in the line of their duty, received revelations, and came to know their God. While the world around them was in darkness, the morning rays of divine truth were opening their vision to the wonders and glories mortal man might obtain.

It was a preparatory gospel. And it is better to walk in godly paths for fear of the penalties of disobedience than not to walk in them at all.

Out of it have come nearly all the principles of ethics and decency that have been incorporated into our whole system of modern jurisprudence. And lest there be any doubt in anyone's mind as to the excellence and beauty of the Mosaic system, let us ponder this conclusion: Even now, after two thousand years of exposure to the new covenant, there are but few of earth's inhabitants who conform to the standards of decency, excellence, and righteousness that even approach those which God imposed upon his ancient covenant people by the mouth of Moses the great lawgiver.

2. Just as our conformity to gospel standards, while dwelling as lowly mortals apart from our Maker, prepares us to return to his presence with an inheritance of immortal glory, so the Mosaic standards prepared the chosen of Israel to believe and obey that gospel by conformity to which eternal life is won. The law of Moses was an Elias; it prepared the way for something far greater.

Hence, everything connected with the lesser law pointed to the higher law, or in other words it pointed to Christ and his gospel. Each Mosaic performance was so arranged and so set up that it was a type and a shadow of what was to be. Their sacrifices were performed in similitude of the coming sacrifice of their Messiah; the rituals out of which they gained forgiveness of sins were tokens of what was to be in the life of Him whose atonement made forgiveness possible; their every act, every ordinance, every performance — all that they did — pointed the hearts and minds of believing worshipers forward to Jesus Christ and him crucified. All this was understood by those among them who were faithful and true; the rebellious and slothful were like their modern counterparts, unbelieving, nonconforming, unsaved. It is the will of the Lord, and has been from the beginning, that all men everywhere should believe in Christ, accept the fullness of his everlasting gospel, and rely on the merits of his atoning sacrifice for salvation.

Yet the Lord God saw that his people were a stiff-necked people, and he appointed unto them a law, even the law of Moses. And many signs, and wonders, and types, and shadows showed he unto them, concerning his coming; and also, holy prophets spake unto them concerning his coming; and yet they hardened their hearts, and understood not that the law of Moses availeth nothing except it were through the atonement of his blood. " (Mosiah 3: 13 - 15)

With this same theme in mind , Abinadi said : " It was expedient that there should be a law given to the children of Israel , yea , even a very strict law ; for they were a stiff-necked people , quick to do iniquity , and slow to remember the Lord their

God; Therefore there was a law given them, yea, a law of performances and of ordinances, a law which they were to observe strictly from day to day, to keep them in remembrance of God and their duty towards him. But behold, I say unto you, that all these things were types of things to come." (Mosiah 13: 29 - 31.)

Paul named various of the Mosaic ordinances and performances and said they were a " shadow of heavenly things. " (Heb.8: 4 - 5.) The " meats and drinks, and diver's washings, and carnal ordinances, imposed on them until the time of reformation, " he said, were designed as " a figure for the time then present. " He spoke of the various formalities involved in sprinkling blood as " patterns " of things of a much higher nature. " The law, " he said, was " a shadow of good things to come. " (Heb. 9: 1 - 10, 19 - 23; 10: 1.) But perhaps Amulek's statement is the clearest and best of them all. He said: " This is the whole meaning of the law, every whit pointing to that great and last sacrifice; and that great and last sacrifice will be the Son of God, yea, infinite and eternal. " (Alma 34: 1)

Salvation Cannot Come by the Law of Moses, Israel had many wicked kings who led the chosen seed astray.

After some further doctrinal exposition, Abinadi said: " I say unto you that it is expedient that ye should keep the law of Moses as yet; but I say unto you, that the time shall come when it shall no more be expedient to keep the law of Moses. And moreover, I say unto you, that salvation doth not come by the law alone; and were it not for the atonement, which God himself shall make for the sins and iniquities of his people, that they must unavoidably perish, notwithstanding the law of Moses. " Following this he spoke of the strict and straitened nature of the restrictions and performances imposed in the law, and of how others, in addition to these false priests of Noah, had not understood the law; " And now, ought ye not to tremble and repent of your sins, and remember that only in and through Christ ye can be saved? Therefore, if ye teach the law of Moses, also teach that it is a shadow of those things which are to come — Teach them that redemption cometh through Christ the Lord, who is the very Eternal Father. " (Mosiah 13, 14, 15, and 16.)

Nephites Followed Both Moses and Christ but, they did so with a proper understanding, knowing that salvation was in Christ who should come and that " the law of Moses was a type of his coming. "

Law of Moses Fulfilled in Christ

If Jesus Christ was the promised Messiah, then the law of Moses was fulfilled in his coming. If he was not the Son of God, then the law of Moses is still in force, and we and all who seek religious truth should be engaged in a diligent performance of all its rites and ordinances.

Since all the sacrifices and performances of the law looked forward to and were in similitude of his atoning sacrifice, it follows that once he had shed his blood for the sins of repentant men, sacrifices should cease. In spite of these plain declarations, there were yet some among them who marveled and wondered concerning the law, and so our Lord climaxed his teachings to them by saying: " Marvel not that I said unto you that old things had passed away, and that all things had become new. Behold, I say unto you that the law is fulfilled that was given unto Moses. Behold, I am he that gave the law, and I am he who covenanted with my people Israel; therefore, the law in me is fulfilled, for I have come to fulfill the law; therefore, it hath an end. Behold, I do not destroy the prophets, for as many as have not been fulfilled in me, verily I say unto you, shall all be fulfilled.

And because I said unto you that old things have passed away, I do not destroy that which hath been spoken concerning things which are to come. For behold, the covenant which I have made with my people is not all fulfilled; but the law which was given unto Moses hath an end in me. Behold, I am the law, and the light. Look unto me, and endure to the end, and ye shall live; for unto him that endureth to the end will I give eternal life. Behold, I have given unto you the commandments; therefore, keep my commandments. And this is the law and the prophets, for they truly testified of me. " (3 Ne. 15: 2 - 10.) From all of this, can we do other than to conclude that if the law of Moses was divine, then Jesus Christ is the Messiah?

Sacrifice — A Form of Worship Sacrifice was a way of worship in Israel. The divine decree, given to Adam, that men should repent and call upon God in the name of the Son forevermore, was still in force among them. Compliance with that decree still required them to " offer the firstlings of their flocks " as sacrifices in " similitude of the sacrifice of the Only Begotten of the Father. " (Moses 5: 5 - 8.) In addition, through Moses they had received an intricate, extensive, and detailed sacrificial system, a system of performances and ordinances that called upon them to pledge new allegiance to the Lord each day of their lives. They did not inherit their sacrificial rites from their pagan neighbors, nor did they perform them in imitation of what other peoples were doing in that day and age.

Feast of the Passover — A Type of Christ Three times each year all male Israelites were commanded to appear before the Lord, at a place appointed, to worship him and renew their covenants. The first of these was the Feast of the Passover (including the Feast of Unleavened Bread); the Passover portion of the feast lasted one day, with the Feast of Unleavened Bread continuing for an additional seven. It was to celebrate the Passover that Joseph and Mary took the boy Jesus when he, having attained the age of twelve, was considered to be " a son of the law, " one upon whom its obligations then rested. It was there that he confounded the learned doctors of the law with his heaven - sent wisdom; it was there that he bore the first testimony, of which we have record, of his own divine Sonship. (Luke 2: 41 - 50)

Among other procedures, the Lord commanded, as found in Exodus 12:   1. " Your lamb shall be without blemish, a male of the first year, " signifying that the Lamb of God, pure and perfect, without spot or blemish, in the prime of his life, as the Paschal Lamb, would be slain for the sins of the world.   2. They were to take of the blood of the lamb and sprinkle it upon the doorposts of their houses , having this promise as a result: " And the blood shall be to you for a token upon the houses where ye are: and when I see the blood, I will pass over you, and the plague shall not be upon you to destroy you, " signifying that the blood of Christ, which should fall as drops in Gethsemane and flow in a stream from a pierced side as he hung on the cross, would cleanse and save the faithful; and that , as those in Israel were saved temporally because the blood of a sacrificial lamb was sprinkled on the doorposts of their houses , so the faithful of all ages would wash their garments in the blood of the Eternal Lamb and from him receive an eternal salvation . And may we say that as the angel of death passed by the families of Israel because of their faith — as Paul said of Moses, " through faith he kept the Passover, and the sprinkling of blood, lest he that destroyed the firstborn should touch them " (Heb. 11: 28) — even so shall the Angel of Life give eternal life to all those who rely on the blood of the Lamb.   3. As to the sacrifice of the lamb, the decree was, " Neither shall ye break a bone thereof, " signifying that when the Lamb of God was sacrificed on the cross, though they broke the legs of the two thieves to induce death, yet they brake not the bones of the Crucified One " that the scripture should be fulfilled, A bone of him shall not be broken. " (John 19: 31 - 36.)   4. As to eating the flesh of the sacrificial lamb, the divine word was, " No uncircumcised person shall eat thereof, " signifying that the blessings of the gospel are reserved for those who come into the fold of Israel, who join the Church, who carry their part of the burden in bearing off the kingdom; signifying also that those who eat his flesh and drink his blood, as he said, shall have eternal life and he will raise them up at the last day. (John 6: 54.)   5. As " the Lord smote all the firstborn in the land of Egypt " because they believed not the word of the Lord delivered to them by Moses and Aaron, even so should the Firstborn of the Father, who brings life to all who believe in his holy name, destroy worldly people at the last day, destroy all those who are in the Egypt of darkness, whose hearts are hardened as were those of Pharaoh and his minions.   6. On the first and seventh days of the Feast of Unleavened Bread, the Israelites were commanded to hold holy convocations in which no work might be done except the preparation of their food. These were occasions for preaching and explaining and exhorting and testifying. We go to sacrament meetings to be built up in faith and in testimony. Ancient Israel attended holy convocations for the same purposes. Knowing that all things operate by faith, would it be amiss to draw the conclusion that it is as easy for us to look to Christ and his spilt blood for eternal salvation as it was for them of old to look to the blood of a sacrificed lamb, sprinkled on doorposts, to give temporal salvation, when the angel of death swept through the land of Egypt? It was, of course, while Jesus and the Twelve were keeping the Feast of the Passover that our Lord instituted the ordinance of the sacrament, to serve essentially the same purposes served by the sacrifices of the preceding four millenniums. After that final Passover day and its attendant lifting up upon the cross of the true Paschal Lamb, the day for the proper celebration of the ancient feast ceased. After that Paul was able to say: " Christ our Passover is sacrificed for us, " and to give the natural exhortation that flowed therefrom: " Therefore let us keep the feast, not with old leaven, neither with the leaven of malice and wickedness; but with the unleavened bread of sincerity and truth. " (1 Cor. 5: 7 - 8.)

The Day of Atonement — A Type of Christ Now we come to the heart and core and center of the whole Mosaic structure, namely, the atonement of the Lord Jesus Christ. This is what the law of Moses is all about. The law itself was given so that men might believe in Christ and know that salvation comes in and through his atoning sacrifice and in no other way. Every principle, every precept, every doctrinal teaching, every rite, ordinance, and performance, every word and act — all that appertained to, was revealed in, and grew out of the ministry of Moses, and all the prophets who followed him — all of it was designed and prepared to enable men to believe in Christ, to submit to his laws, and to gain the full blessings of that atonement which he alone could accomplish. And the chief symbolisms, the most perfect similitudes, the types and shadows without peer, were displayed before all the people once each year, on the Day of Atonement.

On one day each year — the tenth day of the seventh month — Israel's high priest of the Levitical order, the one who sat in Aaron's seat, was privileged to enter the Holy of Holies in the house of the Lord, to enter as it were the presence of Jehovah, and there make an atonement for the sins of the people. In the course of much sacrificial symbolism, he cleansed himself, the sanctuary itself, the priesthood bearers as a whole, and all of the people. Sacrificial animals were slain and their blood sprinkled on the mercy seat and before the altar; incense was burned, and all of the imagery and symbolism of the ransoming ordinances was carried out. One thing, applicable to this day only, is of great moment. Two goats were selected, lots were cast, and the name of Jehovah was placed upon one goat; the other was called Azazel, the scapegoat. The Lord's goat was then sacrificed as the Great Jehovah would be in due course, but upon the scapegoat were placed all of the sins of the people, which burden the scapegoat then carried away into the wilderness. The high priest, as the law required, " lay both his hands upon the head of the live goat " and confessed " over him all the iniquities of the children of Israel, and all their transgressions in all their sins, putting them upon the head of the goat. " The goat then bore upon him " all their iniquities unto a land not inhabited, " even as the Promised Messiah should bear the sins of many. " For on that day shall the priest make an atonement for you, to cleanse you, " Moses said, " that ye may be clean from all your sins before the Lord. " (Lev. 16.)

The old covenant was but " a shadow of good things to come, . . . For it is not possible that the blood of bulls and of goats should take away sins. . . .But this man, after he had offered one sacrifice for sins forever, sat down on the right hand of God. " (Heb. 9 and 10) How perfectly the Mosaic ordinances testify of Him by whom salvation comes and in whose holy name all men are commanded to worship the Eternal Father forevermore!

Moses — Mediator of the Old Covenant

Moses — Mediator of the Old Covenant It has pleased God to make covenants with his people, from time to time, according to the heed and diligence that they give unto him. Those who devote themselves to righteousness receive more of his word and inherit greater rewards; those who harden their hearts and stiffen their necks are denied what otherwise would be theirs. Covenants are contracts. Gospel covenants are made between God in heaven and men on earth. These covenants are the solemn promises of Deity to pour out specified blessings upon all those who keep the terms and conditions upon which their receipt is predicated. The new and everlasting covenant is the fullness of the gospel; it is new in every age and to every people to whom it comes; it is everlasting in that from eternity to eternity it is the same, and its laws and conditions never change. From Adam to Moses, righteous men received and rejoiced in the everlasting covenant. It was offered to and rejected by Israel as a nation, and in its stead came a lesser law, a law of ordinances and performances designed to prepare them for the eventual receipt of the fullness of the gospel. Thus, when the original covenant of salvation was revealed anew by Christ in his day, it was called the new covenant or new testament, in contrast to the old covenant or old testament to which the people had been subject for the preceding fifteen hundred years. For each covenant — the old covenant and the new — there is both a revelator and a mediator. The revelator makes known the mind and will of the Lord, which the people are then privileged to accept or reject. The mediator stands between the Giver of the covenant and the people to mediate their differences; he interposes himself between the two parties of the covenant when they are at variance; he seeks to reconcile them to each other, to bring them into agreement. Moses was the mediator of the old covenant; Jesus is the mediator of the new covenant.

Moses ' struggles and sorrows as a revelator and a mediator are seen in the sad story of the golden calf. Because he was so long gone from them into the holy mountain, where he received the Ten Commandments and the law of the gospel, backsliding Israel prevailed upon Aaron to make a calf of gold, like unto the gods of Egypt. " These be thy gods, O Israel, which brought thee up out of the land of Egypt, " they then said, and — unbelievably — they worshiped and offered sacrifices to this molten idol. While Moses was yet on the mount, the Lord told him of the idolatrous worship and revelry going on in the camp. " I have seen this people, and, behold, it is a stiff-necked people, " the Lord said. " Now therefore let me alone, that my wrath may wax hot against them, and that I may consume them: and I will make of thee a great nation. " (Ex. 32:1 - 10.) Thereupon Moses pled for the people. Among other things he said to the Lord: " Wherefore should the Egyptians speak, and say, For mischief did he bring them out, to slay them in the mountains, and to consume them from the face of the earth? Turn from thy fierce wrath. Thy people will repent of this evil; therefore, come thou not out against them. " Then Moses reminded the Lord of the promises made to Abraham, Isaac, and Jacob concerning their seed, and the Lord, relenting, said to Moses: " If they will repent of the evil which they have done, I will spare them, and turn away my fierce wrath; but, behold, thou shalt execute my judgment upon all that will not repent of this evil this day. Therefore, see thou do this thing that I have commanded thee, or I will execute all that which I had thought to do unto my people. " (JST Ex. 32: 12 - 14) Returning to the camp, Moses in righteous anger brake the two tablets of stone on which the law was written; destroyed the calf; sent forth the cry, " Who is on the Lord's side "; accepted the offer of the Levites, and sent them forth to slay three thousand of the wicked in Israel. On the morrow, Moses said to Israel: " Ye have sinned a great sin: and now I will go up unto the Lord; peradventure I shall make an atonement for your sin. And Moses returned unto the Lord, and said, Oh, this people have sinned a great sin, and have made them gods of gold. Yet now, if thou wilt forgive their sins —; and if not, blot me, I pray thee, out of thy book which thou hast written. And the Lord said unto Moses, whosoever hath sinned against me, him will I blot out of my book. " (Ex. 32: 15 - 35; 33: 13; 34: 9; Deut. 5: 5; 9: 24 - 29; 10: 10; Ps. 106: 23.)

Jesus — Mediator of the New Covenant

Knowing that Moses was the mediator of the old covenant gives meaning to the scriptural passages which speak of Jesus as the mediator of the new covenant.

Moses' status as a mediator thus becomes — as all things in the law of Moses were — a type and shadow of a greater mediatory labor that was to be when the Messiah of whom Moses testified came to work out the infinite and eternal atonement.

Now Christ is the mediator of life; for this is the promise which God made unto Abraham. " (JST Gal. 3: 19 - 20.) Also: " For this is good and acceptable in the sight of God our Savior; Who is willing to have all men to be saved, and to come unto the knowledge of the truth which is in Christ Jesus, who is the Only Begotten Son of God, and ordained to be a Mediator between God and man; who is one God, and hath power over all men. For there is one God, and one mediator between God and men, the man Christ Jesus; Who gave himself a ransom for all, to be testified in due time. " (JST 1 Tim. 2: 3 - 6.)

" Consider the Apostle and High Priest of our profession, " Paul says, " Christ Jesus; Who was faithful to him that appointed him, as also Moses was faithful in all his house. For this man was counted worthy of more glory than Moses, inasmuch as he who hath builded the house hath more honor than the house. For every house is builded by some man; but he that built all things is God. And Moses verily was faithful in all his house, as a servant, for a testimony of those things which were to be spoken after; But Christ as a son over his own house; whose house are we, if we hold fast the confidence and the rejoicing of the hope firm unto the end. " (Heb. 3: 1 - 6.) Christ, thus, hath " obtained a more excellent ministry, by how much also he is the mediator of a better covenant, which was established upon better promises. " (Heb. 8: 6.)

Why Messiah Ministered among Mortals

To minister is to act in the name and place and stead of another in teaching those truths and performing those acts which are necessary for the salvation of those on whose behalf the ministerial service is rendered.

1. He came to atone for the sins of the world. 2. He came to reveal his Father. 3. He came to testify of himself. 4. He came to set a perfect example for all men. 5. He came to teach the gospel, set up the kingdom, bless those among whom he ministered, and perform the ordinances of salvation.

A God Dies!

Interwoven into every concept presented throughout this whole work is the great reality that God himself must die for man; that the Almighty Jehovah, the Creator of all things from the beginning, the Mighty Messiah, Israel's Deliverer, must lay down his life; that the Lord Jesus Christ, the very Son of God, came into the world — above all other reasons — to die, to die upon the cross, to die as he suffered more than man can suffer. The death of a God! The great Creator dies! Not only does he die — he is slain, crucified, pierced. Nails are driven through his hands and feet. A Roman spear is hurled into his side. He hangs in agony upon a cross, feeling again the weight of the sorrow he bore in Gethsemane. A God dies and the rocks rend; a God dies and all creation shudders; a God dies and all the hosts of heaven both sorrow and rejoice. A God dies that he may live again; that he may come forth from the tomb as the first fruits of them that sleep; that he may bring immortality to all and eternal life to those who believe and obey. A God dies that all the terms and conditions of the Father's plan may be fulfilled. A God descends below all things that he may rise to heights above the stars; he lives again, as all men shall; and the infinite and eternal atonement is complete. The will of the Son is swallowed up in the will of the Father. The will of the Father in all things from the beginning is done! All these things have been known in greater or lesser degree by prophets and saints in all dispensations. The nature of this work is such that we have referred to many things concerning the Lord Messiah's death as we have dealt with the various Messianic concepts. It is now, however, our privilege to collate and comment upon the Messianic utterances relative to his death as such, so that we may have before us the wondrous things known by the ancients about Him who is our Deliverer.

Jehovah, Israel's God, Shall Die. We are aware that the ancient prophets and saints knew that their Messiah must die. He is spoken of as " the Lamb slain from the foundation of the world " (Rev. 13: 8), meaning his sacrificial death was planned and foreordained from the beginning as part of the Father's plan.

The angelic pronouncement to Adam that his sacrificial performances were in " similitude of the sacrifice of the Only Begotten of the Father " (Moses 5: 7) carries with it the verity that the Only Begotten will lay down his life in sacrifice.

Messiah Shall Be Crucified

It did not suffice for the Messianic prophecies to set forth that Christ should die to redeem his people. It pleased God to show beforehand the way and manner of his death, a death on a cross, a death by cruel crucifixion. The very manner in which his redeeming blood was shed was itself a means of teaching great truths connected with the atonement.

" No man taketh it from me, " he said, " but I lay it down of myself. I have power to lay it down, and I have power to take it again. This commandment have I received of my Father. " (John 10: 18.) " All things must be fulfilled, which were written in the law of Moses, and in the prophets, and in the psalms, concerning me, " the risen Lord said to the assembled saints in the upper room. (Luke 24: 44)

Cleopas and another disciple, on the Emmaus road, the resurrected Jesus said: " O fools, and slow of heart to believe all that the prophets have spoken: Ought not Christ to have suffered these things, and to enter into his glory? And beginning at Moses and all the prophets, he expounded unto them in all the scriptures the things concerning himself. " (Luke 24: 25 - 27.) Surely those things we shall now quote from the Psalms — pointed express, detailed utterances about his sufferings, death, and atoning sacrifice — were included in those things which he expounded unto them.

Other Psalms also revealed, before the events, additional specifics that would attend or be associated with the cross of Christ and the agonizing death he would suffer thereon. With reference to the conniving and conspiring plots incident to our Lord's arrest and judicial trials the prophecy was: " They took counsel together against me, they devised to take away my life. " (Ps. 31: 13.) As to the role of Judas in those conspiracies, the Psalmist says: " Mine own familiar friend, in whom I trusted, which did eat of my bread, hath lifted up his heel against me. " (Ps 41: 9.) On that occasion when he washed their feet, Jesus spoke in laudatory terms of the twelve, but, said he, " I speak not of you all " for a moment later he was to say, " one of you shall betray me. " " I know whom I have chosen, " he continued, " but that the scripture may be fulfilled, "He that eateth bread with me hath lifted up his heel against me." Now I tell you before it come, that, when it is come to pass, ye may believe that I am he. " After a few more words, he dipped the sop and gave it to Judas, thus identifying the traitor in their midst. (John 13: 18 - 30.)

Prophets Reveal Signs of Messiah's Death

One of Israel's prophets, Zenos, whose writings have been lost to us, but which were on the brass plates of Laban and were thus preserved for Nephite usage, did speak of the destructions that would attend our Lord's death. " He spake concerning the three days of darkness, " we are told, " which should be a sign given of his death unto those who should inhabit the isles of the sea, " and which should be " more especially given unto those who are of the house of Israel. " That is to say, the portions of Israel far removed from Jerusalem and Canaan and who would not see the Messiah personally, or hear the testimony of those who did, were destined to receive special signs of his death and the atoning ransom that came thereby.

Samuel the Lamanite, centuries later and a bare forty years before the crucifixion, rehearsed in detail to the Nephites the destructions and desolations that would attend that event. " In that day that he shall suffer death, " the Lamanite prophet said, " the sun shall be darkened and refuse to give his light unto you; and also, the moon and the stars; and there shall be no light upon the face of this land, even from the time that he shall suffer death, for the space of three days, to the time that he shall rise again from the dead. " While our Lord's body lay in the tomb, while his eternal Spirit preached among the righteous dead, darkness enshrouded the Americas.

Far removed though they were from the criminal events, no Nephite and no Lamanite would be unaware that their prophets had foretold the death of their Messiah and said that it would be known by three days of dooming darkness. Where else in all the history of the earth have continents been enveloped in darkness for three days? How could such an event do aught but witness the truth of the promised event?

And he said unto me that while the thunder and the lightning lasted, and the tempest, that these things should be, and that darkness should cover the face of the whole earth for the space of three days. "

for the time that there should be darkness for the space of three days over the face of the land. And there began to be great doubtings and disputations among the people, notwithstanding so many signs had been given. And it came to pass in the thirty and fourth year, in the first month, on the fourth day of the month, there arose a great storm, such a one as never had been known in all the land.

" And it came to pass that it did last for the space of three days that there was no light seen; and there was great mourning and howling and weeping among all the people continually;

Messiah Shall Be Buried in a Sepulcher

Crucified criminals and other victims of Roman vengeance were often left on their crosses to rot away as signs and warnings to others. Blasphemers and others who were stoned to death among the Jews often had their bodies dumped unceremoniously in the Valley of Hinnom outside Jerusalem where the fires of Gehenna burned everlastingly. Decent burial was a mark of honor and respect. Reverence for those who passed on was unbounded. Abraham purchased the cave of Machpelah from the sons of Heth as a resting place for his beloved Sarah.

Joseph of Arimathea, a rich man who had an expensive tomb hewn from the rock, a tomb in which no man had lain, entreated Pilate that he might have the body of the deceased Christ. Pilate, after receiving the assurance of the centurion that Jesus was in fact dead, and because it was contrary to the Jewish custom for one of their people to hang on the cross on the

Sabbath, granted the Arimathean's request. Nicodemus, another rich and influential Jew, brought myrrh and aloes in large amounts for the embalming. The faithful women embalmed and clothed the body that soon was to rise from death, wrapping it carefully in linen clothes as was the custom among the Jews. Then it was placed in the tomb, which was sealed with a large stone, and a guard was placed, lest Jesus' followers steal the body and claim he had risen on the third day as he had promised to do.

Isaiah said, " He made his grave with the wicked, and with the rich in his death " (Isa. 53: 9), both of which promises were fulfilled. Zenos said he would " be buried in a sepulcher. " (1 Ne. 19: 10.) Nephi gave this promise: " They will crucify him; and after he is laid in a sepulcher for the space of three days he shall rise from the dead. " (2 Ne. 25: 13.)

The prophet Jonah's unparalleled experience in being swallowed and then vomited up by a great fish was all done in similitude of and to teach the fact of our Lord's burial and resurrection. When the Jews sought from Jesus a sign, he condemned them as " an evil and adulterous generation, " and said, " There shall no sign be given to it, but the sign of the prophet Jonas: For as Jonas was three days and three nights in the whale's belly; so shall the Son of man be three days and three nights in the heart of the earth. " (Matt. 12: 38 - 40.)

Truly, " He was crucified, died, and rose again the third day. " (D & C 20: 23.)

Ye know that after two days is the feast of the Passover, and the Son of man is betrayed to be crucified. Specifying that it is two days before the Passover preserves for us the chronology and continuity of the events of the week of his passion; the statement about his betrayal and crucifixion reveals the subject that was uppermost in the minds of all of them as the climax of the one perfect ministry approached.

1. At the first Passover. Three years before, at the Passover, as he began his early Judean ministry, Jesus made the first such declaration of which we know. After the first cleansing of the temple, and in answer to the Jewish demands as to his authority for so doing, he said: " Destroy this temple " —as John says, " he spake of the temple of his body " — " and in three days I will raise it up. "

2. To Nicodemus. In the great Born - Again Sermon, delivered, as we suppose, in the home of John in Jerusalem, Jesus told Nicodemus, a friendly Sanhedrist: " As Moses lifted up the serpent in the wilderness, even so must the Son of man be lifted up. " (John 3: 14.) How apt are the figures and how plain the similitudes that bear record of Him!

4. To the sign - seeking scribes and Pharisees. " For as Jonas was three days and three nights in the whale's belly; so shall the Son of man be three days and three nights in the heart of the earth, " he said as he excoriated them for their evil and adulterous lives. (Matt. 12: 38 - 40.) Again, we are left to suppose that many people thereafter saw in the miraculous experience of Jonah a sign and a type of their Messiah.

After Peter's solemn and Spirit - born confession, Matthew says: " From that time forth began Jesus to shew unto his disciples, how that he must go unto Jerusalem, and suffer many things of the elders and chief priests and scribes, and be killed, and be raised again the third day. " (Matt. 16: 21.) From this it appears that both then and on many subsequent occasions Jesus spoke in plainness to his chosen and favored ones of his death and resurrection.

After Peter's solemn and Spirit - born confession, Matthew says: " From that time forth began Jesus to shew unto his disciples, how that he must go unto Jerusalem, and suffer many things of the elders and chief priests and scribes, and be killed, and be raised again the third day. " (Matt. 16: 21) From this it appears that both then and on many subsequent occasions Jesus spoke in plainness to his chosen and favored ones of his death and resurrection.

Jesus said unto them, The Son of man shall be betrayed into the hands of men: And they shall kill him, and the third day he shall be raised again.

And shall deliver him to the Gentiles to mock, and to scourge, and to crucify him: and the third day he shall rise again. " (Matt. 20: 17 - 19.)

We cannot believe that all these sayings — given as allusions, as similitudes, and in plain words — constituted a tithe, or a hundredth, or a thousandth part of what the Blessed One said of his coming death and crucifixion and of his resurrection on the third day.

In the fourteenth day of the first month at even [between the two evenings] is the Lord's Passover. (Lev. 23: 5.) Your lamb shall be without blemish, . . . And ye shall keep it up until the fourteenth day of the same month: and . . . shall kill it in the evening [between the two evenings] . . . . And they shall eat the flesh in that night, roast with fire, and unleavened bread; and with bitter herbs they shall eat it . . . . It is the Lord's Passover . (Ex. 12: 5 - 11.)

And so, on Thursday morning, knowing that the preparations must be made to eat the Passover meal, the disciples ask Jesus: " Where wilt thou that we go and prepare that thou mayest eat the Passover? " Will it be in blessed Bethany, which was designated by Rabbinical authority as part of Jerusalem for the purposes of the feast, or back in the city proper? Only a few hours remain in which the needed lamb could be slain in the temple; what arrangements, therefore, shall they make?

But now at this Passover, he made one provision with reference to the guest chamber; it was to be " my Katalyma. " His purpose was to eat his last meal alone with his apostles. None of his other followers were to be present — not even his Blessed Mother, nor Mary Magdalene, who had so often traveled with the Twelve in their missionary journeys, nor Mary who worshipped at his feet in Bethany. He and the Twelve were more than the minimum of ten needed for the Passover meal, and he and they had sacred ordinances to perform before he went to Gethsemane to take upon himself the combined weight of all the sins of all men.

(Matthew 26: 20; Mark 14: 17; Luke 22: 14) Peter and John have now done their work; they and the homeowner have made ready the guest chamber. The lamb has been roasted on a pomegranate spit; the unleavened cakes, the bitter herbs, the dish with vinegar — all are in place. Such items of food as needed are on the movable table; the festive lamps are lit; it is even time, and the meal is ready. " It was probably as the sun was beginning to decline in the horizon that Jesus and the other ten disciples descended once more over the Mount of Olives into the Holy City. Before them lay Jerusalem in her festive attire. All around pilgrims were hastening towards it. White tents dotted the sward, gay with the bright flowers of early spring, or peered out from the gardens or the darker foliage of the olive plantations. From the gorgeous Temple buildings, dazzling in their snow - white marble and gold, on which the slanting rays of the sun were reflected, rose the smoke of the altar of burnt - offering.

BOOK REVIEWS

Based on the excerpt provided, the book seems to be well-written with a strong focus on conveying the significance of Jesus Christ's atoning sacrifice in human history. The language used is articulate and meaningful, emphasizing the foundational role of this event in the gospel and salvation. The text effectively communicates complex theological concepts in a clear and compelling manner, making it accessible to readers interested in spiritual and religious themes. Gordon's ability to convey the importance of the plan of salvation and the role of Jesus Christ as the redeemer showcases a deep understanding of the subject matter. Overall, the book appears to be thoughtfully crafted and engaging for readers seeking a profound exploration of faith and redemption.

SAM Andrews

Christian Book Editor

The book mentioned in the text seems to hold significant importance in providing a comprehensive understanding of the chronology of the Passover and the gospel. Its insights into scripture, ancient history, and modern revelation may attract readers interested in religious studies and biblical interpretations. The book's potential for sales would likely depend on the target audience and the effectiveness of its message in addressing controversy surrounding Passover.

Andrew Taylor

a popular news journalist and current anchor on World News Tonight.

Gordon, the author, exhibits a commendable command of grammar and sentence structure, conveying complex ideas with clarity and precision. Their writing flows smoothly, aided by well-structured sentences that enhance readability. The author's attention to detail in grammar and sentence construction contributes to the overall cohesiveness and intelligibility of the text.

JOEL MICHAELS

a most recognizable news reporter in America

The text discusses the notion that God is a source of truth and harmony, emphasizing the importance of following performances and ordinances in the gospel precisely. It explores how details in the Passover portion of the Law to Moses were fulfilled by Jesus Christ, highlighting the shift from a 12-day celebration to a 7-day observance that has led to controversy surrounding the Passover. Joseph Smith, a figure in the last days, is presented as having received the Book of Mormon as part of his divine calling. He emphasizes the importance of understanding scripture through the Spirit of God and asserts that the gospel, its ordinances, and its officers have remained consistent throughout time. The book mentioned in the text aims to harmonize the four gospels into the chronology outlined in the Law of Moses, drawing on various sources including ancient history, modern revelation, and research from different sects. It suggests that controversy surrounding the Passover can be resolved by organizing prophetic information within the context of the 12-day Passover as prescribed in the Law of Moses.

KIM Thompson

Media Literary Excellence Editor